A READING OF

# Jane Austen

Barbara Hardy

THE ATHLONE PRESS
London & Atlantic Highlands, N.J.

Published by
THE ATHLONE PRESS
1 Park Drive, London NW11 7SG
and 165 First Avenue,
Atlantic Highlands, NJ 07716

First edition (Peter Owen Ltd) 1975

First paperback edition,
with corrections (The Athlone Press) 1979
Reprinted 1997

© Barbara Hardy 1975, 1979
British Library Cataloguing in Publication Data
*A catalogue record for this book is available
from the British Library*

ISBN 0 485 12032 1

Printed and bound in Great Britain by
Short Run Press Ltd, Exeter

# A READING OF JANE AUSTEN

TO BETTY

# CONTENTS

# ACKNOWLEDGEMENTS

I am very grateful to Jean Elliott and Barbara Pinsker for their generous work on a difficult manuscript. Jean Elliott also gave valuable advice and criticism. I must also thank Alasdair Aston for his suggestions. I am indebted to students at Royal Holloway College, and Birkbeck College, for their listening and talking over the past ten years. Veronica Wilson-Tagoe will find traces of conversations we had while she was working on her M.Phil. thesis. I have profited from agreements and disagreements with many Jane Austen scholars, but am particularly indebted to the work of R. W. Chapman, Brian Southam, Mary Lascelles, Howard Babb, A. Walton Litz, and Stuart Tave.

This book is a study of Jane Austen's major novels, and does not include a discussion of the juvenilia or the unfinished works.

B.H.

The text used in this book is that of R. W. Chapman's edition of the novels, Oxford Universiy Press, third edition, 1932-4, and his edition of the *Minor Works*, Oxford University Press, 1954.

The following abbreviations are used in the text:

| | | |
|---|---|---|
| *NA* | *Northanger Abbey* | (Composed between 1798 and 1803; sold to Crosby & Co. 1803; published 1817). |
| *SS* | *Sense and Sensibility* | (Composed between *c.* 1795 and 1811; published 1811). |
| *PP* | *Pride and Prejudice* | (Composed between 1796 and 1813; published 1813). |
| *MP* | *Mansfield Park* | (Published 1814). |
| *E* | *Emma* | (Published 1815). |
| *P* | *Persuasion* | (Published 1817). |
| *MW* | *Minor Works* | (Reference is made to *Evelyn* and *Catharine, or the Bower*, composed between *c.* 1788–1809, and the fragment *Sanditon*, composed January–March 1817, published 1925). |

# I

# The Flexible Medium

Good artists work within their chosen genre, great artists transform it. The art of fiction has been radically changed by the novels of Richardson, Sterne, Henry James, James Joyce and Samuel Beckett. These writers presented themselves as innovators. What is astonishing about Jane Austen is that, while making no claims to innovation, she too transformed the art of fiction.[1] Indeed she may be said to have created the modern novel. She combined what Ian Watt calls 'the internal and the external approaches to character', embodying her unified sense of character and society in a flexible language[2] and form. Unlike the other great experimental novelists who have changed the face of fiction, she introduced no conspicuously new formal devices comparable to Richardson's introspective epistle-writing 'to the moment', Sterne's comic dislocations of narrative time, James's concentrated dramatic developments, and Joyce's fundamental experiments in analogues and monologues.

Unlike these others, who were introspective about their own art either within their novels or in literary criticism, she did not analyse, judge, or in any way publicize her own achievement. Nor was her slow and gradual critical reception[3] marked by any early elucidation of her formal achievements, partly because the criticism of fiction

[1] The revolution which Jane Austen created was described by Ian Watt in *The Rise of the Novel* (London, 1957) as the combination of Defoe's and Richardson's subjectivity with Fielding's handling of society as a whole: 'At the same time, Jane Austen varied her narrative point of view sufficiently to give us, not only editorial comment, but much of Defoe's and Richardson's psychological closeness to the subjective world of the characters.' (p. 297)

[2] See particularly Mary Lascelles, *Jane Austen and Her Art* (London, 1939), and Howard S. Babb, *Jane Austen's Novels; the Fabric of Dialogue* (Hamden, Conn., 1967).

[3] See Brian Southam's excellent summary of the critical reception in his introduction to *Jane Austen: The Critical Heritage* (London, 1968).

scarcely concerned itself with form before Henry James started to mature its infantilities, and partly because her formal achievements were muted. Jane Austen took a very long time to attract technical analysis, though she has always been praised, in somewhat general terms, for her artistry. Throughout the nineteenth century she was applauded for craft, finish and neatness. These were features that even her detractors could patronize. Even if she lacked passion, soul, elevation and social range, she was neat, elegant, and tasteful.[4] One of her best Victorian critics, Richard Simpson, wrote in 1870 that 'She is neat, epigrammatic and incisive, but always a lady', and 'art will make up for want of force', adding that her art has 'all the minute attention to detail of the most accomplished miniature-painter'.[5] Her femininity and ladylike elegance, partly inferred from her biographers, partly from her novels, tended to be associated with her finished craft. Her accomplishments as a novelist sometimes even seem to be assimilated to her excellence as a needlewoman. Whether her novels impressed readers or left them feeling that something was missing, her artistry provoked admiration rather than elucidation.

It is irksome to suggest, as we must, that she brought about 'a quiet revolution'[6] in fiction since her quietness has been as over-emphasized as her neatness. Not that she was not neat, or not quiet, but she was many other things as well. Quietness is a word commonly used of the tenor of her life, her attitude to writing, and the novels themselves. The impression of quietness was fixed by her brother Henry Austen, in the 'Biographical Notice' which he published in 1818 as a preface to the four-volume edition of *Northanger Abbey* and *Persuasion*, the posthumously published novels.[7] 'A life of usefulness, literature and religion, was not by any means a life of event.' He speaks of her 'quiet and happy occupations', up to the onset of her illness in 1816, and stresses her tranquillity and placidity. Everyone remembers the peculiar details of her discreet and unobtrusive habits of composition. If the woman novelist's place has commonly had to be in the home, no other woman seems to have gone to such lengths to mask her professional activity in the domestic setting. Her nephew James tells us how she worked in the family sitting-room, 'careful that her occupa-

---

[4] Southam, *Critical Heritage*, loc. cit.

[5] Ibid., pp. 264, 265, 253.

[6] A. Walton Litz, *Jane Austen. A Study of Her Artistic Development* (New York, 1965), p. 53.

[7] Reprinted by Chapman, Vol. V, pp. 3-9.

tion should not be suspected by servants, or visitors, or any persons beyond her own family party. She wrote upon small sheets of paper which could easily be put away, or covered with a piece of blotting paper.'[8]

The small pieces of paper and the covering blotting paper join with her own metaphor of the 'little bit (two Inches wide) of Ivory'[9] to reinforce the ideas of littleness, neatness and modesty. Henry Austen introduced the notion of her reluctance to publish, and the difficulty her friends found in persuading her to face the dreaded notoriety. When the secret of her authorship was out, she declined to be fêted, and refused an invitation to meet Madame de Staël – perhaps no great loss to either when we remember that Madame de Staël thought her novels '*vulgaire*'. We now think of her life as more eventful and varied than her nineteenth-century biographers suggested, but there remains the blank created by her sister Cassandra's censorship – by burning and cutting – of any revealing letters. The limitations and exclusions of her novels, which are confined in class, region and event, complete the picture of quietness. Her self-advertised refusal to 'dwell on guilt and misery', has joined with the biographical details to create a total impression of a sedate and cloistered artistic virtue. The impression has been disturbed by our growing attention to her satire, irony and criticism,[10] but it is true that her art, even as an ironist, steals upon us gently. It is true, too, that *Mansfield Park* and *Persuasion* solicit our interest in mildness and sweet fortitude. It is also true that her social criticism seems compatible with a certain evasion of radically subversive attack. The very elegance and prudence which she consistently admires in her characters must still reinforce her reputation for peace and quiet.

Her revolution was indeed a modest one. Its modesty was more genuine and more important than any other aspect of her so-called quiet life, unobtrusive writing habits, and restrained subject-matter. One of her nieces, writing to tell her about someone's admiration of her novels, said that it was sufficiently whole-hearted to please even

[8] J. E. Austen-Leigh, *A Memoir of Jane Austen* (London, 1886), p. 96. First published in 1870.

[9] *Letters*, ed. R. W. Chapman (Oxford, 1952), p. 469; hereafter referred to as *Letters*.

[10] See especially D. W. Harding, 'Regulated Hatred. An Aspect of the Work of Jane Austen', *Scrutiny*, Vol. viii, No. 4 (March 1940), and Marvin Mudrick, *Jane Austen: Irony as Defense and Discovery* (Princeton, 1952).

Cassandra, 'nothing ever like them before or since'.[11] But to say that there was nothing like them before and nothing like them since obscures her impact. Jane Austen created a new and flexible medium in which the individual and society could be revealed together. The achievement is striking when we approach it from earlier novels, much less so when we approach her novels – as is common – after an acquaintance with the novels of the twentieth century and the novels of the Victorian period.

There are moments in the history of art when we find ourselves face to face with new clearings, heights or depths, after which nothing is quite the same again. I want to look closely at some of the ways in which Jane Austen creates such an epoch in the history of fiction. It is not altogether reckless to suggest that her most singular contribution was what I shall call her flexible medium, a capacity to glide easily from sympathy to detachment, from one mind to many minds, from solitary scenes to social gatherings. It was this medium which she conveyed to her successors and what was for her a triumph won over difficulties, became the novel's stock in trade.

The flexible medium is the dominant gift of her genius. It seems to rely on many powers, dramatic, psychological and stylistic, all of which solve her individual imaginative needs. Her art succeeds in moving in and out of the minds of her people, and in and out of crowds and communities. The combination of such social notation with such analysis of consciousness transforms our sense of what the novel can do. The achievement would be more obvious if we were not so accustomed to taking such a medium for granted in the novels that came after her. We expect the novelist to be profoundly concerned with the human mind and the society. We expect the novel to move fluently from the extreme of inner analysis to that of public life. Moreover, we expect these extremes to meet not simply in the unity of art, but in a pattern of cause and effect which relates the turmoils in the psyche to the portrait of society. The novel accumulates its impressions of society by noting the behaviour of people in social groups, playing social roles, placed in social environments. But such behaviour is made plain by contrasts with private lives.

It may also be hard to think of a picture or a drama of the individual and society, and the individual in society, as a solution to an artistic problem, since we all take it for granted that we have private

[11] Mary Augusta Austen-Leigh, *Personal Aspects of Jane Austen* (London, 1920), p. 53.

and public lives. We will probably be so sophisticatedly aware of the varied functions of our roles and registers of action, relationship and speech, that some of Jane Austen's most original analyses may pass without notice. Only when we go back to Scott, to Fanny Burney, and to the great eighteenth-century novelists, Smollett, Sterne, Fielding, Richardson and Defoe, do we come to realize that the fusion of private and public worlds is a superb achievement. The novelists writing before Jane Austen tend to tilt the balance toward either the private world or the public world. The one may be made implicit in the other, even subordinate to it. If conjunction is attempted, it is made abruptly and jerkily. Characters tend to have *either* public *or* private lives.

Occasionally, we meet a more modern novelist who fails to create a balance. Virginia Woolf complained [12] sharply that in their different ways, and for their different reasons, the novels of Arnold Bennett, John Galsworthy and H. G. Wells failed to give a sense of the individual life, losing it in their preoccupation with the surface or the problems of public life. She was probably unfair to Arnold Bennett, whose ways of implying the individual life were less subtle and less subtly fugitive than her ways; nothing is so difficult for the innovator to appreciate as an old-fashioned version of the innovation being attempted. She was right about Galsworthy's specifications and surfaces, but Wells affords a more useful instance, since his social surveys and arguments need to sacrifice, sentimentalize, or simplify the life of the individual. Like Wells, George Orwell may strike us as brilliant but bizarre in his very generalization of the public world. Novelists who fail to join the individual life with their analysis of society may collapse in imaginative failure, like so many best-sellers, but they may deliberately create an art of social surfaces because their concern, like that of Wells and Orwell, is essentially polemic, using the arts of fiction for political tracts, social studies, ideological fable and documentaries. But what we are chiefly accustomed to in the great novelists who come after Jane Austen is a controlled and profound imaginative grasp of the individual life and the collective life.

Those novelists who are specialists in solitude, and who move away from the patterns of society to the isolated individual life, cannot entirely dispense with society. There is probably no more thoroughgoing and consistent essay in human isolation than Samuel Beckett's

[12] 'Mr Bennett and Mrs Brown', *The Captain's Death Bed* (London, 1950). Reprinted in *Collected Essays*, Vol. I (London, 1966).

*Lessness.* It is a very brief novel, because Beckett is perhaps no more capable of keeping up such moving and chilling solitude throughout a long narrative than George Eliot and Joyce were of making whole novels out of the limited imaginative materials analysed in the stories of *Scenes of Clerical Life* and *Dubliners. Lessness* has to forgo the usual time and space expected of novels for its reduction of the usual quantity of social life to such lessness. Moreover, in this sparest of fictions, the very absence of society relies somewhat on the expectations of its presence, as it does in Beckett's more populous novel *How It Is* or in Sartre's *La Nausée.* In Beckett's mud or Sartre's sickness there is a deviation from normal social life, but relationships persist, intense, hostile, remote, mechanical, bewildered, minimal, or unreal. The proportions of solitude and social relationship are disconcertingly shifted, but it is hard to dispense with the public world, especially in novels.

In modern novels before Beckett, we find the customary balance and junction of private and public worlds. D. H. Lawrence shifts us constantly from intense visionary moments to substantial happenings in everyday life. At the wedding of Will and Anna Brangwen in *The Rainbow*, we hear the family jokes and gossip, but we also see the vision of Tom Brangwen's symbolic sense of himself as a diminished figure in the immense plain of existences. Paul Morel in *Sons and Lovers* burns the bread, and feels his kinship with grass and water. Joyce deals most lavishly with inner and outer life in *Dubliners* and *Stephen Hero,* and in *A Portrait of the Artist as a Young Man* relies on the movements outwards and inwards, while controlling the shape of the public world by the consciousness of his Stephen Dedalus. In *Ulysses,* most private and yet most social of all novels, we sometimes jump disconcertingly from Bloom's private fantasies and sensations to the outer skin of streets and passers-by. Joyce seems to turn away from smooth motion, switching from inner to outer experience in a deliberated primitivism. Such primitive juxtapositions rely on a long tradition of adroit joinings. Lawrence and Joyce reject the old stable ego of the Victorian fiction, but still depend on its characteristic bird's-eye view of society and God's-eye view of the human heart. The dialogue of the mind with itself sounds to the novel-reader's ear against the hubbub of social chorus. We follow the characters of Dickens, Thackeray, George Eliot, Meredith, Hardy and Henry James through shifts from the lonely self to the social self, in contrasts, ironies, contradictions, contractions, expansions, pains, pleasures, perils, tests, causes and effects.

We take it for granted when reading George Eliot's *The Mill on the Floss* that we can be one moment with Maggie Tulliver's turbulent desolations in her attic, the next at the Easter dinner-table with the solidarity and discord of the Tullivers, Gleggs, Pullets and Deans. We find nothing extraordinary in going from the drama of a polite afternoon visit to Uncle and Aunt Dean, with its substantial treats and trials of wiped feet, housemaid, avuncular condescensions, musical-box and cousinly relations, to Maggie's pursuits of impossible wildness, freedom and power. In *Middlemarch* the flexible medium of George Eliot's narrative presents the public occasion of Mr Brooke's dinner-party at Tipton Manor, where Celia Brooke hankers mildly after Sir James Chettam, who talks agricultural chemistry for the benefit of Dorothea, who is impressed by Casaubon, who does his bewildered best to be polite to his scatter-brained host. The next episode goes deeply into Dorothea's mind, as she revises the recent scene in the public world in accordance with the desires of her own fertile and fervent fantasies. In Henry James's *The Portrait of a Lady* we stare through Isabel Archer's eyes in Gilbert Osmond's drawing-room, where he sits and Madame Merle stands. The public and external position is engraved so deeply on Isabel's imagination that she spends the night alone before the fire, stimulated by her reading of the social scene to re-live and review her contractions of spirit. In *Bleak House* Dickens moves us from Esther Summerson's bleak childhood, where repression and joylessness are normal, to the bleakness of the London streets. Thackeray moves in and out of Henry Esmond's loyalties, longings, jealousies and ambitions, to the court, the battlefield, and the coffeehouse. And this oscillation is the rhythm we expect, so customary that we have ceased to find it remarkable. It was not always the customary rhythm of novels.

In her critical study, *The Art of Jane Austen*, Mary Lascelles makes only one comment I find hard to accept. She suggests that Jane Austen may have given up the epistolary form [13] because it allowed for too great a shift in viewpoint, uncongenial to Jane Austen's preference for a steady and sustained centre of consciousness. The epistolary novel does not have to use many correspondents, as we can see from the first part of *Pamela* and from Fanny Burney's *Evelina*, where infrequent interruptions show the effectiveness of keeping to a concentrated viewpoint. Despite the examples of *Clarissa, Sir Charles*

---

[13] Op. cit., p. 203.

*Grandison* and *Humphrey Clinker*, it was certainly open to Jane Austen to write epistolary novels, or first-person novels, like those of Defoe, without deviating from the single centre. What Jane Austen seems to have needed more than such concentration through one viewpoint was the combination of extroverted and introverted actions. Neither the epistolary nor the autobiographical forms were sufficiently flexible for this double emphasis. While the story of *Robinson Crusoe* or *Clarissa* is being told, even though it includes social scenes and dialogues, it presents all its action from single points of view. Defoe presents and even criticizes society, showing his protagonists in public life, in streets, shops, houses, inns, brothels and prisons. However busily his heroes and heroines move through life they remain essentially alone, and it is through their eyes that we see society. Defoe is in fact rather attached to Beckett-like solitudes. The prodigal son of a tradesman, who preferred to go to sea and to leave the middle station of life, Robinson Crusoe inhabits his desert island. What society gradually comes into his novel and its sequel is inconsiderable in size, interest and complexity, compared with his engrossing vitality. Moll Flanders's husbands and lovers, and Roxana's intimates and acquaintances are shadowy. Defoe's novels are conceived in the first person singular, and however vivid their impressions of society, typical or strange, their worlds are all like islands with a single inhabitant. In the more sociable novels, *Moll Flanders* and *Roxana*, the narrator's record of experience is the single thread which ties the individual life to society. Moll Flanders's response to prison seems to represent what moral Defoe needed her to feel, as she voices her shock at finding herself amongst the appallingly hardened crew of Newgate criminals, but there is no attempt to go beyond her point of view, and life in the prison is as simplified and foreshortened as the characters of Moll's lovers, husbands and companions.

Defoe is a great social novelist, but he filters his view of society through detailed portraits of social types. In *A Journal of the Plague Year* we catch many glimpses of life in plague-stricken London, like the episode where men disinfect an abandoned purse before they dare open it, an action eloquent of the effects of disease and fear on the usual appetites. But such social detail is narrated through description and didacticism. There is nothing comparable to Jane Austen's sustained drama of groups, only glimpses, anecdotes and statistics. Defoe's people all inhabit a kind of desert; we see it through their eyes and their solitude.

Despite her affection for Richardson, Jane Austen may have been more influenced by Fielding. He did not call himself a 'historian' for nothing. But Fielding's exuberant histories also illustrate the lack of a flexible medium, capable of registering social and personal life. Here there is social life in plenty, of all kinds and classes. Fielding animates the drama of life in great houses and hovels, on the road, in inns, among soldiers, gipsies, men and women of fairly easy virtue, in country and city, lodgings, theatres and prisons. The experiences of magistrate and dramatist fuse in a novel's full and incisive rendering of the order and disorder of social life. But at a certain cost. In Fielding's novels it is the human psyche which becomes simplified and stylized. He presents the passions, for instance, through set-pieces of description, mock-heroic or seriously elevated. He contributes to the novel the brilliant theatrical invention of the inner moral scene, where aspects of mind, feeling and moral sense debate crises and conclusions in Black George, Mrs Honour, Sophia or Tom. Such occasions are impressive and startling because of their rarity, but are so schematic that they reduce our sense of the individuality of inner play, and locate particularity in moral conclusions, not in mind or sensibility. Even in the more psychologized action of his last novel, *Amelia*, we find types, not complex individual characters. As he says in *Joseph Andrews*, he describes 'not men, but manners; not an individual, but a species'. (Bk III, Chap. i)

The clear, simple outline of performers and their moral theatre fits as effectively into his pictures of society as Hogarth's rakes and whores into his crowded rooms and streets. The depth of mind and feeling in Fielding belongs to one character only, the narrator. His inner life is a complex stage for thought and impassioned reflection. In *Tom Jones* he moves beneath the surfaces of life in depth and over a wide range, fully sensitive in judgement and passion to love, art, fame and death. The narrator of *Tom Jones* resembles his hero in appetite, candour and learning, but Tom's whole range of experience has nothing to offer which is comparable to the narrator's ironically searching admissions of his double impulse as an artist, the love of fame and the need of sustenance. No other character in Fielding can move us as the narrator does in the imaginative reminder of the artist's energy and mortality, anticipated as the common end in 'a worse-furnished box'. Perhaps the most fully and complexly imaginative of the English novelists before Jane Austen, the closest to George Eliot (who admired him) and to Joyce, Fielding creates novels where there is an ironic comic movement from author to creatures, but neither the heights nor depths of the individual life. The action and character are extroverted, seen almost exclusively in the public world.

At the other extreme are the introverted worlds of Richardson and Sterne. Their first-person narrators and writers also tell about roads, inns, brothels, sponging-houses, churches, cottages and great houses, but they do so from a single vision. In Richardson we build up impressions through different points of view, but each view is highly individual, even idiosyncratic, and we look at the world through private obsessions and experiences, one eye and one mind at a time. Even when the communal life of the family or the crowd is described, it is to express the private vision and dilemma. This is of course a method which is socially informative, but the social information comes via the analysis of the individual mind.

One of the novelists we know Jane Austen greatly admired was Fanny Burney.[14] *Evelina* has the enclosed form of an epistolary novel, *Cecilia* is a third-person narrative, but in both we see an attempt to join social and individual life. Fanny Burney places both Evelina and Cecilia in threatened positions. They are innocent visitors discovering the nature of society in the company of different types and classes, at home and abroad – in shops, theatres, masquerades, visits to town and country houses, slums – in high life and low. Fanny Burney frequently forges her links between the individual and the crowd through comic contrast. The fastidious heroine of *Evelina* is fearfully jostled or marooned in Ranelagh or in the one-shilling gallery at the opera with companions who are clumsy, common, riotous or depraved. Perhaps here we begin to come closer to Jane Austen, but Fanny Burney's social action and her ways of registering passions and intelligence are very simple indeed compared with the imaginative chronicle of Jane Austen's novels. Fanny Burney's heroines learn from their experience of society, very much as Tom Jones and Partridge learn about their own culture and sub-cultures, as they illustrate the quotation from Horace which stands as epigraph to *Tom Jones: 'Mores hominum multorum vidit'*. But Fanny Burney's habit is to set the heroine quite apart from the social scenes in which she appears. Heroines and social types are painted in different colours, constructed from different materials. Her picture of society is a collage, and the joins show.

[14] See *Letters*, pp. 9, 13, 14, 64, 180, 254, 334, 388, 438. See also Frank W. Bradbrook, *Jane Austen and Her Predecessors* (Cambridge, 1966), Chap. 6.

It is hard to think of a busier social world than Jane Austen's, though she (notoriously) kept her social range much narrower than any of the previous novelists I have mentioned. The scenes and aspects of social life which she does show are active, crowded, and often noisy. But as we think of the busy social life in her novels and of the fully-occupied social lives of her characters, we also remember silence, solitude, isolation and privacy. We move from the innermost recesses of the heart and mind to the most extrovert social occasions. And we move from one to the other with perfect ease and smoothness. It is this formal balance, ease and harmony which is scarcely found before Jane Austen, though frequently afterwards.

Not one of Jane Austen's heroines, who are her most interesting, complex and important characters, lives alone. In this respect they are quite unlike many of their predecessors, female and male.[15] Moll Flanders and Roxana make their own way. Robinson Crusoe and the Saddler are sequestered. Pamela and Clarissa are less physically alone than they like, but are separated from family and friends. Sophia leaves her father's house in search of Tom Jones with only her maid as a companion. Amelia has to fend for herself while her husband is in prison. Cecilia endures solitude, and privation and danger among strangers. Jane Austen's heroines are never without some friend or relation, and their physical perils and privations are not extreme, judged by earlier standards. They do suffer from perils, privations and inner isolation, however, and it is often in the groups and coteries of social life that Jane Austen locates these ordeals.

On her sensitive scales, little things weigh heavy. The weight of social experiences in her novels is what restores reality to the trials of being a heroine. It is embarrassing, unnerving, exciting and risky to go to your first ball. Fanny Burney inflicts public humiliation and embarrassment on Evelina who is doubly impeded by ignorance and irresistible charm; but even though her ballrooms are a long way from Richardson's perilous great houses or houses of ill-fame, they are also a long way from the world of Jane Austen. In some ways the problems of etiquette and manners are common to both novelists. In Fanny Burney's ballroom the dazzling heroine is in danger of inflicting grave offence and receiving gross insult. In Jane Austen the worst that can happen is overhearing a casual rude remark made by a young man who doesn't ask you to dance, being afraid of the wrong man asking

[15] Heroines of Gothic novels had a very bad time, but I confine myself to fiction making some attempt to show character and society.

you to dance before the right one does, being the third in the company of two who are company for each other, being taken for a wallflower when you are merely waiting for your partner, sitting at a table with strangers. In *Northanger Abbey* there is a famous scene in which Catherine Morland and Mrs Allen are in the tea-room:

Every body was shortly in motion for tea, and they must squeeze out like the rest. Catherine began to feel something of disappointment—she was tired of being continually pressed against by people, the generality of whose faces possessed nothing to interest, and with all of whom she was so wholly unacquainted, that she could not relieve the irksomeness of imprisonment by the exchange of a syllable with any of her fellow captives; and when at last arrived in the tea-room, she felt yet more the awkwardness of having no party to join, no acquaintance to claim, no gentleman to assist them.—They saw nothing of Mr. Allen; and after looking about them in vain for a more eligible situation, were obliged to sit down at the end of a table, at which a large party were already placed, without having any thing to do there, or any body to speak to, except each other.

Mrs. Allen congratulated herself, as soon as they were seated, on having preserved her gown from injury. 'It would have been very shocking to have it torn,' said she, 'would it not?—It is such a delicate muslin.—For my part I have not seen any thing I like so well in the whole room, I assure you.'

'How uncomfortable it is,' whispered Catherine, 'not to have a single acquaintance here!'

'Yes, my dear,' replied Mrs. Allen, with perfect serenity, 'it is very uncomfortable indeed.'

'What shall we do?—The gentlemen and ladies at this table look as if they wondered why we came here—we seem forcing ourselves into their party.'

'Aye, so we do.—That is very disagreeable. I wish we had a large acquaintance here.'

'I wish we had *any*;—it would be somebody to go to.'

'Very true, my dear; and if we knew anybody we would join them directly. The Skinners were here last year—I wish they were here now.'

'Had not we better go away as it is?—Here are no tea things for us, you see.'

'No more there are, indeed.—How very provoking! But I think we had better sit still, for one gets so tumbled in such a crowd! How is my head, my dear?—Somebody gave me a push that has hurt it I am afraid.'

'No, indeed, it looks very nice.—But, dear Mrs. Allen, are you sure there is nobody you know in all this multitude of people? I think you *must* know somebody.'

'I don't upon my word—I wish I did. I wish I had a large acquaintance here with all my heart, and then I should get you a partner.—I should be so glad to have you dance. There goes a strange-looking woman! What an

odd gown she has got on!—How old fashioned it is! Look at the back!'
After some time they received an offer of tea from one of their neigh-
bours; it was thankfully accepted, and this introduced a light conversation with the gentleman who offered it, which was the only time that any
body spoke to them during the evening, till they were discovered and
joined by Mr. Allen when the dance was over. (*NA*, pp. 21-3)

In *Cecilia*, the grosser equivalent of this scene is one in which Cecilia
is trying to make tea at a crowded table in Vauxhall:

> Mr. Morrice now brought intelligence that he had secured one side of
> a table which would very well accommodate the ladies; and that the other
> side was only occupied by one gentleman, who, as he was not drinking tea
> himself, would doubtless give up his place when the party appeared.
>
> Miss Larolles then ran back to her own set, and the rest followed Mr.
> Morrice; Mrs. Harrel, Mrs. Mears and Cecilia took their places. The
> gentleman opposite to them proved to be Mr. Meadows: Morrice, there-
> fore, was much deceived in his expectations, for, far from giving up his
> place, he had flung himself all along upon the form in such a lounging
> posture, while he rested one arm upon the table, that not contented with
> merely keeping his own seat, he filled up a space meant for three.
>
> *
>
> The task of making tea fell upon Cecilia, who being somewhat incom-
> moded by the vicinity of her neighbours, Mrs. Mears called out to Mr.
> Meadows, 'Do pray, sir, be so good as to make room for one of us at your
> side.'
>
> Mr. Meadows, who was indolently picking his teeth, and examining
> them with a tooth-pick-case glass, did not, at first, seem to hear her; and
> when she repeated her request, he only looked at her, and said 'Umph?'
>
> 'Now really, Mr. Meadows,' said she, 'when you see any ladies in such
> distress, I wonder how you can forbear helping them.'
>
> 'In distress, are you?' cried he, with a vacant smile, 'pray what's the
> matter?'
>
> 'Don't you see? we are so crowded we can hardly sit.'
>
> 'Can't you?' cried he, 'upon my honour it's very shameful that these
> people don't contrive some seats more convenient.'
>
> 'Yes,' said Mrs. Mears; 'but if you would be so kind as to let somebody
> else sit by you we should not want any contrivance.'
>
> Here Mr. Meadows was seized with a furious fit of yawning, which as
> much diverted Cecilia and Mr. Gosport, as it offended Mrs. Mears, who
> with great displeasure added, 'Indeed, Mr. Meadows, it's very strange
> that you never hear what's said to you.'
>
> 'I beg your pardon,' said he, 'were you speaking to me?' and again
> began picking his teeth.
>
> Morrice, eager to contrast his civility with the inattention of Mr.
> Meadows, now flew round to the other side of the table, and calling out
> 'let *me* help you, Miss Beverley, I can make tea better than anybody,' he

leant over that part of the form which Mr. Meadows had occupied with one of his feet, in order to pour it out himself: but Mr. Meadows, by an unfortunate removal of his foot, bringing him forwarder that he was prepared to go, the tea-pot and its contents were overturned immediately opposite to Cecilia.

Young Delvile, who saw the impending evil, from an impetuous impulse to prevent her suffering by it, hastily drew her back, and bending down before her, secured her preservation by receiving the mischief with which she was threatened. (Vol. I, Bk IV, Chap. ii)

Fanny Burney's scene is at once a display of manners and a farcical exposure of the heroine's dismay. It doesn't matter whether we like to regard Jane Austen's version as a sensitive re-working of Fanny Burney's scene, or an independent instance of a typical social embarrassment. Jane Austen is clearly using a slighter, less comic and less violent event[16] for the purposes of her realistic chronicle of inner and outer life.

The differences in such social chronicles point to one of the chief sources of Jane Austen's flexibility. She applies a very gentle pressure to bring out the minute but real problems of social life. Such nuances can equally divide the interest between the psychological response and the social surface of conduct. In Fanny Burney, the humour and humours of the scene are so strong and prominent – and successfully so for her broad effects – that the heroine's responses are made glaringly obvious. Such social suffering lies on the surface. No one would like to have steaming tea poured over them, and neither the threat nor the rescue conveys anything peculiar to Cecilia alone. But Catherine Morland's diffidence and shyness, companioned by Mrs Allen's bland indifference to anything except the crushing of her gown, is created through small ripples in her mind and feelings. There are no vast disappointments or triumphs, but a faithful record of social responses in this society and for these people.

This notation of nuance is more constant and continuous than the enlarged and emphatic scenes of farce or comedy of manners and humours in *Evelina*, *Cecilia* and *Camilla*. Jane Austen builds up her social surface as steadily and carefully as her characters, through the observation of many such small occasions. We get a much clearer and truer impression of what it must have felt like to make one's début in Bath from the delicately amused record of Catherine's appearance

---

[16] A similar comparison is that of John Thorpe's attentions to Catherine with Dubster's attentions to Camilla.

in the Pump room, than from the grotesque actions in Fanny Burney. Jane Austen's restraint allows for some rudeness and grossness, in John Thorpe for instance, but if we compare him with Fanny Burney's boors, we recognize Jane Austen's fainter, more muted and more naturalistic use of similar materials. Manners are differentiated in *Northanger Abbey* and *Pride and Prejudice* as in *Evelina* or *Camilla*. Politeness, Courtesy, Good Manners, Flirtation, Affectation and Indifference make their appearance in Jane Austen's Bath as in Fanny Burney's London and Bristol. The man who will not dance, the harassed or neglected beauty, the unwantedly attentive gallant, the partner one really longs for, are all present in Fanny Burney's farce and caricatures as in Jane Austen's sensitive analysis.[17] Fops, rakes, quizzes, rattles, boors and flirts surround the superior heroine in the action of both novelists.

D. W. Harding observes[18] that Jane Austen joins caricature and character. It is worth observing the means by which she achieves this fusion since these are essential aspects of her skilled art of modulation. Fanny Burney too could be described as joining caricature and character. (So could Ben Jonson and Congreve.) Cecilia, Evelina and Camilla are the characters in an environment of almost unrelieved caricature. Evelina and Cecilia, though embarrassed, uncertain, fearful, and at times made to look mistaken, awkward and silly, on the whole behave reasonably and sensitively. Everyone else behaves insensitively and stupidly. It is the irrationalities which are caricatured, and the result is a gap which we cross every time we move to the broad humours of the social group. Jane Austen consistently makes a real relationship between her heroines and her more comic characters. The heroine is less impeccable than Fanny Burney's, and the surrounding characters are less grotesque.

The relationship between major and lesser characters in Jane Austen's novels is intricate. The heroines do not stand apart from the group in morally impressive positions, passive or commanding, but partake of its deficiencies. In *Northanger Abbey*, when John Thorpe, Isabella Thorpe and Captain Tilney variously offend against good manners and delicacy, Catherine is brought into close connection with their social sins. Their offences create mild or invisible disturbances in the public scene. Their defections or deviations from good taste and proper conduct weigh heavily on Jane Austen's delicate

[17] Some of them are also present in the real-life anecdotes of the *Letters*.
[18] Op. cit.

scales, but are slight compared with the violence of Fanny Burney's aggressive attentions, assaults and duels. Catherine is amazed when Isabella affects a fidelity to the absent lover, then immediately defects to a new partner, and her innocence is as amusing and at least as instructive as her friend's specious arguments and generous susceptibilities. John Thorpe's assumptions that he has engaged Catherine as a partner are no more ludicrous than her efforts not to attract his attention in the hope that Henry Tilney will get in first. Her praise of Henry Tilney's dancing and her questions to Eleanor Tilney about his partner, 'Do you think her pretty?', are not only as comically vulnerable as anything else that happens in this social drama, but are brought into visible connection with the discords, fears, flirtations, sexual vanities, predatoriness and clandestine energies of the elegant assembly. Jane Austen's dances have been flatteringly elevated by symbolic interpretation [19] but are composed of men and women more or less gracefully chasing and hunting partners. Catherine is no more purely interested in the dance and politeness than anyone else, but she is less hypocritical and fresher in feeling. She even knows that she has 'no fixed opinions', but she is not noticeably less self-deceived in practice than some of the others, and her self-deceptions are made, however gently, the object of satire. Fielding and Fanny Burney usually involve the heroines in the social comedy while at the same time exempting them from strong criticism, satire, or farce. In Jane Austen, everyone is involved and vulnerable. Even the experienced and intelligent Henry Tilney objects to John Thorpe's distractions and interferences and is perhaps not totally in command of himself as he suggestively propounds the famous analogy between the dance and marriage.

Subdued action and vulnerable characters make for flexibility. Even more important is Jane Austen's continuity of feeling. On her début Catherine responds in embarrassment, anxiety, shyness, expectation, pleasure, mild disappointment and relief. The initial stages of her response to Bath merge in a general sense of novelty, enthusiasm and delight which is, as Henry Tilney approvingly declares, the opposite of the prevailing fashionable *ennui*. At the same time, therefore, we become acquainted with the manners of Bath society and with Catherine's sensibility. Her responses are seen and said to be genuine, fresh and unaffected. Her progress of passion

[19] David Daiches, 'Jane Austen, Karl Marx, and the Aristocratic Dance', *American Scholar*, XVII (1947-48), pp. 289-96.

includes a response to social life. Moreover, her feelings are always available, not held up, put aside or generalized while the social scene takes place. They may not always be very strong feelings; Jane Austen truthfully chronicles the realities of mild dismay, disappointment and pleasure in Catherine's first assembly. But such pale feelings are made part of an intelligible and consistent response. They have variety, shape and likelihood. Jane Austen knew, as well as E. M. Forster, that strong feeling is not always called for, nor always available when called for.

There are a few social scenes where the heroine is absent, like the Dashwoods' cupiditinous duet in *Sense and Sensibility*, but the chronicle of feeling is usually a continuous sequence of the heroine's responses in private and public life. There is a typically implicit but emphatic analysis in *Emma*, which illustrates the flexible nature of emotional continuity:

> *She* would notice her; she would improve her; she would detach her from her bad acquaintance, and introduce her into good society; she would form her opinions and her manners. It would be an interesting, and certainly a very kind undertaking; highly becoming her own situation in life, her leisure, and powers.
>
> She was so busy in admiring those soft blue eyes, in talking and listening, and forming all these schemes in the in-betweens, that the evening flew away at a very unusual rate; and the supper-table, which always closed such parties, and for which she had been used to sit and watch the due time, was all set out and ready, and moved forwards to the fire, before she was aware. With an alacrity beyond the common impulse of a spirit which yet was never indifferent to the credit of doing every thing well and attentively, with the real good-will of a mind delighted with its own ideas, did she then do all the honours of the meal. . . . (*E*, pp. 23-4)

Emma has been talking to Harriet Smith while her father entertains the older guests; we are deep in her excitement and pleasure as she begins to fill the emptiness left by Miss Taylor's marriage with her intentions of improving Harriet. She is so absorbed that for once she forgets to notice the time. Being Emma, socially adroit and considerate, she has to move swiftly out of her private fantasy and attend to the guests. She needs all her energy and tact in order to counter her father's valetudinarian hospitality, which is intent on discouraging the pleasures of the traditional, attractive but perilous supper-table. Jane Austen not only keeps up Emma's feelings of pleasure and interest in her schemes but gives them shape in the demands of the social scene, observing that she is especially energetic and elated as a hostess because of the headiness of new projects. It is a quiet registration of cause and effect, beautifully characteristic of Jane Austen's way of changing the focus. She does not switch feeling on and off, but diverts it from private to social life, marking its course, character, cause and effect. Her social scenes are accordingly characterized by the private feeling, as they are linked to inner life in a real observation of the shifts and causes of roles and responses. Jane Austen marks the raptness of Emma's imaginative enterprise. The inner life is swept with excitement, so she throws herself into social activity. Just as her heroines are not exempt from the social comedy, but forced to make their contribution to satire or humour, so they are also carefully designed to carry the life of personal feelings into the social scene. There are not social feelings and personal feelings, but the responses of individual characters to social and personal relationships. Social life is psychologized. Private life is related to environment. Implicit in the evening party at Hartfield is the analysis of Emma's imaginative history. It may seem a far cry from a scene of hospitality to fantasies of power, but to connect the two is the business of Jane Austen's imagination. Such occasions, such needs and such solutions have helped to encourage Emma in her self-flattering energies and creations. Virginia Woolf showed the kinship between the artist's and the hostess's unifying powers in Mrs Dalloway's party-giving and Mrs Ramsay's strenuously created harmony at the dinner-table. Less inclined to flatter her heroine and the feats of hospitality, Jane Austen draws a similar analogy and then goes beyond analogy to mark cause and effect.

Jane Austen's profound interest in social roles and functions links her individual portraits with her presentation of society in *Mansfield Park*. We move from a clash of interests and tempers during the discussion of the Mansfield theatricals:

'Fanny,' cried Tom Bertram, from the other table, where the conference was eagerly carrying on, and the conversation incessant, 'we want your services.'

Fanny was up in a moment, expecting some errand, for the habit of employing her in that way was not yet overcome in spite of all that Edmund could do.

'Oh! we do not want to disturb you from your seat. We do not want your *present* services. We shall only want you in our play. You must be Cottager's wife.'

'Me!' cried Fanny, sitting down again with a most frightened look. 'Indeed you must excuse me. I could not act any thing if you were to give me the world. No, indeed, I cannot act.'

'Indeed but you must, for we cannot excuse you. It need not frighten you; it is a nothing of a part, a mere nothing, not above half a dozen speeches altogether, and it will not much signify if nobody hears a word you say, so you may be as creepmouse as you like, but we must have you to look at.'

'If you are afraid of half a dozen speeches,' cried Mr. Rushworth, 'what would you do with such a part as mine? I have forty-two to learn.'

'It is not that I am afraid of learning by heart,' said Fanny, shocked to find herself at that moment the only speaker in the room, and to feel that almost every eye was upon her; 'but I really cannot act.' (*MP*, pp. 145-6)

The scene is not only a typically incisive piece of social drama and criticism, but turns on the analysis of social roles. Mrs Norris is always insisting that Fanny should play the role of the poor relation, humble, grateful, helpful, obedient, even servile. On this occasion Tom more covertly makes the same suggestion. It is a lowly role and small part he asks Fanny to play, and it is a part of Fanny's problem that she has been encouraged in such low expectations. She is Emma's opposite, never flattered by her own powers and superiority, but accepting the powers and patronage of her spoilt cousins and despotic aunt with genuine gratitude, modesty and timidity. This occasion presents a crisis, and involves the first conflict about her social role. To be a creepmouse might be to obey, or to retreat from publicity. Her diffidence makes it almost unimaginable for her to perform, compounded as it is of an integrity which cannot assume roles, and a fearfulness which dare not act in public. But her diffidence also partakes of her habitual gratitude and timidity. This refusal marks an important stage in her process of growing up, showing through action and symbol that she can shed servility.

But Jane Austen makes it very difficult for us to chart her heroine's progress. She confuses the issue, refuses to elevate Fanny and eventually shows her agreeing to act. Fanny cannot be entirely exempt from powerful social pressures, though her author kindly rescues her from action, contriving the arrival of Sir Thomas Bertram to make the performance unnecessary.[20] This capitulation prepares us for the author's insistence that Fanny would have married Henry Crawford if Edmund had married Mary. Both suggestions of social compromise

[20] See Stuart M. Tave, *Some Words of Jane Austen* (Chicago and London, 1973), p. 192.

bring this not-too-perfect heroine into the highroad of public life. Fanny retreats into her solitary East room, to reflect and choose, perhaps the first [21] of a long line of nineteenth-century heroines who make such moral retreats into privacy – Jane Eyre, Lucy Snowe, Maggie Tulliver, Dorothea Brooke and Isabel Archer. It is typical of Jane Austen to show the call from society to solitude, where oppression is relieved, space made for reflection and decision.

But Fanny's solitude is furnished with social symbols and is, therefore, no pure retreat or sanctuary. In the East room are the reminders and relics of the family's childhood, the discarded stool, the transparencies, and Tom's promiscuously generous presents – the table covered with workboxes. Drawn up like the ranks of an opposing army are the things that represent Fanny's independence, her books, plants and works of charity.[22] Jane Austen's flexible medium is not simply made up of a continuous track of feeling. She shows Fanny's deep stream of feeling in the social conflict in the warm drawing-room and the social conflict alive in the cold East room. Her heroine cannot retire from social pressures or dispense with social symbols.

When Marianne Dashwood breaks down at the evening party in John Dashwood's house in Harley Street, it is because she has made a desperate effort to come straight from her unrestrained, wretched solitude to the social scene. She is at best disinclined to make polite efforts in society, preferring books or music to polite conversation and cards, and she is here at her worst, edging a little further beyond the pale of social propriety. She had behaved badly on other social occasions, and justified the behaviour with a mixture of valid criticism and self-indulgent superiority. This breakdown marks the climax of her social subversions. It is fully intelligible because we have seen her in the strain and ease of solitude. Marianne's privacies of grief have been no preparation for society, and collapse is inevitable. The handling of the psychology of social response is typically complex. It is Marianne's consistent refusal to control herself and com-

---

[21] The habit of reflection begins very early, in *Catharine, or the Bower, Volume the Third, MW*, ed. R. W. Chapman (Oxford, 1954): 'To this Bower, which terminated in a very pleasant and retired walk in her Aunt's Garden she always wandered whenever anything disturbed her, and it possessed such a charm over her senses, as constantly to tranquillize her mind and quiet her spirits—Solitude & reflection might perhaps have had the same effect in her Bed Chamber, yet Habit had so strengthened the idea which Fancy had first suggested, that such a thought never occurred to Kitty, who was firmly persuaded that her Bower alone could restore her to herself.' (p. 193)　　　　[22] See p. 154 below.

promise her romantic radicalism in society that has made self-control impossible, in solitude or in her sister's company. We are probably inclined to welcome the subversive scene which effectively breaks the smooth and specious surface of decorum and falsehood. But Jane Austen refuses to let us share Marianne's complacency. If we are tempted to applaud her for explosively destroying polite hypocrisy and acquisitiveness, we are held back by the knowledge that Marianne's violence, like some of its political analogues, hurts guilty and innocent alike.

Richard Simpson acknowledged Jane Austen's sense of the individual as a social being:

> It is her thorough consciousness that man is a social being, and that apart from society there is not even the individual. She was too great a realist to abstract and isolate the individual, and to give a portrait of him in the manner of Theophrastus or La Bruyère. Even as a unit, man is only known to her in the process of his formation by social influences.
>
> (*Critical Heritage*, No. 44, p. 249)

Solitude and society are set side by side, ensuring reflection on the response to both, and on the connections between responses. Between the public scenes which analyse many kinds of structure and relationship, Jane Austen places the conversations of kin and friendship. The novelist's concern with the social narrative makes a strong link between solitude, intimate conversation and the crowd.

Covert aggressions run through the conversation of the evening party, and the confidences which Lucy Steele forces on Elinor. The well-meaning and indiscreet outbursts of Marianne and her mother are part of the continuity of event and argument. Flattery, gossip, idle chat, boast, innuendo and insult mark the morality of the group or the crowd in essentially social ways, conveniently covered by the surface of pleasure and politeness, stimulated by sociability and performance. Mary Crawford is too polite to say outright that Mrs Norris is being hostile to Fanny, so takes refuge in a euphemism which Fanny will read as sympathetic: 'this *place* is too hot for me'.(*MP*, p. 147) Her social self, which can be perfectly generous when generosity costs nothing, or self-excusingly grasping when kindness would be too expensive, is seen as making good use of that wit which on other occasions is cheap and insensitive, ('. . . my home at my uncle's brought me acquainted with a circle of admirals. Of *Rears*, and *Vices*, I saw enough' [*MP*, p. 60]). The individual styles of feeling run through the social and the intimate conversations. The social conversation may be charged with private complicity and persuasion. Captain Wentworth asks Anne to stay behind at Lyme Regis and help to nurse Louisa, Elizabeth Bennet and her aunt talk to the housekeeper at Pemberley, Anne tries to draw out Admiral Croft about Captain Wentworth's response to Louisa's engagement, Lucy Steele listens to Sir John Middleton teasing Elinor about the beau whose name begins with F, and Anne and Captain Wentworth talk about music in the interval of the concert in Bath. These conversations have the form and content of perfectly conventional gossip, chat, teasing and news, but their discourse is charged with the private meanings the reader has learnt to impute to these speakers and listeners.

The subtexts of social occasion were not invented by Jane Austen, but she makes a fuller and more subtle use of them than anyone since Shakespeare. Sometimes she draws attention to the private thoughts and feelings, as when we are told what Anne was thinking when she questioned Admiral Croft. Sometimes we make the inference for ourselves. The author does not tell us what Julia Bertram was thinking when she joked about the altar in Sotherton chapel, why Edward Ferrars exclaimed 'Devonshire!' at the beginning of *Sense and Sensibility* (p. 25), and why Mr Knightley was so angry with Emma's idle expectations of Frank Churchill. Jane Austen uses explicitness and implication, unspectacularly and quietly. We have only to compare the thinness of the social dialogues in Fanny Burney, and even in Richardson, to see what density she adds to the psychology of the social scene.

The social groups are variously structured. Jane Austen restricted her presentation and analysis of society, but her group-dramas often make implicit analyses of social response and interaction. She composes her groups of minds, feelings, morals and styles, and sets them in action. They interact to offend, match, compromise and change each other. The group is examined, not merely displayed, but her examination is overt and implicit. Her groups are never shaped by the simple conflicts or convergences of humours as they are in Richardson and Fanny Burney, and the comic drama of the eighteenth and seventeenth centuries. She is concerned to compare the behaviour of the individual in the group with his behaviour when he is alone or with his intimates. Some of Jane Austen's characters are only vital in groups, like the simplified, almost caricatured figures of Mr and Mrs John Dashwood, Mr and Mrs Elton, Mrs Norris and Miss Bates. We should hesitate to call these caricatures or humours. They are characterized by some kind of inner life and do not simply answer to Ben Jonson's formula of 'some one peculiar quality'[23] which distorts and simplifies the whole affective life. They do show a tendency to behave in a predictable, bizarre and biased fashion, and their behaviour is wholly public. The hollow Dashwoods, Steeles and Eltons are happily composed in pairs. The pairing aids social generalization but also gives them companionship in monstrosity, and an appearance of human relationship. Jane Austen knows that Fanny Dashwood is a 'strong caricature' of her husband and so encourages him in callousness and meanness. She creates a whole scene to show how this can come about, but its ends are not totally satiric. It manages to convince us that the 'caricatures' are wholly dynamic, made of alterable flesh and blood, and not 'cut in marble'[24] any more than the realistic heroines and heroes. The Eltons suggest a hideous if amusing renewal and doubling in their marital complicity, but this too is more than the comedy of humours. They seem so very married that we have a sense of congeniality and invigorated relationship. Both are affected, mercenary, vulgar and aggressive. Both are proud, in different ways, of their association with Mr Knightley. Mrs Elton's fuss about knowing what her 'caro sposo' and 'Knightley' are doing in their parish meeting has the true ring of possessive, ingratiating and ambitious wifehood. We are thus reminded that Mr Elton did have a professional life, and was different, as Mr Knightley told Emma, in the company of men. (One supposes him to have substituted boastfulness for the crude flattery and hypocrisy which makes Emma wince – and makes us wince more subtly as we see what she is willing to accept for Harriet.)[25] We know what is in Emma's mind when she acutely imagines – and she does not always misuse her imagination – what Mr Elton will have told his bride about her and Harriet. The sense of their marital intimacy makes them more complicated, and more deeply and animatedly unpleasant. The social types have a fringe of life, implicit but not shown, which trails the suggestion of complex experience.

The same fringe of reality is trailed by more attractive and engaging characters like Miss Bates. She has some kinship with Fanny

---

[23] *Everyman Out of His Humour.*

[24] George Eliot, *Middlemarch*, Chap. 72.

[25] See Ronald Blythe's introduction to the Penguin edition of *Emma* (Harmondsworth, 1966), p. 20.

Price in appealing through a degree of self-knowledge: 'I am rather a talker, you know'. After Emma's insult she reflects painfully on what it is to be a bore; if she did not, Emma's offensiveness would not be so serious. It is not only her kindness and good nature, but the sense that we are given of an inner life, which makes her quite distinct from the humours of Richardson, Fanny Burney or even Dickens. It is such shadowed depths which make the fusion of major and minor characters successful. These creatures of comedy or satire are a little more than caricatures, and the surplus life makes a vast difference. It makes for a continuity of character, even amongst those who are never actually seen in private. We feel that they are all capable of an inner life.

Jane Austen's analysis of the private life depends largely on the projection of social feeling, and her presentation of the public life on continuities and implications of analysis and presentation. But there is another strand in the web of social and solitary life. Jane Austen's creation of environment depends very much less than any later novelist on description.[26] The visible world is presented to us almost exclusively through the responses of the characters, and these responses fully suggest the presence of streets, buildings, rooms and objects. The private life, as we have seen in Fanny's retreat to the East room, is given a social environment solidly and specifically substantiated. The environment is not made up of people alone. It is a peopled universe, but as the narrator in Samuel Beckett's most abstract novel, *The Unnameable*, knows, where there are men there are objects. The shared environment is a set, with scenery and properties. The dramatic analogy isn't quite good enough, since it suggests only the common ground and things that form and link the private person and the communal life, but not the personal penumbra. Each private person carries with him a collection of things, his roof, his home or homelessness, his furniture and private possessions. Each person carries with him an implacable reminder of his social existence. He creates personal symbols – Harriet's precious treasures of the courtplaster and pencil stub, Fanny's geranium, Mary's harp. These things are all commodities, even though some are purely social accessories, others more private symbols. This is a world of purchase. It is also a world where the individual communicates with others, even in

---

[26] Her advice to her niece Anna Austen is well known, '. . . your descriptions are often more minute than will be liked. You give too many particulars of right hand & left'. (*Letters*, p. 401)

the most intimate relations, through manufactured things. Harriet's treasures are filched, not given, like her love. Emma's picture of Harriet is as imperfect in execution, as it is dubious in purpose. Frank Churchill's present of the pianoforte is a frivolous, self-regarding gift, like the thoughtless alibi of the London hair-cut which he manufactures to cover it. These things give the novel its solidity of specification and link people through the social actions of purchase, donation, acquisition and display. The most private relic or fetish has its social significance.

Throughout the solitary and the social scene, the author is in charge. She is probably the most discreet guide in the English novel. She describes sparingly, and generalizes only on a very limited number of topics. Such modesty seemed strange to Victorian readers accustomed to the uninhibited emotional and moral flights of Thackeray, Dickens and George Eliot, at their best and worst. A reviewer of 1866 said that she had no 'maternal love' for her characters,[27] and Mrs Oliphant, in 1870, suggested that 'she can scarcely be said to be sorry for them'.[28] Jane Austen's voice has a steadiness, neutrality and flexibility which allows her most unobtrusively to present the private and public world. She can say briefly, in a parenthesis and aside, where George Eliot would give a paragraph: 'Her happiness on this occasion was very much à-la-mortal, finely chequered.' (*MP*, p. 274) The restraint of the passing remark shows a social tact and ease in understatement which does not pass over the poignancy of its admission. That poignancy, sharply observed, is not dwelt on but accepted. This is what life is like, it says more gracefully, why expect anything different? It goes without saying any more than five words, edged into a sentence whose business is descriptive. The tones of this unexcited voice are heard in some comments which are more conspicuously placed, like the famous opening sentence of *Pride and Prejudice*: 'It is a truth universally acknowledged, that a single man in possession of a good fortune, must be in want of a wife.' Here the author's voice totally engrosses the ironic generalization. It is of that species of irony which appears to take for granted an amusing or appalling opinion. After she occupies a whole first sentence, the narrator quickly moves to share the responsibility with her characters. Mr Bennet speaks for all the irony of the admission, and his wife represents all its face-value:

[27] Southam, *Critical Heritage*, p. 213.
[28] Ibid., p. 216.

'A single man of large fortune. . . . What a fine thing for our girls!'
'How so? how can it affect them?'
'My dear Mr. Bennet,' replied his wife, 'how can you be so tiresome!
You must know that I am thinking of his marrying one of them.'
'Is that his design in settling here?'

The first sentence of *Mansfield Park* is even quieter:

About thirty years ago, Miss Maria Ward of Huntingdon, with only seven
thousand pounds, had the good luck to captivate Sir Thomas Bertram, of
Mansfield Park, in the county of Northampton, and to be thereby raised
to the rank of a baronet's lady, with all the comforts and consequences of
an handsome house and large income.

It injects its ironic and moral viewpoint into four inserted words,
'good luck to captivate'. The narrator's responsibility is transferred
and irony deepened as the true and specious values go their all too
separate ways:

All Huntingdon exclaimed on the greatness of the match, and her uncle,
the lawyer, himself, allowed her to be at least three thousand pound short
of any equitable claim to it.

After Jane Austen, George Eliot was to develop a dramatized
version of such irony for similar purposes of generalizing and rebuking
a social response. Jane Austen criticizes society through the drama of
complex and particular types and groups, and the shy or sly irony of
her rare authorial comments helps her to state a viewpoint without
occupying too much space. Her moral comments are weighty, but
never heavy. In her narrative voice, in the free indirect style in which
she shares commentary with the characters, and in her habit of quick,
vivid summary, she moves lightly and unobtrusively from character
to group, close-up to distance. Like all the threads that join her private
and public worlds, that of her commentary is so fine that its stitches
scarcely show. But the fineness is the product of great and delicate
skill.

# II

# The Feelings and the Passions

'The Passions are perfectly unknown to her', wrote Charlotte Brontë to W. S. Williams, publisher's reader for Smith and Elder, in April 1850. She went on: 'she rejects even a speaking acquaintance with that stormy Sisterhood; even to the Feelings she vouchsafes no more than an occasional graceful but distant recognition.'[1] George Henry Lewes had tried in vain to convince Charlotte Brontë of her predecessor's genius, but even he, who declared in 1847 that Fielding and Jane Austen were our greatest novelists, and in 1852 that Jane Austen was 'the greatest artist' who had ever written, admitted that she could only be thought of as Shakespeare's 'younger sister' if we 'set aside his passion'.[2] Throughout the nineteenth century, when passion was assumed to be a required constituent of novels, and indeed in the twentieth century too, we can find repeated complaints that it was not to be found in Jane Austen. Strong feeling, emotional depth, sublimity, elevation, and soul, critics objected or admitted, are absent in her six major novels. Although recent critics have more thoughtfully scrutinized her powers, it is her rational and intellectual genius which has attracted most analytical attention, even in such thoroughly argued and felt appreciations as those of D. W. Harding and Tony Tanner.[3]

Jane Austen frequently laughs at the affectations of feeling, as Dickens was to do even more loudly after her, though the attack on protestations of Heart is scarcely a sign of heartlessness. She jokes about the Novel of Passion through one of her most brilliantly silly

[1] Southam, *Critical Heritage*, p. 128.

[2] Ibid., pp. 124, 140, 130.

[3] See Harding, op. cit. Also his introduction to the Penguin edition of *Persuasion* (Harmondsworth, 1965) and Tony Tanner's introduction to the Penguin edition of *Pride and Prejudice* (Harmondsworth, 1972). Two exceptions are the American critics, Howard Babb (*Jane Austen's Novels; the Fabric of Dialogue*, Hamden, Conn., 1967) and Stuart Tave, op. cit.

characters, Sir Edward Denham in *Sanditon*, who contrives to make
even Mr Collins of *Pride and Prejudice* appear capable of argument
and illustration: 'The Novels which I approve are such . . . as exhibit
the progress of strong Passion from the first Germ of incipient
Susceptibility to the utmost Energies of Reason half-dethroned. . . .'
(*MW*, p. 403) On the only important occasion when Reason is
threatened in Jane Austen, in the almost willed and self-destructive
delirium of Marianne Dashwood in *Sense and Sensibility*, it is most
clear that there is nothing admirable in the sickness. The common
cases of dethroned Reason are like those of Mr Collins, Mrs Bennet, or
Lady Catherine de Bourgh, whose lack of feeling is made plain by
their lack of mind. Such characters have a disguised feeling for self,
but the feelings they display are dishonest and pretentious. Jane
Austen does indeed create a progress of passion, which can be
described in a cooler version of Sir Edward's description as a development from the first germ of sensibility to the utmost energies of feeling. It is a development of passion inevitably accompanied by an
intellectual growth. Jane Austen could no more ignore passion than
any other great novelist, but she was consistently and lucidly interested in people possessed both of strong feeling and a knowledge of
their feelings. To be able to be rational and passionate, and to look
rationally at the passions, was her ideal requirement. As well as being
a stern requirement, it is a highly imaginative one. Sir Edward Denham, who is as intellectually deficient as he is emotionally vacuous,
merely mimics passion, almost as funnily and feebly as Mr Collins
when he neatly rounds off his proposal to Elizabeth with the
announced intention of assuring her 'in the most animated language
of the violence of my affection'.

Dickens's criticism of affected feeling is often unfortunately self-
accusatory; his somewhat uneven powers of expressing emotional
energy, especially the sexual feelings of desire, affection and esteem,
are often all too glaringly illuminated by the piercing light of his own
satire. His ridiculous aspirants to passion, like Augustus Moddle in
*Martin Chuzzlewit*, or Mrs Skewton in *Dombey and Son*, speak an
intense, affected, and lofty language which is dangerously close to the
style of his more sincere characters, like Tom Pinch or Florence
Dombey. Jane Austen discriminates with crystalline clarity between
false and real passions. Real feeling is never unintelligent, even in
Catherine Morland or Marianne Dashwood, where it may occasionally gather force from a warped or suspended judgement. The energy

of feeling is always dramatized in people who have minds,[4] even if they may be doing their best, as Marianne does, not to use them fully, scrupulously, and sustainedly. It is admittedly very hard to overstate Jane Austen's emphasis on rational control: she not only anticipates George Eliot's insistent and central concern for self-knowledge, but also her total analysis of intelligence. But whatever the importance of argument and idea in the novel's action, and however imperatively argument and idea are demanded of the central character, Jane Austen's people are always creatures of strong feeling.

The heroines and heroes are not specialists in feeling. Humours are reserved for the irrational. Jane Austen never thinks of her heroines as 'frail vessels', as George Eliot and Henry James did, and they are all capable of strengths of feeling. The feeling she is most concerned with is sexual love, but never exclusively. The course of true love defines the course of the passions in each novel, but she takes care to diffuse her passionate energies. The heroines and heroes are strong in family feeling, pity, jealousy, and various other less definable elations. It is hard to be selective when trying to illustrate the passions in Jane Austen, as in any great novelist. The novel at its best does not turn on the passions one at a time, like some of the more simple catalogues allowed in drama or poetry. Collins's 'The Passions: an Ode for Music', for instance, is an influential list of feelings – Fear, Anger, Despair, Grief, Hope, Pleasure, Revenge, Woe, Pity, Jealousy, Love, Melancholy, Cheerfulness, Joy – who all throng round Music:

> Exulting, trembling, raging, fainting,
> Possest beyond the Muse's Painting;
> By turns they felt the glowing Mind,
> Disturb'd, delighted, rais'd, refin'd.

The 'real' novelist, as D. H. Lawrence was to insist, educates us by showing a life of feeling so complex that classification is defied and denied. It may seem perverse to invoke Lawrence here, since he notoriously thought of Jane Austen as 'that old maid . . . knowing in apartness' (*A Propos of Lady Chatterley's Lover*), but he also spoke of her more admiringly, even going so far as to call her emotions vivid. Jane Austen anticipates Lawrence – also John Stuart Mill, George Eliot and E. M. Forster – in her implicit insistence that education must attend to heart as well as head. Lawrence maintained that the

---

[4] I hope the apparent exception of Lady Charlotte Bertram's, 'Dear Fanny, now I shall be comfortable,' supports my argument.

likeliest vehicle for emotional instruction was the novel – the 'real' novel – and Jane Austen is one of the real novelists who make his meaning clear.

'Listen in,' Lawrence advises in his essay 'The Novel and the Feelings' (published in *Phoenix*, 1936), 'listen to . . . the low, calling cries of the characters, as they wander in the dark woods of their destiny.' In the novels of Jane Austen the characters sometimes wander in dark woods, wildernesses, shrubberies, and hedgerows, but their low calls of feeling are often heard – low indeed – in the noise and glare of pump rooms, drawing-rooms and dining-rooms. They call, unmistakably, in expressions of feeling which are diffuse, confused, bewildered, generating more feeling but also generating reflection and question. They are no doubt often too cerebral and analytic for Lawrence's tastes, but the intensity and growing-power of their progress of passion depends on exactly that complexity which Lawrence had in mind when he spoke of the dangers of simplifying and trying to frame, tame, and name the passions:

> We see love, like a woolly lamb; or like a decorative decadent panther in Paris clothes: according as it is sacred or profane. We see hate, like a dog chained to a kennel. We see fear, like a shivering monkey. We see anger, like a bull with a ring through his nose, and greed, like a pig. Our emotions are our domesticated animals, noble like the horse, timid like the rabbit, but all completely at our service. The rabbit goes into the pot, and the horse into the shafts.

Jane Austen occasionally makes unpleasant characters subject to ruling passions or humours. Greed and Anger rule Mrs Norris, Pride determines every act and speech of Lady Catherine de Bourgh. These are perversions of feeling. Such caricatures of human spirit are outlined in terms of hardened and narrowed feeling, which impel and imprison the human being. This hard and fast feeling usefully defines and surrounds the more open emotional life of the other characters. When Fanny comes up against Mrs Norris, or Elizabeth Bennet confronts Lady Catherine, there is a contrast and clash of free with fixed feelings, as well as of mind with mindlessness. More common in Jane Austen are those characters whose feelings have been constricted or inhibited rather than taken over by a ruling passion. Neither Mr Bennet nor Sir Thomas Bertram is shown as a passionate man, but rather as one who has been forced to reduce and control feeling. The conventionality of the one, and the satirical self-indulgence of the other, ought not to blind us to the cause and effect implicit in their similar emotional careers. Jane Austen makes very little explicit reference to their sexual passions, but we know them both to be very intelligent men who have married very stupid women. This tells us something of the cause and effect of their restricted emotions. The reign of reason in each case goes beyond the suggestions of intellectual make-up and social background. Jane Austen knew more about her characters than she showed explicitly. Although we should resist the temptation to speculate too widely about the vitality of characters in fiction, such speculation can usefully suggest the depths that lie beneath the revealed surface. Even Jane Austen's relatively simple characters may be created so completely that they answer to a whole range of psychologically speculative questions. Jane Austen had thoroughly imagined the progress of feeling that led to, and led from, these two unfortunate and unfortunately typical marriages.

The heroines are surrounded by characters whose life of feeling is hardened, perverted, or affected, but the effect is not simply that of psychological contrast. The opposition of characters sets surface against depth; it also attempts to define and display enough cases to create a sense of social typicality. Perversions of feeling impersonate an environment, and against it we study the hard life of true feeling. Jane Austen, again like Dickens, shows an acquisitive, mercenary, and socially stratified society, where feeling is a highly priced commodity, greatly praised but not greatly valued. This commodity is almost entirely designed for the marriage-market, but Jane Austen's portrait of a culture goes beyond the institution of marriage. Affectations of love go together with other affectations – in art, education, and social intercourse. Since the world she presents is so much a woman's world, it is tempting to see the analysis of feeling as centred in sexual feeling, and to set all the corruptions of the heart in the context of her love-stories, as permutations of the central theme of marriage. Although we can know a society by its myths of love, we can only appreciate Jane Austen's opposition to the values of her society if we look hard at the apparent balance of cause and effect. The society that markets sexual feeling, markets other kinds of feeling too; the feeling for nature, for religion, for the poor, and for learning and art are all suspect. If love is affected, so also may be pity, enthusiasm, piety, and admiration.

Jane Austen is chiefly concerned to tell a love-story, to show the dangers and difficulties of being a heroine. D. W. Harding praises her success in bringing together the character and the caricature, as I have said, and one reason for success in this hard enterprise seems to lie in her power to suggest and sustain the course of feeling.

The so-called caricatures are analysed and dramatized so as to suggest a potentially full emotional life which has been distorted and restricted. At the beginning of *Persuasion,* for example, the sharp, clear-outlined caricature of Sir Walter Elliot makes it very plain that we have before us a case of the perversion of feeling, the channelling of various emotions in one too narrow but powerfully flowing current: Sir Walter reads his favourite book, the Baronetage, where 'he found occupation for an idle hour'. There follows a list of his diverted emotions:

> Sir Walter Elliot, of Kellynch Hall, in Somersetshire, was a man who, for his own amusement, never took up any book but the Baronetage; there he found occupation for an idle hour, and consolation in a distressed one; there his faculties were roused into admiration and respect, by contemplating the limited remnant of the earliest patents; there any unwelcome sensations, arising from domestic affairs, changed naturally into pity and contempt, as he turned over the almost endless creations of the last century—and there, if every other leaf were powerless, he could read his own history with an interest which never failed. . . . (*P,* p. 3)

Like the beginning of *Volpone* it shows a clear case of the single passion absorbing the normal emotional energies of distress, admiration, respect, pity, and contempt. The less conspicuously monstrous case of Elizabeth, introduced three or four pages later, is also analysed in terms of feeling:

> Elizabeth did not quite equal her father in personal contentment. Thirteen years had seen her mistress of Kellynch Hall, presiding and directing with a self-possession and decision which could never have given the idea of her being younger than she was. For thirteen years had she been doing the honours, and laying down the domestic law at home, and leading the way to the chaise and four, and walking immediately after Lady Russell out of all the drawing-rooms and dining-rooms in the country. Thirteen winters' revolving frosts had seen her opening every ball of credit which a scanty neighbourhood afforded; and thirteen springs shewn their blossoms, as she travelled up to London with her father, for a few weeks annual enjoyment of the great world. She had the remembrance of all this; she had the consciousness of being nine-and-twenty, to give her some regrets and some apprehensions. She was fully satisfied of being still quite as handsome as ever; but she felt her approach to the years of danger, and would have rejoiced to be certain of being properly

solicited by baronet-blood within the next twelvemonth or two. Then might she again take up the book of books with as much enjoyment as in her early youth; but now she liked it not. Always to be presented with the date of her own birth, and see no marriage follow but that of a youngest sister, made the book an evil; and more than once, when her father had left it open on the table near her, had she closed it, with averted eyes, and pushed it away. (*P*, pp. 6-7)

'Regrets', 'apprehensions', 'satisfied', 'felt her approach to the years of danger', 'rejoiced', 'enjoyment', 'liked it not' are direct descriptions of feeling. There is also the more subtle implicit account of feeling through action in the 'thirteen winters' revolving frosts' which had seen her opening local balls, and the 'averted eyes' with which she closes the Baronetage and pushes it away. Feeling is stated and acted.

The characters who play a central part in the novels are those whose emotional progress is shown in most detail and with most drama. Their progress of feeling, which moves like a blood-vessel through the novels' action, is continuous in circulation. In neither form nor feeling do we find anything resembling Sir Edward Denham's Reason half-dethroned, but in both there is strong emotion or passion. Feelings may be private or secret but move eventually into relationships, passion finding resonance in reciprocity. Jane Austen is very far from 'knowing in apartness'. On the contrary, she blends thinking with feeling, valuing the passionate mind, showing its development as an outward movement towards outlets and unions. Although it is true that her strongest passions are usually solitary and private, inner and hidden, the conclusions and culminations of the novels make it plain that emotional solitude is an undesirable and painful deprivation. The life and progress of feelings are essentially social in the novels of Jane Austen.

In all the novels the stream of feeling is sufficiently marked in its private moments for us to be aware of its constant motion beneath the formal social surfaces. In assemblies, balls, dances, dinner-parties, suppers, parties of pleasure, visits and chance meetings, the bland and polite conventions are threatened. Passion is subversive. Marianne bursts into tears when Mrs Ferrars, rich old enemy of love, snubs Elinor. The drama of strain and breakdown plays realistically into the hands of social criticism. Jane Austen here uses a collapse of nerve and formality to suggest, most decorously, the shams and distortions which uphold decorum. Marianne moves half-consciously to attack the acquisitiveness of which she is an unknowing victim:

'Hum'—said Mrs. Ferrars—'very pretty,'—and without regarding them at all, returned them to her daughter.

Perhaps Fanny thought for a moment that her mother had been quite rude enough,—for, colouring a little, she immediately said,

'They are very pretty, ma'am—an't they?' But then again, the dread of having been too civil, too encouraging herself, probably came over her, for she presently added,

'Do you not think they are something in Miss Morton's style of paint-ing, ma'am?—*She does* paint most delightfully!—How beautifully her last landscape is done!'

'Beautifully indeed! But *she* does every thing well.'

Marianne could not bear this.—She was already greatly displeased with Mrs. Ferrars; and such ill-timed praise of another, at Elinor's expense, though she had not any notion of what was principally meant by it, provoked her immediately to say with warmth,

'This is admiration of a very particular kind!—what is Miss Morton to us?—who knows, or who cares, for her?—it is Elinor of whom *we* think and speak.'

And so saying, she took the screens out of her sister-in-law's hands, to admire them herself as they ought to be admired.

Mrs. Ferrars looked exceedingly angry, and drawing herself up more stiffly than ever, pronounced in retort this bitter phillippic; 'Miss Morton is Lord Morton's daughter.'

Fanny looked very angry too, and her husband was all in a fright at his sister's audacity. Elinor was much more hurt by Marianne's warmth, than she had been by what produced it; but Colonel Brandon's eyes, as they were fixed on Marianne, declared that he noticed only what was amiable in it, the affectionate heart which could not bear to see a sister slighted in the smallest point.

Marianne's feelings did not stop here. The cold insolence of Mrs. Ferrars's general behaviour to her sister, seemed, to her, to foretel such difficulties and distresses to Elinor, as her own wounded heart taught her to think of with horror; and urged by a strong impulse of affectionate sensibility, she moved, after a moment, to her sister's chair, and putting one arm round her neck, and one cheek close to her's, said in a low, but eager, voice,

'Dear, dear Elinor, don't mind them. Don't let them make *you* un-happy.'

She could say no more; her spirits were quite overcome, and hiding her face on Elinor's shoulder, she burst into tears. (*SS*, pp. 235-6)

Jane Fairfax turns, like other women in these novels, to Nature and the open view of the sweet English scene, and has abruptly to leave the party at Donwell Abbey, and run off in the heat of the day from Mrs Elton's patronage and her own clandestine griefs and anxieties:

'Will you be so kind,' said she, 'when I am missed, as to say that I am gone home?—I am going this moment.—My aunt is not aware how late it is, nor how long we have been absent—but I am sure we shall be wanted, and I am determined to go directly.—I have said nothing about it to any body. It would only be giving trouble and distress. Some are gone to the ponds, and some to the lime walk. Till they all come in I shall not be missed; and when they do, will you have the goodness to say that I am gone?'

'Certainly, if you wish it;—but you are not going to walk to Highbury alone?'

'Yes—what should hurt me?—I walk fast. I shall be at home in twenty minutes.'

'But it is too far, indeed it is, to be walking quite alone. Let my father's servant go with you.—Let me order the carriage. It can be round in five minutes.'

'Thank you, thank you—but on no account.—I would rather walk.— And for *me* to be afraid of walking alone!—I, who may so soon have to guard others!'

She spoke with great agitation; and Emma very feelingly replied, 'That can be no reason for your being exposed to danger now. I must order the carriage. The heat even would be danger.—You are fatigued already.'

'I am'—she answered—'I am fatigued; but it is not the sort of fatigue— quick walking will refresh me.—Miss Woodhouse, we all know at times what it is to be wearied in spirits. Mine, I confess, are exhausted. The greatest kindness you can show me, will be to let me have my own way, and only say that I am gone when it is necessary.' (*E*, pp. 362-3)

At Box Hill Frank Churchill's nervous innuendo and flirtation infect Emma. One failure in control leads to another, offensiveness and discord sadly disrupting the festive intentions of leisure, play, harmony and exploration. Jane Austen, like that later great satirist and social chronicler, Thackeray, knew that the heightened and heady air of parties, even such unorgiastic ones of Highbury and Donwell, could stimulate revulsions and revolutions of feelings. The festive occasion gives scope to the clandestine, the artful, the over-playful play of feeling and false feeling.

When they all sat down it was better; to her taste a great deal better, for Frank Churchill grew talkative and gay, making her his first object. Every distinguishing attention that could be paid, was paid to her. To amuse her, and be agreeable in her eyes, seemed all that he cared for— and Emma, glad to be enlivened, not sorry to be flattered, was gay and easy too, and gave him all the friendly encouragement, the admission to be gallant, which she had ever given in the first and most animating period of their acquaintance; but which now, in her own estimation, meant nothing, though in the judgment of most people looking on it must have had such an appearance as no English word but flirtation could very

well describe. 'Mr. Frank Churchill and Miss Woodhouse flirted together
excessively.' They were laying themselves open to that very phrase – and
to having it sent off in a letter to Maple Grove by one lady, to Ireland by
another. Not that Emma was gay and thoughtless from any real felicity;
it was rather because she felt less happy than she had expected. She
laughed because she was disappointed; and though she liked him for his
attentions, and thought them all, whether in friendship, admiration, or
playfulness, extremely judicious, they were not winning back her heart.
She still intended him for her friend. (*E*, pp. 367-8)

Mr Weston's good wine stimulates Mr Elton, the party leaves in
disarray, and he is left alone with Emma for their disturbing home-
ward drive:

> To restrain him as much as might be, by her own manners, she was
> immediately preparing to speak with exquisite calmness and gravity of
> the weather and the night; but scarcely had she begun, scarcely had they
> passed the sweep-gate and joined the other carriage, than she found her
> subject cut up—her hand seized—her attention demanded, and Mr. Elton
> actually making violent love to her: availing himself of the precious
> opportunity, declaring sentiments which must be already well known,
> hoping—fearing—adoring—ready to die if she refused him; but flattering
> himself that his ardent attachment and unequalled love and unexampled
> passion could not fail of having some effect, and in short, very much
> resolved on being seriously accepted as soon as possible. It really was so.
> Without scruple—without apology—without much apparent diffidence,
> Mr. Elton, the lover of Harriet, was professing himself *her* lover. She
> tried to stop him; but vainly; he would go on, and say it all. Angry as she
> was, the thought of the moment made her resolve to restrain herself when
> she did speak. (*E*, p. 129)

> 'Good heaven!' cried Mr. Elton, 'what can be the meaning of this?—
> Miss Smith!—I never thought of Miss Smith in the whole course of my
> existence—never paid her any attentions, but as your friend: never cared
> whether she were dead or alive, but as your friend. If she has fancied
> otherwise, her own wishes have misled her, and I am very sorry—
> extremely sorry—But, Miss Smith, indeed!—Oh! Miss Woodhouse! who
> can think of Miss Smith, when Miss Woodhouse is near! No, upon my
> honour, there is no unsteadiness of character. I have thought only of you.
> I protest against having paid the smallest attention to any one else. Every
> thing that I have said or done, for many weeks past, has been with the
> sole view of marking my adoration of yourself. You cannot really,
> seriously, doubt it. No!—(in an accent meant to be insinuating)—I am
> sure you have seen and understood me.'
> It would be impossible to say what Emma felt, on hearing this—which
> of all her unpleasant sensations was uppermost. She was too completely
> overpowered to be immediately able to reply: and two moments of silence

being ample encouragement for Mr. Elton's sanguine state of mind, he tried to take her hand again, as he joyously exclaimed—

'Charming Miss Woodhouse! allow me to interpret this interesting silence. It confesses that you have long understood me.'

'No, sir,' cried Emma, 'it confesses no such thing.' (*E*, pp. 130-1)

> He was too angry to say another word; her manner too decided to invite supplication; and in this state of swelling resentment, and mutually deep mortification they had to continue together a few minutes longer, for the fears of Mr. Woodhouse had confined them to a foot pace. If there had not been so much anger, there would have been desperate awkwardness; but their straight-forward emotions left no room for the little zigzags of embarrassment. (*E*, p. 132)

We should not sense the underground strength of feeling which often makes itself felt beneath the surface without breaking out, were it not for the revelations of inner action, the moments of feeling unbared in privacy and solitude and silence. Elinor Dashwood's inner life of passion is contained by her code of fortitude, self-command and consideration, but it is marked by strength, vivacity and variety and happily lacks the over-formal and often humourless ponderousness of the rhetoric of her public speech. This inner life is intense and 'natural' in its longings, griefs, jealousies and curiosities, capable even of humour and self-deprecation, as when she observes, in her talk to herself, that the curative properties of Mrs Jennings's rare old Constantia may as well be tested on her heart as on her sister's. Indeed, perhaps one of the difficulties of *Sense and Sensibility* comes from its failure [5] to move as fully into Marianne's track of feeling as it does into Elinor's. The quality of wry rationality, the capacity to try to look neutrally and reasonably at one's passions, even in their throes, is expressed profoundly, humorously and realistically. There is something akin to Elinor's own rational register of feeling in the concluding neutrality that observes Willoughby's wretchedness and his survival. Without anterior experience of low expectations and fortitude turned towards the self, the conclusion of the novel might seem too punitive, too destructive of feeling, too anti-romantic:

> Willoughby could not hear of her marriage without a pang; and his punishment was soon afterwards complete in the voluntary forgiveness of Mrs. Smith, who, by stating his marriage with a woman of character, as

---

[5] Stuart Tave (op. cit., p. 96) insists that we see *Sense and Sensibility* as Elinor's story, but even if we accept the subordination of Marianne as a necessary part of the novel's scope and shape, it has some disadvantages.

the source of her clemency, gave him reason for believing that had he behaved with honour towards Marianne, he might at once have been happy and rich. That his repentance of misconduct, which thus brought its own punishment, was sincere, need not be doubted;—nor that he long thought of Colonel Brandon with envy, and of Marianne with regret. But that he was for ever inconsolable, that he fled from society, or contracted an habitual gloom of temper, or died of a broken heart, must not be depended on—for he did neither. He lived to exert, and frequently to enjoy himself. His wife was not always out of humour, nor his home always uncomfortable; and in his breed of horses and dogs, and in sporting of every kind, he found no inconsiderable degree of domestic felicity.

(*SS*, p. 379)

In *Northanger Abbey* Catherine is startled by meeting Henry Tilney, crying 'Good God' when she emerges from his mother's room, not because she has been prying, but because he has broken into the disappointment and shame of her secret fantasy. That fantasy is revealed in inner drama, just as her more profound fears, anxieties, suspicions and repugnance are later thrown into relief, on the night before she has to leave Northanger, by our previous deep acquaintance with the more detached, literary, and unreal rehearsals and performances of Gothic feeling.

In Jane Austen's novels love tends to approach slowly and gradually. Marianne comes closer to the romantic ideal of love at first sight than the other heroines, though Elizabeth Bennet is charmed quickly – if more mildly – by Wickham's appearance and manner. Emma is reckless as she cleverly perceives that Mr and Mrs Weston would rather like to make a match for her with Frank Churchill, and hastens to anticipate them in imagination. Her love for Mr Knightley is perceived late, suddenly, but as an unadmitted long-standing attachment. The progression of feeling in Anne Elliot is barely shown; its beginnings are vividly but quickly summarized, lying as they do in the novel's memory, and not its present. Elinor's feelings for Edward also begin, in the novel's time, as well-established. The three heroines whose progress in love we observe from the beginning to the happy end are Catherine Morland, Elizabeth Bennet and Fanny Price.

The progress of Catherine's feelings is cleverly and conveniently screened by two burlesques of feeling: Isabella Thorpe's vision of a Bath full of amorous young men – with a little leftover interest to spare for her friend – and Henry Tilney's comic affectations of novelistic feeling. Isabella assures Catherine that her feeling for Henry is love at first sight, but it comes on much more slowly than that. Jane

Austen teases the reader by refusing to reveal Catherine's dreams after that first dance, in case they might give away anything as indecorous as night thoughts about a stranger. Jane Austen is able to be implicit about Catherine's susceptibility to Henry, which is undoubtedly present from the beginning, under such cover, and although the end explicitly declares that Henry was first drawn to Catherine by her interest in him, this judgement is too crude. He has always been shown as encouragingly flirtatious, and moved by Catherine's fresh feelings. Catherine and Henry are perhaps the most lightly sketched of Jane Austen's couples, and the obstacles to their attachment are mostly external; but they show one important thing, less analytically but as lucidly as any of the other pairs of lovers, the generation of feeling by feeling. No previous novelist that I can think of treated love quite like this. Richardson's characters love each other for merit, or supposed merit, but he doesn't show feeling responding to feeling. Clarissa feels something like love for Lovelace, but it is not a response to his feelings. Fanny Burney's heroines fall in love rather fixedly, with fairly static characters, and even though time may be needed for discovery and disclosure to be made, especially in *Cecilia*, where the love-story may have suggested certain aspects of the progress of Elizabeth and Darcy, there is no response to response.

This mutuality of feeling, in which interest, attraction and antagonism have their parts to play, is best shown in *Pride and Prejudice*. It is made fully, but not coldly, explicit in Elizabeth's changing feelings for Darcy. The best implicit presentation of the beginnings of love is that of Fanny in *Mansfield Park*. Most readers, even after several readings, must be hard put to it to determine the moment when Fanny is felt to love Edmund. There is no such moment. Jane Austen apparently does not want to fix on one. Love grows from gratitude, esteem and proximity, as Mrs Norris, to whom esteem and gratitude are unknown feelings, but who contemplates proximity, assures Sir Thomas Bertram it cannot possibly do: 'It is a moral impossibility'. It is a moral probability. Fanny's progress in feeling makes perfect sense, if we want to analyse compatibility, dependence, gratitude and esteem, but Jane Austen leaves us to do all that for ourselves, contenting herself with one or two brief overt remarks delicately inserted in the course of the action. When Edmund replaces the 'old grey poney' with his new mare, Jane Austen uses the convenient device, of which Defoe was a master, of describing feelings beyond expression:

... her delight in Edmund's mare was far beyond any former pleasure of the sort; and the addition it was ever receiving in the consideration of that kindness from which her pleasure sprung, was beyond all her words to express. She regarded her cousin as an example of every thing good and great, as possessing worth, which no one but herself could ever appreciate, and as entitled to such gratitude from her, as no feelings could be strong enough to pay. Her sentiments towards him were compounded of all that was respectful, grateful, confiding, and tender. (*MP*, p. 37)

When Edmund plans to stay at home with Lady Bertram so that Fanny can go on the expedition to Sotherton, her affection is described with suitable vagueness. Once more it is fondness which is inseparable from gratitude: 'She felt Edmund's kindness with all, and more than all, the sensibility which he, unsuspicious of her fond attachment, could be aware of.' (*MP*, p. 79) Such occasional comments are sufficient, and appropriately quiet. Fanny's love is gradual, and not made explicit for a long time, even in her reflections. She takes it for granted, but we see it emerge from the response to Edmund's almost consistent kindness, which she appreciates and returns, in fondness. When the kindness stops, as it does briefly when he lends the mare to Mary Crawford, Jane Austen makes very clear Fanny's jealousy, depression, disapproval and distaste for her own bad feelings. One of the necessary moments of physical jealousy in the novel occurs when Fanny sees Edmund helping Mary on the horse, and sees him take her hand: 'she saw it, or the imagination supplied what the eye could not reach' (*MP*, p. 67).

The novels, like most great novels, are introspective. They succeed more realistically than any previous novels in showing an introverted passional life, at the same time being subtly self-descriptive. Jane Austen's qualities of toughness and neutrality, which are shown in her capacity to make comic and tough reflections on the passions, are fully demonstrated and tested within her characters. Elizabeth Bennet [6] is engaged in the fatiguing process of thinking and re-thinking. But her epistemological essays and discoveries are parts of the progress of her feeling. She first begins to scrutinize these feelings, without too much pain and unease, when her aunt suggests that she should be on guard against being too much in love with Wickham:

'At present I am not in love with Mr. Wickham; no, I certainly am not. But he is, beyond all comparison, the most agreeable man I ever saw—

---

[6] See Tony Tanner's introduction to the Penguin edition of *Pride and Prejudice*, op. cit.

and if he becomes really attached to me—I believe it will be better that he should not. I see the imprudence of it.—Oh! *that* abominable Mr. Darcy!—My father's opinion of me does me the greatest honor; and I should be miserable to forfeit it. My father, however, is partial to Mr. Wickham. In short, my dear aunt I should be very sorry to be the means of making any of you unhappy; but since we see every day that where there is affection, young people are seldom withheld by immediate want of fortune, from entering into engagements with each other, how can I promise to be wiser than so many of my fellow creatures if I am tempted, or how am I even to know that it would be wisdom to resist? All that I can promise you, therefore, is not to be in a hurry. I will not be in a hurry to believe myself his first object. When I am in company with him, I will not be wishing. In short, I will do my best.' (*PP*, pp. 144-5)

. These early reflections and observations are much more simple and certain than her later analysis of the feeling for Darcy, and the feelings generated by reflections are not pleasant, but perfectly bearable. With subtlety and poignancy, we are shown the human heart trying to know itself in all the throes of strong feeling, with all its resources of courage, curiosity and candour; but we see it first in easy exercises. When Elizabeth reflects on the feeling for Wickham, or when Emma analyses the fantasy-life in which Frank Churchill is a central but unsuccessful suitor, they analyse language, mood and conduct to draw a simple and accurate conclusion: they cannot be much in love. When passion is involved, there is confusion, bewilderment, fatigue, tension, hardship. These self-possessed and poised heroines, so well-endowed, the one with her creator's wit and satire, the other with her brilliant imagination, each come to the fearful point of discovering that wit, satire and imaginative penetration can disintegrate in the solvent of strong feeling. Such is the self-analysis of Elizabeth, whose feeling for Darcy is just beginning to look like love. The very persistence of her reasoning shows the strength of feeling. It also shows the inadequacies of causal analysis, definition and classification as the attempts at naming feeling deny, frustrate, and defeat themselves. We can say that Elizabeth reasons herself into loving, but this is too crude and not quite accurate. In her analysis there is too little ease and command, because the reasoning is under pressure from the feeling it tries to analyse. Hers is a creative and passionate reflection. It borrows the action of intellectual classification for an analysis which is imperfect as explanation, but a valuable and liberating imaginative entertainment of possibilities. Jane Austen knew very well and could show how reason can encourage passion as well as restrain it, how the mind can rouse as well as dampen strong feeling. She knew too, as Lawrence knew so well, how attempts to name feeling fail. Elizabeth senses something like the fatigue that Birkin feels when reasoning has to stop in *Women in Love*. She is forced into a half-desired capitulation. As a monument in the passionate analysis of passion, this is perfect:

> As for Elizabeth, her thoughts were at Pemberley this evening more than the last; and the evening, though as it passed it seemed long, was not long enough to determine her feelings towards *one* in that mansion; and she lay awake two whole hours, endeavouring to make them out. She certainly did not hate him. No; hatred had vanished long ago, and she had almost as long been ashamed of ever feeling a dislike against him, that could be so called. The respect created by the conviction of his valuable qualities, though at first unwillingly admitted, had for some time ceased to be repugnant to her feelings; and it was now heightened into somewhat of a friendlier nature, by the testimony so highly in his favour, and bringing forward his disposition in so amiable a light, which yesterday had produced. But above all, above respect and esteem, there was a motive within her of good will which could not be overlooked. It was gratitude.— Gratitude, not merely for having once loved her, but for loving her still well enough, to forgive all the petulance and acrimony of her manner in rejecting him, and all the unjust accusations accompanying her rejection. He who, she had been persuaded, would avoid her as his greatest enemy, seemed, on this accidental meeting, most eager to preserve the acquaintance, and without any indelicate display of regard, or any peculiarity of of manner, where their two selves only were concerned, was soliciting the good opinion of her friends, and bent on making her known to his sister. Such a change in a man of so much pride, excited not only astonishment but gratitude—for to love, ardent love, it must be attributed; and as such its impression on her was of a sort to be encouraged, as by no means unpleasing, though it could not be exactly defined. She respected, she esteemed, she was grateful to him, she felt a real interest in his welfare; and she only wanted to know how far she wished that welfare to depend upon herself, and how far it would be for the happiness of both that she should employ the power, which her fancy told her she still possessed, of bringing on the renewal of his addresses. (*PP*, pp. 265-6)

The analysis casts back to an earlier stage which it rejects, not coldly, but emotionally: Elizabeth is ashamed of having felt a dislike that could be called hating; she is no longer repelled by the respect she first felt unwillingly, which has grown warmer than respect, 'somewhat of a friendlier nature'; esteem is slipped in, without comment, and then joined by gratitude, with the rational explanation, an explanation which brings in a warmer word, that of love. Not yet in love, she sees herself as 'grateful' for his past and continued loving, despite her conduct. His love is analysed a little, seen as forgiving her acrimony. As she speculates about his feelings, hers change. She feels astonished and then grateful for his forgiveness. We move into the deliberate vagueness of impressions not to be exactly defined. There then follows a recapitulation, and a crescendo: 'She respected, she esteemed, she was grateful to him, she felt a real interest in his welfare . . .'.The sentence is as elaborate and precise in refinement and qualification as a sentence of Henry James, and for reasons he would respect. Elizabeth is inspecting, delicately skirting and questioning, with honesty, goodwill, nuance and scruple, those feelings which she cannot yet quite call love. The shifting of the names of feeling is true not only to her bewilderment, but to the shyness both of the recognition and the admission, and – above all – to the greater shyness of energetic antipathy humbling itself. The chapter ends with a brief statement of a further small movement, in her pleasure at the thought of the morning call, a statement which still hesitates to enlarge and explain: 'Elizabeth was pleased, though, when she asked herself the reason, she had very little to say in reply.' This is the dialogue not only of the mind with itself, but of the whole affective consciousness.

The successive waves of feeling and reflection on feeling are characteristic of Jane Austen and utterly central in each novel. In each novel there is a prevailing register of feeling, coloured by character and theme. Elizabeth's has assurance, shyness, humour; Anne Elliot's is brave but agitated and anxious; Elinor's is sad but relatively serene and stable. The word 'agitation' occurs frequently in *Persuasion*, where the action is one of regret, loss, deprivation, shock, doubt and tension. There are common elements in each novel's analysis: for Elizabeth, Emma, and Anne, the passionate declaration of love is followed by the sense that privacy and solitude are necessary for recovery and repose, perhaps for recognition and consolidation. In Anne's case there is without any doubt a religious aspect in her final meditative retreat, prayerful and graceful, an emotional conclusion to the long history. The stream of passion flows deep but always moves into the public world, and in many ways. The passionate inspection of the passions produces the fine inevitability of the final reunion of Darcy and Elizabeth, Anne and Captain Wentworth.

Despite the guard kept on feeling, the characters are all surprised and shocked by their own and other people's feeling. Elinor is alarmed and compassionate when Willoughby bursts in to enquire about Marianne's dangerous fever and then to unfold his story. When Darcy startles Elizabeth Bennet, her mind and ours have been concerned with chagrin and sympathy for Jane, and resentment of Darcy after Fitzwilliam's innocent disclosures. Darcy is supposedly safely at Rosings in the enclosure and formality of one of Lady Catherine's dinner-parties, the last kind of social occasion from which one could ever imagine anyone slipping away.

When Elizabeth is startled by Darcy's very abrupt declaration she is overcome with mixed feelings, including some gratification and sense of compliment and even compassion, but chiefly composed of anger, scorn, and contempt:

> In spite of her deeply-rooted dislike, she could not be insensible to the compliment of such a man's affection, and though her intentions did not vary for an instant, she was at first sorry for the pain he was to receive; till, roused to resentment by his subsequent language, she lost all compassion in anger. She tried, however, to compose herself to answer him with patience, when he should have done. (*PP*, p. 189)

When he realizes that she is really rejecting him, his feeling too gathers itself into an equal anger, taking some of its strength from hurt and surprise, as we see, some from love, and some from the sense of injustice, as we do not immediately see. Their angers clash together promisingly:

> 'The feelings which, you tell me, have long prevented the acknowledgment of your regard, can have little difficulty in overcoming it after this explanation.'
>
> Mr. Darcy, who was leaning against the mantle-piece with his eyes fixed on her face, seemed to catch her words with no less resentment than surprise. His complexion became pale with anger, and the disturbance of his mind was visible in every feature. He was struggling for the appearance of composure, and would not open his lips, till he believed himself to have attained it. The pause was to Elizabeth's feelings dreadful. At length, in a voice of forced calmness, he said,
>
> 'And this is all the reply which I am to have the honour of expecting! I might, perhaps, wish to be informed why, with so little *endeavour* at civility, I am thus rejected. But it is of small importance.'
>
> 'I might as well enquire,' replied she, 'why with so evident a design of offending and insulting me, you chose to tell me that you liked me against your will, against your reason, and even against your character? Was not this some excuse for incivility, if I *was* uncivil? But I have other provocations. You know I have. Had not my own feelings decided against you, had they been indifferent, or had they even been favourable, do you think that any consideration would tempt me to accept the man, who has been the means of ruining, perhaps for ever, the happiness of a most beloved sister?'

As she pronounced these words, Mr. Darcy changed colour; but the emotion was short, and he listened without attempting to interrupt her while she continued.

'I have every reason in the world to think ill of you. No motive can excuse the unjust and ungenerous part you acted *there*. You dare not, you cannot deny that you have been the principal, if not the only means of dividing them from each other, of exposing one to the censure of the world for caprice and instability, the other to its derision for disappointed hopes, and involving them both in misery of the acutest kind.'

She paused and saw with no slight indignation that he was listening with an air which proved him wholly unmoved by any feeling of remorse. He even looked at her with a smile of affected incredulity. (*PP*, pp. 190-1)

The action of strong passion is a relationship, even an intimacy, and of course the *odi* leads to *amo*, as in similar passionate conflicts between Beatrice and Benedict or Mrs Gaskell's Margaret Hale and Mr Thornton in *North and South*. When Elizabeth is informed and astonished once more by Darcy's letter, the anger is modified and changed by the sense of injustice, which is in its turn bound up with shame, and self-reproach, not only for her mistake about Darcy, but for her mistake about Wickham. We see the intimacy of anger and reproach rising into that of affection. But the movement is slow and complex, forming part of the whole chronicle of feeling which shows the passions at play both in solitude and in public. In all these cases physical surprise intensifies passion, the feeling coming violently upon us. One of the best examples of this intensification in a small space is Emma's passionate self-discovery 'darting through her with the speed of an arrow'. Perhaps the most striking union of feelings, inevitable rather than surprising, is that in *Persuasion*. Anne Elliot and Frederick Wentworth are the lovers who communicate silently and painfully throughout the novel, never once alone until the declaration is written, in a public and crowded hotel room. The contrast between Jane Austen's final version of this scene and the original,[7] where the public nature of the lovers' meetings is broken before the declaration, brings out the importance of the tension and the relief of solitude and climax. The final and superior version makes a movement from separation to intimacy, as well as containing a much more moving and plausible precipitation in Anne's rhapsodic defence of woman's constancy, overheard by Captain Wentworth though not designed for his ears.

[7] Reprinted in the Chapman edition, pp. 253-63.

For Anne, like Elizabeth and Fanny, is capable of the rhapsodic, even the Sublime. Rather faint in *Pride and Prejudice*, slightly stronger in *Emma*, and at their most energetic in *Mansfield Park* and *Persuasion*, are outbursts of feeling not directly connected with the love-stories. Such bursts of passion are isolated, stylized, framed, and focused. They bring us close to the romantic ode, being rhapsodies – or almost rhapsodies – on a natural scene, marked by the conjunction of sense and symbol, and the relation of outer and inner experience. Jane Austen's use of sympathetic weather is conspicuous but delicate. It is a depressingly cold and stormy July day when Emma feels sure she has lost Knightley, but a brilliant morning that brings them together. The capriciousness of the English spring and summer is affectionately invoked and exploited on several occasions. The novelist never rhapsodizes about nature, though she carefully allows her characters to be more ecstatic. She dramatizes both the outer world and the character's sensibility, with an explicitness of interpretation which is lucid but subtle enough to leave some things unsaid. Such rhapsodies offer the closest approach to that elevation which some of the Victorians found lacking in Jane Austen. Jane Austen, unlike George Eliot and Hardy, does not aspire to a numinous vision. Although her piety is in evidence in her novels, they keep us firmly in the phenomenal world, in which we live. Her landscape lacks those Alpine peaks to which Dickens and George Eliot aspire and sometimes climb, but also lacks their failures in sublimity, the mechanically conceived Alps in *David Copperfield*, or some of the strained visions in *Romola* or *Daniel Deronda*. Nature may have been more sublime for Jane Austen than we can imagine, but her human passions seldom or never go beyond the sensuous world. She keeps a tight hold on rhapsody, as we might expect from the creator of Sir Edward Denham:

'Do you remember, said he, Scott's beautiful lines on the Sea?—Oh! what a description they convey!—They are never out of my Thoughts when I walk here.—That Man who can read them unmoved must have the nerves of an Assassin!—Heaven defend me from meeting such a Man un-armed.' 'What description do you mean?—said Charlotte. I remember none at this moment, of the Sea, in either of Scott's Poems.' 'Do you not·indeed?—Nor can I exactly recall the beginning at this moment—But—you cannot have forgotten his description of Woman!—
       "Oh! Woman in our Hours of Ease—"
Delicious! Delicious! Had he written nothing more, he would have been Immortal.' (*MW*, p. 396)

Jane Austen required her characters to be precise and concrete even in the moment of rhapsody, unlike Sir Edward, but perhaps not totally unlike Wordsworth or Keats, and very like Rousseau. She is a novelist, not a poet, and in her rhapsodies she places the inner and outer experience typical of the ode in character, marking the confines of personal experience and the larger world that lies outside that experience. There is something like an ode in *Persuasion*:

> Anne's object was, not to be in the way of any body, and where the narrow paths across the fields made many separations necessary, to keep with her brother and sister. Her *pleasure* in the walk must arise from the exercise and the day, from the view of the last smiles of the year upon the tawny leaves and withered hedges, and from repeating to herself some few of the thousand poetical descriptions extant of autumn, that season of peculiar and inexhaustible influence on the mind of taste and tenderness, that season which has drawn from every poet, worthy of being read, some attempt at description, or some lines of feeling. She occupied her mind as much as possible in such like musings and quotations. . . .
>
> (*P*, p. 84)

> Anne could not immediately fall into a quotation again. The sweet scenes of autumn were for a while put by—unless some tender sonnet, fraught with the apt analogy of the declining year, with declining happiness, and the images of youth and hope, and spring, all gone together, blessed her memory. She roused herself to say, as they struck by order into another path, 'Is not this one of the ways to Winthrop?' But nobody heard, or, at least, nobody answered her.
>
> Winthrop, however, or its environs—for young men are, sometimes, to be met with, strolling about near home, was their destination; and after another half mile of gradual ascent through large enclosures, where the ploughs at work, and the fresh-made path spoke the farmer, counteracting the sweets of poetical despondence, and meaning to have spring again, they gained the summit of the most considerable hill, which parted Uppercross and Winthrop, and soon commanded a full view of the latter, at the foot of the hill on the other side. (*P*, p. 85)

We do not forget the scene, the exercise and the walk. Jane Austen is writing about poetry instead of writing poetry, so she describes and does not enact her effects: 'season of peculiar and inexhaustible influence on the mind of taste and tenderness', but not 'season of mists and mellow fruitfulness'. This is a generalization of poetic response, precisely in accordance with the advice on dangerous and indulgent selective reading which Anne is to give to Harville. But the response is personal and the writing soon becomes more particular, as she hears

Louisa's enthusiastic speech 'If I loved a man', and hears it praised and 'honoured' by Frederick Wentworth. Understandably, she proceeds to select not the poetry of autumn's sweetness but that of its decline. The response is narrated, not lyricized, but at the end the passage rises into a different feeling, which includes but goes beyond Anne's chagrin, and yet is eventually and fully responsive to her stoicism as well as to her 'second spring'. This narration of feeling resembles an Ode to Autumn in three stanzas: the first is fraught with sweetness, in the 'last smiles' of the year upon the leaves and hedges; the second is a sigh for decay, with 'declining happiness, and the images of youth and hope, and spring, all gone together'; and the third is a recovery and an enlargement: '. . . after another half mile of gradual ascent through large enclosures, where the ploughs at work, and the fresh-made path spoke the farmer, counteracting the sweets of poetical despondence, and meaning to have spring again. . . .'

This nearly lyric episode is important not just as a statement of theme, but as a reflection of feeling and a moral expansion of the emotional state. It places Anne in relation to her as-yet-unanticipated happy ending, but goes beyond this to bring in the world beyond poetry, and beyond passion. It involves the larger world in which we live and feel, not in apartness. It uses Anne's passions, then expands to leave those passions behind. But its enlargement is responsive to the sense of sympathy and community which Anne consistently shows, generous, benevolent, and responsible as she is.

Mary Crawford, who is not at all like an old maid, lives in social apartness. She is surprised not to get a horse and cart to transport her harp in the middle of the late hay harvest, puts on an irrational woman's charming act of intuition, insisting that furlongs are miles, or that black clouds mean rain, because it suits her needs and desires. 'South or North, I know a black cloud when I see one', she says, echoing Hamlet with a more than Hamlet-like irrationality. But Fanny Price's vision of Nature is grounded in attentive and careful observation: 'But they are passed over . . . I have been watching them. This weather is all from the south.'

Fanny is the greatest rhapsodist in Jane Austen. In Portsmouth we see her in a rapturous natural scene where, like Anne, she is perceived as well as perceiver. We see her with Henry Crawford by the sea, feeling 'many a tender reverie' (its subject is unstated, but we know it is not Henry). Jane Austen makes clear her 'openness' to nature, her enjoyment, physical animation, and her carelessness 'of the conditions'. The 'carelessness' means she isn't worried by resting on Henry's arm, an important carelessness for Fanny:

> The day was uncommonly lovely. It was really March; but it was April in its mild air, brisk soft wind, and bright sun, occasionally clouded for a minute; and every thing looked so beautiful under the influence of such a sky, the effects of the shadows pursuing each other, on the ships at Spithead and the island beyond, with the ever-varying hues of the sea now at high water, dancing in its glee and dashing against the ramparts with so fine a sound, produced altogether such a combination of charms for Fanny, as made her gradually almost careless of the circumstances under which she felt them.
>
>                     \*
>
> The loveliness of the day, and of the view, he felt like herself. They often stopt with the same sentiment and taste, leaning against the wall, some minutes, to look and admire; and considering he was not Edmund, Fanny could not but allow that he was sufficiently open to the charms of nature, and very well able to express his admiration. She had a few tender reveries now and then, which he could sometimes take advantage of, to look in her face without detection. . . . (*MP*, p. 409)

> It was sad to Fanny to lose all the pleasures of spring. She had not known before what pleasures she *had* to lose in passing March and April in a town. She had not known before, how much the beginnings and progress of vegetation had delighted her.—What animation both of body and mind, she had derived from watching the advance of that season which cannot, in spite of its capriciousness, be unlovely, and seeing its increasing beauties, from the earliest flowers, in the warmest divisions of her aunt's garden, to the opening of leaves of her uncle's plantations, and the glory of his woods.—To be losing such pleasures was no trifle; to be losing them, because she was in the midst of closeness and noise, to have confinement, bad air, bad smells, substituted for liberty, freshness, fragrance, and verdure, was infinitely worse;—but even these incitements to regret, were feeble, compared with what arose from the conviction of being missed, by her best friends, and the longing to be useful to those who were wanting her! (*MP*, pp. 431-2)

Fanny's attitude to nature is personal, even domestic, but her spontaneity and vitality are defined by it, as Henry Crawford observes.

Fanny's most elaborate rhapsody is a twofold one, on the evergreen and the human memory. The two exclamations of wonder are linked by her recollection of the Parsonage garden (in the old Norris days) before its shrubbery existed, and the link is strengthened through the quality of endurance shared by tree and mind:

. . . in the midst of some tender ejaculation of Fanny's, on the sweets of so protracted an autumn, they were forced by the sudden swell of a cold gust shaking down the last few yellow leaves about them, to jump up and walk for warmth.

'This is pretty—very pretty,' said Fanny, looking around her as they were thus sitting together one day: 'Every time I come into this shrubbery I am more struck with its growth and beauty. Three years ago, this was nothing but a rough hedgerow along the upper side of the field, never thought of as any thing, or capable of becoming any thing; and now it is converted into a walk, and it would be difficult to say whether most valuable as a convenience or an ornament; and perhaps in another three years we may be forgetting—almost forgetting what it was before. How wonderful, how very wonderful the operations of time, and the changes of the human mind!' And following the latter train of thought, she soon afterwards added: 'If any one faculty of our nature may be called *more* wonderful than the rest, I do think it is memory. There seems something more speakingly incomprehensible in the powers, the failures, the inequalities of memory, than in any other of our intelligences. The memory is sometimes so rententive, so serviceable, so obedient—at others so bewildered and so weak—and at others again, so tyrannic, so beyond control!—We are to be sure a miracle every way—but our powers of recollecting and of forgetting, do seem peculiarly past finding out.'

Miss Crawford, untouched and inattentive, had nothing to say; and Fanny, perceiving it, brought back her own mind to what she thought must interest.

'It may seem impertinent in *me* to praise, but I must admire the taste Mrs. Grant has shewn in all this. There is such a quiet simplicity in the plan of the walk! not too much attempted!'

'Yes,' replied Miss Crawford carelessly, 'it does very well for a place of this sort. One does not think of extent *here*—and between ourselves, till I came to Mansfield, I had not imagined a country parson ever aspired to a shrubbery or any thing of the kind.'

'I am so glad to see the evergreens thrive!' said Fanny in reply. 'My uncle's gardener always says the soil here is better than his own, and so it appears from the growth of the laurels and evergreens in general.—The evergreen!—How beautiful, how welcome, how wonderful the ever-green!—When one thinks of it, how astonishing a variety of nature!—In some countries we know the tree that sheds its leaf is the variety, but that does not make it less amazing, that the same soil and the same sun should nurture plants differing in the first rule and law of their existence. You will think me rhapsodizing; but when I am out of doors, especially when I am sitting out of doors, I am very apt to get into this sort of wondering strain. One cannot fix one's eyes on the commonest natural production without finding food for a rambling fancy.'

'To say the truth,' replied Miss Crawford, 'I am something like the famous Doge at the court of Lewis XIV; and may declare that I see no wonder in this shrubbery equal to seeing myself in it.' (*MP*, pp. 208-10)

It is characteristic of Fanny to utter a double praise of the human and the natural. She thinks of Mansfield Park as her aunt's garden and uncle's woods, and here responds to the Parsonage shrubbery. This is her Romanticism, grounded in sense and science,[8] like her author's insistence in *Persuasion* on the farmer 'meaning to have spring again'. The rhapsody is typically prim but endearing in its pedantry, and, most important, in its reliable sense of audience, the modesty, the apology in 'You will think me rhapsodizing'. We do. This is an openness, to what is beyond the self.

Jane Austen is explicitly contrasting this openness with Mary's apartness, her egocentric and entirely unromantic lack of intellectual and imaginative concern for anything beyond the self. We see a closed and an open mind, both warm, but Fanny's is the movement of imagination – into the larger world. Not only is Fanny meditating on the properties of mind and nature, in praise and reflective analysis, but she is doing so in a very testing situation, where she might be forgiven for self-absorption. The modern meditation is in context not unlike Hamlet's 'What a piece of work is man', in the moral strength of its break from a passion which possesses and obsesses. Like Shakespeare, Jane Austen can demonstrate the mind's power to draw on the strength and intensity of the private passion for an enlarged act of sensibility and rational appraisal:

Fanny spoke her feelings. 'Here's harmony!' said she, 'Here's repose! Here's what may leave all painting and all music behind, and what poetry only can attempt to describe. Here's what may tranquillize every care, and lift the heart to rapture! When I look out on such a night as this, I feel as if there could be neither wickedness nor sorrow in the world; and there certainly would be less of both if the sublimity of Nature were more attended to, and people were carried more out of themselves by contemplating such a scene.'

'I like to hear your enthusiasm, Fanny. It is a lovely night, and they are much to be pitied who have not been taught to feel in some degree as you do—who have not at least been given a taste for nature in early life. They lose a great deal.'

'*You* taught me to think and feel on the subject, cousin.'

'I had a very apt scholar. There's Arcturus looking very bright.'

'Yes, and the bear. I wish I could see Cassiopeia.'

'We must go out on the lawn for that, Should you be afraid?'

'Not in the least. It is a great while since we have had any star-gazing.'

---

[8] The combination is very reminiscent of Rousseau, especially in *Les rêveries du promeneur solitaire*. It is just possible that Jane Austen's fondness for the term 'reverie' derives from Rousseau.

'Yes, I do not know how it has happened.' (*MP*, p. 113)

This is also in character, precise, pedantic, sententious, even slightly priggish. Her appeal is religious, ecstatic, strong, and persuades Edmund to look away for a moment from the pianoforte, candles and Mary Crawford.

Mary's is the indoor world, and hers are the indoor arts and lights: candles not stars, music not poetry. The implied disparagement of music is also in character,[9] for we know that Fanny likes literature but not music and painting, and there are moral and social implications. This novel discusses education and seems at times to criticize music and painting as typically alluring accomplishments, while seeing literature, at least locally, as a serious part of moral education. Of course Jane Austen doesn't suggest that literary taste is a guarantee of virtue – Henry Crawford's reading is as exhibitionist and seductive as Mary's harp-playing. Fanny's æsthetic and moved rapture at the stars and her overt defence of the Sublime, are amorous too, though privately and discreetly so. The amorousness is there in the 'Not in the least. It is a great while since we have had any star-gazing', but also implicit, if not conscious, in: 'if people were carried more out of themselves'. Edmund himself is not so carried away, but still ruled by his present feeling for Mary, when his reply 'I like to hear your enthusiasm' reverts to 'they are much to be pitied . . .'. He almost goes out to look at Cassiopeia, invisible from the open window, moved by Fanny to look with her, at the stars and at their past star-gazing. Jane Austen underlines the amorous beauty of the scene by something very rare in her, though common enough in other evocations of intense passion, like the image of Ruth in 'The Ode to the Nightingale', in a reinforcement of associations that link this rapture with another pair of lovers, another image of harmony, on another starlit night:

> The moon shines bright. In such a night as this. . . .

> How sweet the moonlight sleeps upon this bank!
> Here will we sit, and let the sounds of music
> Creep in our ears—soft stillness and the night
> Become the touches of sweet harmony:
> Sit Jessica,—look how the floor of heaven

---

[9] It is also a local emphasis; in other novels Jane Austen makes no attempt to disparage music. Anne Elliot's music is quite different from Mary Crawford's.

Is thick inlaid with patens of bright gold. . . .
                    *(The Merchant of Venice)*

The strongest echo is not in the imagery but in the echo of Shakespeare's many times repeated 'in such a night'.[10]

Poetry and rapture are not isolated. This rhapsody is less like an
ode than a refusal to write an ode: 'Fanny sighed alone at the window
till scolded away by Mrs Norris's threats of catching cold.' It is a
novel, not a poem. The passions exist in intensity and strength; they
are part of the creation of character, part of the moral definition, and
part of the action. Although Jane Austen's novels do not anæsthetize
the heart, as Bergson tells us comedy must, her passions have to
inhabit the ordinary world. Their poetry – if we can ever call them
poetic – is only a transient exaltation and heightening of prose, and
lacks the isolation from character, history, judgement, which the
romantic ode delights in, and possesses. The 'Ode to the Nightingale'
can end on the modulation into doubt and question its own language
in, 'Forlorn! the word is like . . .' but it cannot ever smile at its
passions.

Fanny's celebration of nature has a moral significance that is more
than a superior act of penetrating imagination. It is part of her
capacity to ask, see, and judge, to appreciate, spontaneously, crea-
tively and genuinely. Readers of Victorian novels, where the response
to nature is either less important than the response to the human
world, or closely related to that response through sensibility and
symbol, may well find a lack of social passion and elevation in Jane
Austen, think her raptures uncomfortably sealed off from the larger
world. We all know the honest – perhaps too honest – observations in
*Northanger Abbey*, 'from politics it was an easy step to silence' (*NA*, p.
111), a comment which is particularly resounding for being placed
after Catherine's delighted initiation into good conversation, on the
subjects of nature, painting and literature. Catherine, like Emma and
Fanny, is praised for her responsiveness and 'fresh feelings'. She is
indeed initiated into the horrors of social fact – injustice, mercenariness, tyranny and duplicity – through General Tilney with his
unspecified larger duties which keep him up late studying for the good
of the nation. But there is no suggestion that Jane Austen wants to
take this heroine beyond the fresh appraisal of her immediate environment. Emma is not especially open to æsthetic rapture, and the

[10] See Frank W. Bradbrook, op. cit., p. 78.

grounds of Donwell and its Abbey please her chiefly for what they represent in social solidity of standing and possession. Nor is Emma remarkable for her social passion, despite her goodness and sympathy to the poor, and the candid lack of cant afterwards : ' ". . . I hope it may be allowed that if compassion has produced exertion and relief to the sufferers, it has done all that is truly important. If we feel for the wretched, enough to do all we can for them, the rest is empty sympathy, only distressing to ourselves." ' (*E*, p. 87) This is scarcely the full flow of social love, though a reasonable and honest attitude.[11]

Catherine's lack of interest and Emma's strictly practical social sympathy highlight Fanny's sensibility. It is only a detail but eloquent in its context, much more eloquent, for instance, than Jane Fairfax's fuller comment on the slave-trade, for Fanny speaks as one whose flow of passion we know. 'Did you not hear me ask him about the slave-trade last night?' she says to Edmund soon after the return of Sir Thomas from Antigua. Interesting too is her reason for not 'following the question' with others, as Edmund would have liked, because it would have looked like display and rebuke to the silently bored Maria and Julia. Jane Austen knew that politics could be boring, and those who think Fanny's priggishness excessive should reflect on her insight, unusual in prigs, into the dangers of being boring and morally superior. Her sensibility is contrasted with Maria's and Julia's early schoolroom boasts about their useless young ladies' syllabus, as they reel off the metals, semi-metals, planets and distinguished philosophers, and with Mary Crawford's amazement that she can't get transport for her harp in the middle of the late hay harvest. Fanny has not only acquired some knowledge of literature, geography, and astronomy, but like Sissy Jupes or Dorothea Brooke, she is directed both by imagination and a sense of local relevance. Her uncle has been across the Atlantic and back (despite Mary's wishes for a calm), and has had his problems in the West Indies, perhaps even arising out of the emancipation of the slaves in 1807.[12] Fanny's question is one about the world outside Mansfield Park, but it is also a niece's question about her uncle's world. Like her knowledge of coniferous and deciduous trees, the constellations and Cowper, her questioning is part of her sensibility, which harmonizes the impulses to know, to wonder, and to love. She is a figure in Jane Austen's romantic sensibility, one

[11] It is like Jane Austen's remarks on charity in the *Letters*, p. 295.
[12] See Avrom Fleishman, *A Reading of Mansfield Park* (Minneapolis, 1967), pp. 36-9.

of the most complete Romantic heroines, and her social sensibility links her with Rousseau, Wordsworth, Byron and Keats. Like the poets, Fanny finds objects sacred, and is moved imaginatively to relate all her sacred objects to each other and to the world outside the self. Jane Austen's moments of deepest feeling show something strikingly close to Shelley's thinking in *The Defence of Poetry*:

> Man is an instrument over which a series of external and internal impress-ions are driven, like the alternations of an ever-changing wind over an Æolian lyre, which move it by their motion to ever-changing melody. But there is a principle within all sentient beings, which acts otherwise than in the lyre, and produces not melody alone, but harmony, by an internal adjustment of the sounds or motions thus excited to the impressions which excite them. It is as if the lyre could accommodate its chords to the motions of that which strikes them, in a determined proportion of sound. . . .

Jane Austen is not an extroverted social novelist, interested chiefly in the series of external impressions, but conceives her heroines as imaginative beings, able to accommodate their responses to the move-ments of the larger world.

# III

# The Storytellers

## 1: Continuity, Climax and Conclusion

Each of Jane Austen's novels has a continuity of feeling. It also has its flow of telling and listening.[1] Like all novelists writing in the third person, Jane Austen depends on a variety of viewpoints, a number of internal narrators who carry much of the narrative responsibility, formally and informally.

When we contemplate the narrator in fiction, we tend to invoke the idea of a dominant voice. This voice may present itself as engaged in writing or editing letters, memoirs, autobiography, reminiscence or self-proclaimed fiction, but no single narrator, real or imaginary, tells the whole of the story. The external narrator's stance is maintained in Jane Austen's novels, though it is neither very insistent nor very conspicuous, because the stories she tells are made up of many acts of telling and listening. The passions of her people move within them and without, and their storytelling too is both private and public. The density and the vitality of great novels depend on the abundance of internal narrative, which repeats and sustains the narrative activity outside novels, and at the same time creates character, action, dialogue and argument. Internal narrative is at once means and end. The unit of narration is as important a unit in the structure of a novel as an image. The large narrative that we call the novel proceeds through inner telling and listening, in an interwoven chain of discourse.

Jane Austen's internal narrative sometimes takes the form of ambitious, formal and lengthy exposition. The stories of Willoughby, Lucy Steele, Wickham, Darcy, Frank Churchill and Captain Wentworth are extensive, reporting their past lives, truthfully or untruthfully. Narratives may be fragmentary and allusive, as in the brief, incoherent or piecemeal narratives of Marianne Dashwood, Edward

[1] See my general discussion of this topic in *Tellers and Listeners: The Narrative Imagination* (Athlone Press, 1975).

Ferrars or Henry Crawford, who offer brief histories of the past or projects for the future. At its most reduced, narrative can reside in a few words, like Lady Bertram's effortless but unusually vivid revelation to the returning Sir Thomas that they 'have been all alive with acting'. Like this brief account it may be utterly direct, telling explicitly and clearly what past or future events have been or may be. It may be indirect, forming the subtext of Fanny's lyrical outburst on the subject of the stars, or of Mary Crawford's murmur of masked wit against the hostilities directed at Fanny in the Mansfield drawing-room: 'this *place* is too hot for me'. It may be public, addressed to willing, unwilling, eager, abstracted or uncomprehending listeners. It may be interior and silent, like the repressed and reserved story of Elinor Dashwood, which Marianne thinks can't exist because it doesn't get told, or the constant play of memory and reflection in the fine mind of Anne Elliot, who has had no one to listen to her since she found and lost the perfect listener eight years before the novel's story began. (She has Lady Russell, and appreciates her company, but she cannot tell her the whole story of the past.)

From beginning to end, the novel weaves its constantly shifting pattern of internal narrative. There is always someone telling and someone listening. We move from the private to the public life through the constant narrative motion, utterances are joined with silences, and events become reflections. Within the public talk, however brilliantly extroverted the conversation may be, there are always two sets of narration going on, for the spoken words are accompanied, enlarged, qualified and contradicted by the words that are thought. While Captain Wentworth talks to amuse, inform and charm the Musgrove sisters, Anne Elliot listens, remembering how he had once talked to her. She compares the stories of the sea he had told her then, with those he is telling now to others, and feels the difference between the listening of the present and that of eight years ago:

From this time Captain Wentworth and Anne Elliot were repeatedly in the same circle. They were soon dining in company together at Mr. Musgrove's, for the little boy's state could no longer supply his aunt with a pretence for absenting herself; and this was but the beginning of other dinings and other meetings.

Whether former feelings were to be renewed, must be brought to the proof; former times must undoubtedly be brought to the recollection of each; *they* could not but be reverted to; the year of their engagement could not but be named by him, in the little narratives or descriptions which conversation called forth. His profession qualified him, his disposition led him, to talk; and 'That was in the year six;' 'That happened before I went to sea in the year six,' occurred in the course of the first evening they spent together: and though his voice did not falter, and though she had no reason to suppose his eye wandering towards her while he spoke, Anne felt the utter impossibility, from her knowledge of his mind, that he could be unvisited by remembrance any more than herself. There must be the same immediate association of thought, though she was very far from conceiving it to be of equal pain.

They had no conversation together, no intercourse but what the commonest civility required. Once so much to each other! Now nothing. There *had* been a time, when of all the large party now filling the drawing-room at Uppercross, they would have found it most difficult to cease to speak to one another. With the exception, perhaps, of Admiral and Mrs. Croft, who seemed particularly attached and happy, (Anne could allow no other exception even among the married couples) there could have been no two hearts so open, no tastes so similar, no feelings so in unison, no countenances so beloved. Now they were as strangers; nay, worse than strangers, for they could never become acquainted. It was a perpetual estrangement.

When he talked, she heard the same voice, and discerned the same mind. There was a very general ignorance of all naval matters throughout the party; and he was very much questioned, and especially by the two Miss Musgroves, who seemed hardly to have any eyes but for him, as to the manner of living on board, daily regulations, food, hours, &c.; and their surprise at his accounts, at learning the degree of accommodation and arrangement which was practicable, drew from him some pleasant ridicule, which reminded Anne of the early days when she too had been ignorant, and she too had been accused of supposing sailors to be living on board without any thing to eat, or any cook to dress it if there were, or any servant to wait, or any knife and fork to use. (*P*, pp. 63-4)

'But, Captain Wentworth,' cried Louisa, 'how vexed you must have been when you came to the Asp, to see what an old thing they had given you.'

'I knew pretty well what she was, before that day;' said he, smiling. 'I had no more discoveries to make, than you would have as to the fashion and strength of any old pelisse, which you had seen lent about among half your acquaintance, ever since you could remember, and which at last, on some very wet day, is lent to yourself.—Ah! she was a dear old Asp to me. She did all that I wanted. I knew she would.—I knew that we should either go to the bottom together, or that she would be the making of me; and I never had two days of foul weather all the time I was at sea in her; and after taking privateers enough to be very entertaining, I had the good luck, in my passage home the next autumn, to fall in with the very French frigate I wanted.—I brought her into Plymouth; and here was another instance of luck. We had not been six hours in the Sound, when a gale came on, which lasted four days and nights, and which would have done for poor old Asp, in half the time; our touch with the Great Nation not having much improved our condition. Four-and-twenty hours later, and I should only have been a gallant Captain Wentworth, in a small paragraph at one corner of the newspapers; and being lost in only a sloop, nobody would have thought about me.'

Anne's shudderings were to herself, alone: but the Miss Musgroves could be as open as they were sincere, in their exclamations of pity and horror. (*P*, pp. 65-6)

All the time her imagination is busy with what is going on in the speaker's memory. She has to hear her old lover's new stories silently and uncomfortably, wondering what is in his mind as he easily and wittily adapts his style and tone for the ears of the Musgrove girls, the conventionally good lady listeners. She reads between the lines as he tells the story of his first command and explains that he wanted to be away and doing, or tells of success, dangers and possible death with no one to mourn him. Her listening is intent, agitated, regretful, as it doubles back on the long past and probes the doubtful present.

Like Elinor Dashwood, Anne is a good listener, forced to hold back her own story though it beats persistently inside. There is an interior life beneath the public one. And the public storytelling sometimes tells more than it may seem to. This dipping in and out of public and private story goes to create the elasticity of Jane Austen's narrative medium. The continuity and the density of the novels depend on the constant movement of narrative.

The plot moves on many small hinges of narrative. Telling Sir Thomas about *Lovers' Vows* is a matter of moment, and Tom's confusion is almost a masterpiece of deflection and understatement, only slightly too casual and throwaway. Henry Crawford's visit to Portsmouth gives most pleasure – as he quickly sees – because he can tell Fanny about Mansfield Park. His narrative to her is both passionate and manipulative, increasing intimacy by assuming it. An item in a gossip-column in the newspaper, read out by Mr Price, excellent commentator for the delicate purpose of breaking the news to Fanny ('by G– if she belonged to me, I'd give her the rope's end as long as I could stand over her'), changes the fortunes of many people.

As the course of the novel welds inner and outer narration, the fluent form is, from time to time, interrupted by strong climax or serious crisis. One of Jane Austen's most brilliant gifts is her ability to surprise. Though her art deals in the staple of the novel and the drama – expectation, not surprise – she can astonish and arrest the reader. The astonishment is always profoundly instructive as well as thrilling. Compared with her predecessors in fiction, with the possible exception of Richardson, whose epistolary form solves the problem of continuity in a special way, Jane Austen creates an exceptionally strong and cunning chain, whose firm links must sometimes be violently broken.

The private crisis in feeling, when Elizabeth Bennet or Emma comes to know or acknowledge the truth of the heart, is a recurring moment of change. It has its equivalent in the public world, where something startling is told, to burst with forceful surprise upon the reader outside and the listener inside the novel. Surprise in Jane Austen commonly takes the form of startling news, good or bad, true or false. The news is unexpected. Surprises make the action of the novel constantly interesting – varied, unpredictable and tense. But like all the devices and conventions of a great artist, they enlarge our knowledge as well as excite our interest. They form a part of the story of the feelings. They are not always told lengthily or even directly. Mrs Smith in *Persuasion* astonishes Anne Elliot (after having been herself surprised by Anne's insistence that she doesn't care for her cousin) by telling the story of Mr Elliot's true character, but the surprise for the reader is muted by a detailed and thorough preparation. Mrs Smith's is a hesitating and lengthy confidence, slow to get off the ground, prefaced by doubts, and held up by the search for documentary evidence. But Jane Austen's most stunning surprises work through sudden impassioned narratives that force themselves, unexpectedly, into the narrative action.

In *Northanger Abbey* Jane Austen lightly mocks the convention of the long narrative digression, common in Cervantes and the English eighteenth-century novelists. She tells us that her two-sentence summary of Mrs Thorpe and her family will do instead of 'a long and minute detail from Mrs Thorpe herself, of her past adventures and sufferings, which might otherwise be expected to occupy the three or four following chapters' (*NA*, p. 34). Some of her predecessors, especially Fielding, knew perfectly well that a long inset narrative is best justified by a response from the listener, and when the listeners are Parson Adams in *Joseph Andrews*, Tom Jones and Partridge in *Tom Jones*, and Booth in *Amelia*, their response is carefully characteristic, and their attention thoroughly and effectively imagined. The stories of Fielding's Mr Wilson, the Man of the Hill, and Miss Matthews are not simply narrative embellishments or cadenzas, but are seen to be told for a profound purpose. They are also told for an immediate effect by particular tellers to particular listeners. Such elaborate digressive stories are still and formal, however, like carefully inserted pieces of contrasting material in a static marquetry design, when compared with the confessions, confidences and revelations in Jane Austen. Her inset stories are part of the narrative flow, arresting action in order to thrust it into more powerful motion, buttonholing the characters in order to shatter their feelings, overturn their ideas, and utterly change their lives.

In each novel there comes a piece of transforming news. In *Sense and Sensibility* Lucy Steele's information about her engagement to Edward Ferrars is no less shattering for being unfolded slowly. Lucy takes her time, first prefacing a question about Mrs Ferrars with 'You will think my question an odd one', (Elinor does), and then persisting in spite of Elinor's politely cool refusal to satisfy 'what seemed impertinent curiosity'. Throughout her skirting and scouting we are aware of Lucy's look, which is as sharp, baleful and controlled as Becky Sharp's.[2] She first eyes Elinor attentively, later looks down in amiable bashfulness 'with only one side glance at her companion to observe its effect on her'. Just before coming to the point and announcing her engagement to Mr Robert Ferrars's 'elder brother', she fixes her eyes upon Elinor. But if Lucy is snakelike, Elinor is no rabbit, and Jane Austen sets her this cruel listening test in order to let her powers of control and reserve show the advantage of long practice:

> What felt Elinor at that moment? Astonishment, that would have been as painful as it was strong, had not an immediate disbelief of the assertion attended it. She turned towards Lucy in silent amazement, unable to divine the reason or object of such a declaration, and though her complexion varied, she stood firm in incredulity and felt in no danger of an hysterical fit, or a swoon. (*SS*, p. 129)

What initially helps her to preserve her control is incredulity, but this is succeeded by the desire to question. Then she is in turn shocked, still incredulous, and unpleasantly moved by a certain measure of plausibility in the tale. She feels 'an exertion of spirits, which increased with her increase of emotion'. Elinor's self-command is reinforced by various feelings and allows her to reply with calmness to Lucy's hints

---

[2] I think it likely that Becky owes several of her features – name, eyes and cunning – to Lucy.

at intimacy, especially to the remark that Edward is longing for her picture, and to show no response to the tearful play with the handkerchief. She is even given the self-possession to make the shrewd comment that she is surprised by an unnecessary and unsought confidence: 'You must at least have felt that my being acquainted with it could not add to its safety.' The pointed remark – showing the victim in the ascendant – is accompanied by her earnest look at Lucy. The play of eyes is an important weapon in this duel of aggressive falsehood with sincere reserve. At the end of the first confidence Elinor's stoicism is 'almost overcome – her heart sunk within her, and she could hardly stand', but once more she exerts herself. Despite her defences, the totally unexpected revelation leaves her 'mortified, shocked, confounded'. And the reader shares the shock. Jane Austen's surprises bring reader and character together, if not in a concurrence of feeling, at least in an overlapping response. To say that we comprehend Elinor's feelings is inadequate; we feel the mortification by sharing both shock and incredulity.

Lucy's story is startling to reader and character because it comes out of the blue, as a piece of news no one could anticipate. Even the elder Miss Steele's hints, and Lucy's preference of Elinor, which is innocently, naturally and acceptably interpreted by Elinor as a result of Marianne's intolerance and coldness, cannot act as preparation for Lucy's confidences. It is a perfect analysis of aggressive and spiteful jealousy, emerging as it does from the assumption that Elinor has been made a confidante because she is such a courteous listener. An aggressive woman purrs out the lie which is strengthened by its threads of truths – it is true that she and Edward are engaged, untrue that they love each other; the story is designed to hurt and depress her rival, who has to be tongue-tied. Lucy captures her by her very politeness, and both surprise and submissive listening make a part of the revenge. Jane Austen, as always, enjoys the discrimination of minds, as she pits one intelligence against the other. Each woman knows what is happening, speaks or hears the subtext. Lucy perhaps expects Elinor to respond more openly or crudely – at least to give something away under the pressure of her aggressive confidence and basilisk gaze, but much of the satisfaction of the exchange lies in Elinor's preservation of control, and in her subsequent powerful initiative as she returns to to the confidence, armed with resolutions and questions. Elinor's self-sought sequel, which gives her the advantage after recovery, develops Lucy's suspicious jealousy and controlled curiosity of Elinor in a game of adroit fencing. This is a perfectly contrived social set and scene: Elinor politely collaborates with her rival in the filigree work for the spoilt child Anna Maria, with 'working candles' to bring more light. While the others play their game of cards, Elinor and Lucy play their game of work. The busy kindness of the basket-making masks and permits a tense exchange of innuendo and clash of feeling. It is an essentially *narrative* conflict:

In a firm, though cautious tone, Elinor thus began.

'I should be undeserving of the confidence you have honoured me with, if I felt no desire for its continuance, or no farther curiosity on its subject. I will not apologize therefore for bringing it forward again.'

'Thank you,' cried Lucy warmly, 'for breaking the ice; you have set my heart at ease by it; for I was somehow or other afraid I had offended you by what I told you that Monday.'

'Offended me! How could you suppose so? Believe me,' and Elinor spoke it with the truest sincerity, 'nothing could be farther from my intention, than to give you such an idea. Could you have a motive for the trust, that was not honourable and flattering to me?'

'And yet I do assure you,' replied Lucy, her little sharp eyes full of meaning, 'there seemed to me to be a coldness and displeasure in your manner, that made me quite uncomfortable. I felt sure that you was angry with me; and have been quarrelling with myself ever since, for having took such a liberty as to trouble you with my affairs. But I am very glad to find it was only my own fancy, and that you do not really blame me. If you knew what a consolation it was to me to relieve my heart by speaking to you of what I am always thinking of every moment of my life, your compassion would make you overlook every thing else I am sure.'

'Indeed I can easily believe that it was a very great relief to you, to acknowledge your situation to me, and be assured that you shall never have reason to repent it. Your case is a very unfortunate one; you seem to me to be surrounded with difficulties, and you will have need of all your mutual affection to support you under them. Mr. Ferrars, I believe, is entirely dependent on his mother.'

'He has only two thousand pounds of his own; it would be madness to marry upon that, though for my own part, I could give up every prospect of more without a sigh. I have been always used to a very small income, and could struggle with any poverty for him; but I love him too well to be the selfish means of robbing him, perhaps, of all that his mother might give him if he married to please her. We must wait, it may be for many years. With almost every other man in the world, it would be an alarming prospect; but Edward's affection and constancy nothing can deprive me of I know.'

'That conviction must be every thing to you; and he is undoubtedly supported by the same trust in your's. If the strength of your reciprocal attachment had failed, as between many people and under many circumstances it naturally would during a four years' engagement, your situation would have been pitiable indeed.'

Lucy here looked up; but Elinor was careful in guarding her countenance from every expression that could give her words a suspicious tendency.

'Edward's love for me,' said Lucy, 'has been pretty well put to the test, by our long, very long absence since we were first engaged, and it has stood the trial so well, that I should be unpardonable to doubt it now. I can safely say that he has never gave me one moment's alarm on that account from the first.'

Elinor hardly knew whether to smile or sigh at this assertion.

(*SS*, pp. 146-7)

They were again silent for many minutes. At length Lucy exclaimed with a deep sigh,

'I believe it would be the wisest way to put an end to the business at once by dissolving the engagement. We seem so beset with difficulties on every side, that though it would make us miserable for a time, we should be happier perhaps in the end. But you will not give me your advice, Miss Dashwood?'

'No;' answered Elinor, with a smile, which concealed very agitated feelings, 'on such a subject I certainly will not. You know very well that my opinion would have no weight with you, unless it were on the side of your wishes.'

'Indeed you wrong me,' replied Lucy with great solemnity; 'I know nobody of whose judgment I think so highly as I do of yours; and I do really believe, that if you was to say to me, "I advise you by all means to put an end to your engagement with Edward Ferrars, it will be more for the happiness of both of you," I should resolve upon doing it immediately.'

Elinor blushed for the insincerity of Edward's future wife, and replied, 'This compliment would effectually frighten me from giving any opinion on the subject had I formed one. It raises my influence much too high; the power of dividing two people so tenderly attached is too much for an indifferent person.'

' 'Tis because you are an indifferent person,' said Lucy, with some pique, and laying a particular stress on those words, 'that your judgment might justly have such weight with me. If you could be supposed to be biassed in any respect by your own feelings, your opinion would not be worth having.'

Elinor thought it wisest to make no answer to this, lest they might provoke each other to an unsuitable increase of ease and unreserve. . . .

(*SS*, pp. 149-50)

As Jane Austen relieves, animates, dramatizes and deepens this long narrative, she gives new life to the old form of the confidence. Elinor's politeness, sympathy, reserve and intelligence doom her to be a confidante in painful circumstances. Here is also the ironic position, to be reworked in the cases of Fanny Price and Anne Elliot, of the confidante who has to listen but who has herself no one in whom to confide. *Sense and Sensibility*'s second astonishing story is also told to Elinor. It is Willoughby's confession. Like Lucy's confidence, it also has a full and fully justified emotional urgency. Willoughby bursts in on Elinor as we have seen, when our mind and hers are elsewhere. She is recovering from the agitating fears and hopes of Marianne's fever, and alone at night, is waiting for the sound of her mother's carriage. When she does hear the carriage, rather earlier than she had expected, she looks out and, seeing that it is drawn by four horses instead of two, immediately concludes this to be the reason for her mother's speedy arrival:

> Never in her life had Elinor found it so difficult to be calm, as at that moment. The knowledge of what her mother must be feeling as the carriage stopt at the door,—of her doubt—her dread—perhaps her despair!—and of what *she* had to tell!—with such knowledge it was impossible to be calm. All that remained to be done, was to be speedy; and therefore staying only till she could leave Mrs. Jennings's maid with her sister, she hurried down stairs.
> The bustle in the vestibule, as she passed along an inner lobby, assured her that they were already in the house. She rushed forwards towards the drawing-room,—she entered it,—and saw only Willoughby. (*SS*, p. 316)

In Willoughby's long, impassioned story, Jane Austen's art is delicately and cunningly at work. A long story ought to be varied and broken, so Willoughby is allowed no monolith of narrative. Before even beginning his story he has to make his way against Elinor's reluctance, first to receive and then to hear him. 'Such a beginning as this', she says after hearing about his motives in engaging Marianne's affections 'without any design of returning' them, 'cannot be followed by any thing'. It is of course actually followed by Willoughby's version of that rake's sentimental education which is repeated in more depth and detail with Henry Crawford in *Mansfield Park*. He must tell and she must listen. She interrupts as he claims to have 'lost everything' that could make life a blessing, and is 'a little softened' as she half-asks, half-understands, that he does feel a loss. But her words are guarded, in spite of her sympathy: 'You did then . . . believe yourself at one time attached to her?' The course of her response varies with that of the feelings and events in his story. Embarrassment succeeds sympathy as he is forced to mention – or not mention – Eliza Williams. Jane Austen draws attention to the constant play and change of response during 'the course of this extraordinary conversation', and by the time Willoughby has gone, we are not surprised that Elinor finds herself so shaken. But she is an experienced listener, and this is a vital listening test for both her sense and her sensibility. She is moved, but alive to the knowledge that she is moved by meretricious causes. During the conversation, she feels mixtures and alternations of distaste and pity, withdrawal and approach; there are some beautifully recorded moments, when sympathy is registered in silence, including one 'pause of mutual thoughtfulness'.

The story is astonishing, but the nature of this listener's astonishment is carefully scrutinized. Elinor's self-inspection is typical of her sense and sensibility, rationality and sympathy. She is left feeling oppressed by 'a croud of ideas, widely differing in themselves, but of which sadness was the general result'. Before Willoughby's arrival she and the reader were engrossed by Marianne. After it she is too oppressed 'to think even of her sister'. But shaken and engrossed as she is by his narrative, she is still able to allow for the influence of 'circumstances which ought not in reason to have weight; by that person of uncommon attraction, that open, affectionate, and lively manner which it was no merit to possess; and by that still ardent love for Marianne, which it was not even innocent to indulge'.

Jane Austen's insistence that sense and sensibility must work together is shown in the novel in many ways. Here it is stressed by Elinor's inability to be moved without analysing her response and using her reason to expose its nature, together with her equal inability to obliterate that response. The impact of the storytelling survives analysis and judgement: 'But she felt that it was so, long, long before she could feel his influence less.' We are told later that the effect does wear off, having been given enough time: 'Reflection had given calmness to her judgment, and sobered her own opinion of Willoughby's deserts.' Jane Austen does not forget the strong moments of her emotional action, but keeps them in mind. Continuity is never lost.

The novels are full of such bursts of news, good and bad. Most startling are such inner disclosures which have a double effect, like that just described, within the novel itself. These surprises are almost always narrative revelations. Catherine Morland encounters Henry Tilney coming unexpectedly up a stairway as she is leaving his dead mother's disappointingly well-lit room, and the physical shock is followed by Catherine's forced confession. This surprise meeting is less startling to the reader who knows and expects all, than the later revelation which, though heralded by the Gothic turning of Catherine's doorhandle, is Eleanor's unGothic announcement that General Tilney, a modern villain, is turning the heroine out of Northanger Abbey. Here too there is a combination of physical and mental shock. And here again is a brilliant sense of timing. Jane Austen surprises us when we are looking somewhere else. She interrupts one absorbing story with another. In *Pride and Prejudice* she springs the news of Lydia and Wickham's elopement just when Elizabeth Bennet, and the reader, are engrossed by the renewal of the acquaintance with Darcy. In *Emma* there is a whole series of shocks for the heroine, though the reader is usually prepared for most of them, but the actual news of Emma's attachment to Knightley is an entirely inward surprise, and slightly lowers the impact – as it should – of the startling news of Jane Fairfax's secret engagement to Frank Churchill:

> Harriet was standing at one of the windows. Emma turned round to look at her in consternation, and hastily said,
> 'Have you any idea of Mr. Knightley's returning your affection?'
> 'Yes,' replied Harriet modestly, but not fearfully—'I must say that I have.'
> Emma's eyes were instantly withdrawn; and she sat silently meditating, in a fixed attitude, for a few minutes. A few minutes were sufficient for making her acquainted with her own heart. A mind like her's, once opening to suspicion, made rapid progress. She touched—she admitted—she acknowledged the whole truth. Why was it so much worse that Harriet should be in love with Mr. Knightley, than with Frank Churchill? Why was the evil so dreadfully increased by Harriet's having some hope of a return? It darted through her, with the speed of an arrow, that Mr. Knightley must marry no one but herself! (*E*, pp. 407-8)

> 'Have you indeed no idea?' said Mrs. Weston in a trembling voice. 'Cannot you, my dear Emma—cannot you form a guess as to what you are to hear?'
> 'So far as that it relates to Mr. Frank Churchill, I do guess.'
> 'You are right. It does relate to him, and I will tell you directly;' (resuming her work, and seeming resolved against looking up.) 'He has been here this very morning, on a most extraordinary errand. It is impossible to express our surprise. He came to speak to his father on a subject,— to announce an attachment—'
> She stopped to breathe. Emma thought first of herself, and then of Harriet.
> 'More than an attachment, indeed,' resumed Mrs. Weston; 'an engage-

ment—a positive engagement.—What will you say, Emma—what will anybody say, when it is known that Frank Churchill and Miss Fairfax are engaged; nay, that they have been long engaged!'
    Emma even jumped with surprise;—and, horror-struck, exclaimed, 'Jane Fairfax!—Good God! You are not serious? You do not mean it?'
                                                      (*E*, pp. 394-5)

Anne Elliot, in *Persuasion*, is happily astonished at the news of Louisa Musgrove's engagement to Captain Benwick. The news about Mr Elliot's past, though surprising, is much less of a shock because she has perceived his insincerity and lack of 'seriousness'. But the good news changes her life: 'She had never in her life been more astonished. ... It was almost too wonderful for belief.' (*P*, p. 165)

But such disclosures depend on ignorance, mystery and secrecy. Most of the lovers are unprepared for the final surprise, the joyful revelation at the end, which tells all at last. Jane Austen's conclusions are conventional in outline, but original in particularity. They are also created out of that imaginative art which avoids the mere narration of a story about fictional characters to a reader. Jane Austen tells a story about telling and listening, or even writing and reading. Narrative is made internal; both author and reader are curiously and intimately involved. The effects of this narrative art are therefore never thinly rhetorical, never there just to startle or satisfy us. There is nothing between dramatist and audience, or writer and reader, in those time-honoured and probably valuable modes of pseudo-art, melodrama and pornography, except curious instruments devised for stimulus. Jane Austen had herself sensed and even savoured the rhetorical hollowness of Gothic novels, but her own effects are more profound. She explores sensation and feeling within her characters, and moves us by the exploration. Beginnings are beginnings for all, the author setting out to tell, the characters initiated into new experience, and the reader eager and willing for the journey. The turns and surprises of action are for all. By the time we arrive at the end, we are not the only ones to be told the end of a story.

When Elinor is told the true story (after the false impression) of Lucy's marriage, and the true story (after her ignorance and Lucy's lies) about Edward's past, the story of *Sense and Sensibility* is nearly over. The disposal of Marianne to Colonel Brandon, presented more summarily and remotely than Elinor's destiny, brings the whole novel to an end. Perhaps the common feeling that there is something unsatisfactory about Marianne's share in the conclusion owes something to the lack of that imaginative concurrence of learning and ending for character and reader, which is felt for Elinor and Edward. It is also felt for Catherine Morland and Henry Tilney, Elizabeth and Darcy, Fanny and Edmund, Emma and Knightley, and Anne and Captain Wentworth.

The story that we all learn at the end is not a simple one. The lovers are expected to live happily ever after, because the mysteries in the past – and there are always mysteries about human behaviour in Jane Austen – are so perfectly cleared up. There are no magical transformations, as there are so often in Victorian novels, but there are profound and thorough revelations. We learn what happened between Lucy and Edward, General Tilney and John Thorpe, Darcy, Lydia and Wickham, Maria Rushworth and Henry Crawford, Edmund and Mary, Frank and Jane, Knightley and Harriet, Captain Wentworth, Mr Elliot and Anne. We learn everything. The whole truths are made available, the plot's mysteries are dispelled, events thoroughly explained, problems solved, all looked at in the clear light of day. If we compare such explanations and revelations with, say, the end of a detective story, or a Victorian sensation novel, the difference is clear. The events of Jane Austen's plots are made plain for characters as well as reader. Emotional and intellectual difficulties are elucidated for all who have been ignorant, puzzled or misled within the novel. Although the best thrillers and detective stories go through the motions of presenting the concluding revelatory narrative dramatically, with some attention to individual motive and response, the detective's summary is usually apparent as a device or a convention. In these novels, however, it is absolutely essential for the characters to know what has happened. The disclosures are urgently needed within the story. Catherine is dying to know what made General Tilney turn her out; Elinor has been patient for a long time but desperately wants to know how Edward and Lucy ever came together; Elizabeth Bennet, always curious, but particularly anxious to know how Darcy could have been at her sister's wedding, has to write and find out what has happened from her aunt, once Lydia's inability to keep the secret has tempted and tantalized. Fanny Price must know how Henry Crawford, her declared lover, could have run away with Maria, for whom he had never much cared, and how they could have sinned. She is incredulous, but needs most, though painfully and fearfully, to know what the consequences are for Edmund and Mary, the man she loves and the woman he loves. Anne Elliot –

while needing to know less than most since her speculation and surmise have always been rational and steady, never leaping ahead of
firm evidence – still needs to know, and needs to tell, what has been
happening and why, since she and Wentworth separated in 1805.

Confidences, confessions, blurted-out secrets, transient attempts to
deceive, mark the last part of a Jane Austen novel. The narrative
needs and responses are in character, in every sense of that phrase.
They depend on the novel's past, on our memory of the character's
memories which is guaranteed by the novelist's more faithful memory.
The concluding telling and listening is in character too: timid, bold,
sensible, restrained, joyful, playful, agitated, grateful. And always
loving. The story of the obscured action, the glance back at the rough
path of these true lovers, is inseparable from the final story of happy
love. The lovers' happy-ever-after is perhaps more convincing in Jane
Austen's novels than anywhere else in realistic fiction. It is something
that relies on our sense of congruity in mind and feeling. The development of appropriate and strong conjunctions depends on the whole
of the novel's drive and action, but reaches a consummation at the
end. Love and aggression often find appropriate narrative forms in
fiction. Lucy and Elinor attack, defend and counter-attack as they tell
and listen. Elizabeth Bennet wounds Darcy as she rejects the first story
he tells her of his love, and her refusal to listen appals and insults him
as she feels appalled and insulted. But telling can join as well as
separate, through language, form and content. In each novel the
lovers end by telling each other the common, necessary and all-
engrossing story of how it all began. Tellers and listeners have their
characteristic mode of thinking and feeling, and the telling and listening generate a loving complicity. This is what each has been meaning,
thinking and feeling during the time of doubt and separation.

For Elinor there is a rational judgement, as she and Edward look
back together:

> 'Your behaviour was certainly very wrong,' said she, 'because—to say
> nothing of my own conviction, our relations were all led away by it to
> fancy and expect *what*, as you were *then* situated, could never be.'
> He could only plead an ignorance of his own heart, and a mistaken
> confidence in the force of his engagement.
> 'I was simple enough to think, that because my *faith* was plighted to
> another, there could be no danger of my being with you; and that the
> consciousness of my engagement was to keep my heart as safe and sacred
> as my honour. I felt that I admired you, but I told myself it was only

friendship; and till I began to make comparisons between yourself and Lucy, I did not know how far I was got. After that, I suppose, I *was* wrong in remaining so much in Sussex, and the arguments with which I reconciled myself to the expediency of it, were no better than these:—The danger is my own; I am doing no injury to anybody but myself.'

Elinor smiled, and shook her head. (*SS*, p. 368)

The exchange of histories here is an exchange of mind and feeling. It is made very implicitly. These quiet and rational lovers, distracted though they have at times been shown to be, judge and analyse steadily, but even Jane Austen's summaries of intimate feeling make us aware of the deeper currents. Implicitness is warm, reticence intimate, gentle or tender:

> Edward was now fixed at the cottage at least for a week;—for whatever other claims might be made on him, it was impossible that less than a week should be given up to the enjoyment of Elinor's company, or suffice to say half that was to be said of the past, the present, and the future;— for though a very few hours spent in the hard labour of incessant talking will dispatch more subjects than can really be in common between any two rational creatures,· yet with lovers it is different. Between *them* no subject is finished, no communication is even made, till it has been made at least twenty times over. (*SS*, pp. 363-4)

The restrained conversation sets the pattern for all the novels in its essential exchange of events in the sentimental history, and in its insistence, explicit or implicit, that the exchange itself, almost irrespective of the content, is a delight. It brings teller and listener together, closely and congruously. The sentimental history is related rather briefly here compared with the other novels. But the process is plain.

One thing all the concluding stories have in common is joy. Although Fanny and Edmund's joint declation has had to be postponed, when it does eventually come, Jane Austen's objective, generalized, but delicate description of it in no way lessens its joyous impact:

> Timid, anxious, doubting as she was, it was still impossible that such tenderness as hers should not, at times, hold out the strongest hope of success, though it remained for a later period to tell him the whole delightful and astonishing truth. His happiness in knowing himself to have been so long the beloved of such a heart, must have been great enough to warrant any strength of language in which he could cloathe it to her or to

himself; it must have been a delightful happiness! But there was happiness elsewhere which no description can reach. Let no one presume to give the feelings of a young woman on receiving the assurance of that affection of which she has scarcely allowed herself to entertain a hope.

(*MP*, p. 471)

The staider lovers like Elinor and Edward are delighted; there is a powerful and spontaneous outpouring of feeling in *Emma*; Elizabeth and Darcy are playful, easy, but also grave, beginning their life-long exchange of temperaments; and Anne's always latent humour comes out fully. The concluding exchange of the lovers is both a happy ending and a true taste of the conjugal conversation. As with Charlotte Brontë's re-united Jane Eyre and Rochester, who talk 'all day long', we are made to feel that the conversation of histories is a testimony of affection and candour, a guarantee of passion, like an embrace, and even better than an embrace for suggesting constancy.

The uses of narrative are often joined with their abuses, and these bright endings often have a dark lining. The outsiders and victims have no one to talk to. Willoughby isn't always unhappy, but there are no conversations of love and what he seems most to like to speak of is his admiration for Mrs Brandon. There are some pairs whose dialogue and silences are not comfortable to imagine – Mrs Norris and Maria, for instance, or Lydia and Wickham. And it is a tribute to the thoroughness with which Jane Austen has imagined the telling and listening that we feel we know exactly how these other conversations would go.

IV

# The Storytellers

*2: Imagination and Memory*

Jane Austen's presentation of telling and listening is very much more than a formal device; it is an analysis and an evaluation of the human mind. Like all novelists, Jane Austen has her favourite themes and topics, some of which are common to all literary narrative – in the novel, drama, or poetry – and others which seem to prevail character-istically in her individual art. It is hard to imagine a novel which doesn't record and rely on the simplest form of narrative exchange, in which we tell each other about ourselves. The daily telling is hardly ever purely narrative, but it uses narrative to convey feeling as well as information. The actual telling about deep hopes and wishes is often redundant between intimates, yet it has to go on if intimacy is to last, expressing and generating feeling. In the case of Marianne Dashwood in *Sense and Sensibility*, the story she tells her mother can't be a new one, though it is obviously not stale. It is about the past and about the future, it imagines and remembers:

> 'Nay, mama, if he is not to be animated by Cowper!—but we must allow for difference of taste. Elinor has not my feelings, and therefore she may overlook it, and be happy with him. But it would have broke *my* heart had I loved him, to hear him read with so little sensibility. Mama, the more I know of the world, the more am I convinced that I shall never see a man whom I can really love. I require so much! He must have all Edward's virtues, and his person and manners must ornament his good-ness with every possible charm.'
> 'Remember, my love, that you are not seventeen. It is yet too early in life to despair of such an happiness. Why should you be less fortunate than your mother? In one circumstance only, my Marianne, may your destiny be different from her's!' (*SS*, p. 18)

The story Elinor tells Marianne is new, because it tells about a new acquaintance, but it is obviously part of the continuous, long-standing telling and listening that goes on in the family:

'In my heart I feel little—scarcely any doubt of his preference. But there are other points to be considered besides his inclination. He is very far from being independent. What his mother really is we cannot know; but, from Fanny's occasional mention of her conduct and opinions, we have never been disposed to think her amiable; and I am very much mistaken if Edward is not himself aware that there would be many difficulties in his way, if he were to wish to marry a woman who had not either a great fortune or high rank.'

Marianne was astonished to find how much the imagination of her mother and herself had outstripped the truth.

'And you really are not engaged to him' said she. 'Yet it certainly soon will happen. But two advantages will proceed from this delay. *I* shall not lose you so soon, and Edward will have greater opportunity of improving that natural taste for your favourite pursuit which must be so indispensably necessary to your future felicity. Oh! if he should be so far stimulated by your genius as to learn to draw himself, how delightful it would be!'

(*SS*, pp. 21-2)

The family narrative is not totally unreserved and open. As in all families, even close ones, people talk to each other, about each other, and behind each other's backs. The structure of feeling is revealed and created in such telling. When the Dashwoods have moved to Barton, Marianne confides in her mother a fear that Edward Ferrars is ill, since he hasn't visited them, and her mother replies:

'I rather think you are mistaken, for when I was talking to her yesterday of getting a new grate for the spare bedchamber, she observed that there was no immediate hurry for it, as it was not likely that the room would be wanted for some time.'

'How strange this is! what can be the meaning of it! But the whole of their behaviour to each other has been unaccountable! How cold, how composed were their last adieus! How languid their conversation the last evening of their being together! In Edward's farewell there was no distinction between Elinor and me: it was the good wishes of an affectionate brother to both. Twice did I leave them purposely together in the course of the last morning, and each time did he most unaccountably follow me out of the room. And Elinor, in quitting Norland and Edward, cried not as I did. Even now her self-command is invariable. When is she dejected or melancholy? When does she try to avoid society, or appear restless and dissatisfied in it?' (*SS*, p. 39)

The flow of the domestic novel consists to a very large extent of this kind of speculative exchange, intimate but also ignorant. Jane Austen is reflecting a truth about family life in showing its constant surmise and limited confidence, its secrets, and its isolations. She uses such internal narrations for the purposes of her own larger narrative tension. As the characters speculate, so does the reader. We come to be trusted with certain secrets that members of the family don't know, to exchange curiosity for the stimulus of ironic knowledge. Mrs Dashwood is rash and irrational in her affections and hopes, but has sufficient tact to speak with some reserve about her hopes for Elinor's marriage. When she says discreetly, with that blend of affectionate and amused sharpness characteristic of the family discourse, that 'if Elinor would ever condescend to anticipate enjoyment, she would perhaps expect some from improving her acquaintance with her sister-in-law's family', Elinor can't be as candid as she would like. To tell the whole story is impossible. But she has her own characteristic method of adapting the timing and structure of her telling to the listener, and starts, unsuccessfully, to reveal her secret doubts. Ironic knowledge allows us to appraise both effort and failure:

> Elinor had often wished for an opportunity of attempting to weaken her mother's dependence on the attachment of Edward and herself, that the shock might be the less when the whole truth were revealed, and now on this attack, though almost hopeless of success, she forced herself to begin her design by saying, as calmly as she could, 'I like Edward Ferrars very much, and shall always be glad to see him; but as to the rest of the family, it is a matter of perfect indifference to me, whether I am ever known to them or not.'
>
> Mrs. Dashwood smiled and said nothing. Marianne lifted up her eyes in astonishment, and Elinor conjectured that she might as well have held her tongue. (*SS*, p. 157)

Jane Austen analyses the daily storytelling, but her interest in narrative often strikes us as a particularly professional interest. It is never merely professional. Despite the popularity of artist-novels, novels have a tendency not to be narrowly or directly about novelists. What every novelist knows most about is writing novels, but the analysis of narrative imagination is usually two-headed. It looks towards art, and towards life. We cannot always tell which is primary, the professional or unprofessional, just as we cannot know whether the interest in the life-narrative impels the novelist's career, or develops with the writing. In *Emma*, for instance, the author obviously has some personal and professional interest in describing a heroine who is 'an imaginist, on fire with zeal and speculation'. But Jane Austen never writes a novel about a novelist. She is much more widely concerned with human character. Emma's are the temptations of a human being possessed of fertile narrative imagination, and they are also the temptations of a lazy, rich, clever young woman living in a small village, brought up by weak and amiable people who have let her have things her own way. When Jane Austen wrote *Emma* she seems to have been writing about the strengths and weaknesses of human imagination from a sensibility alerted by professional experience. Perhaps more striking than the major events of the plot is the occasional account of Emma's mind. On this occasion it is revealed when idling, and off-duty. She expects little, and sees little. Both expectation and actuality show the characteristic working of her mind:

> ... Emma went to the door for amusement.—Much could not be hoped from the traffic of even the busiest part of Highbury;—Mr. Perry walking hastily by, Mr. William Cox letting himself in at the office door, Mr. Cole's carriage horses returning from exercise, or a stray letter-boy on an obstinate mule, were the liveliest objects she could presume to expect, and when her eyes fell only on the butcher with his tray, a tidy old woman travelling homewards from shop with her full basket, two curs quarrelling over a dirty bone, and a string of dawdling children round the baker's little bow-window eyeing the gingerbread, she knew she had no reason to complain, and was amused enough; quite enough still to stand at the door. A mind lively and at ease, can do with seeing nothing, and can see nothing that does not answer. (*E*, p. 233)

Jane Austen never really suggests that the highest truth of which the novel is capable, is the goal of most novels, and she knows how sensational fiction can encourage us to distort the expectations of common life. Readers of novels need to distinguish carefully and lucidly between what happens in the novel, allowing for its genre and its arena, and what may happen in their environment, as Henry Tilney tells Catherine in *Northanger Abbey*:

> 'If I understand you rightly, you had formed a surmise of such horror as I have hardly words to——Dear Miss Morland, consider the dreadful nature of the suspicions you have entertained. What have you been judging from? Remember the country and the age in which we live. Remember that we are English, that we are Christians. Consult your own understanding, your own sense of the probable, your own observation of what is passing around you—Does our education prepare us for such atrocities? Do our laws connive at them? Could they be perpetrated without being known, in a country like this, where social and literary intercourse is on such a footing; where every man is surrounded by a neigh-

bourhood of voluntary spies, and where roads and newspapers lay every thing open? Dearest Miss Morland, what ideas have you been admitting?'

(*NA*, pp. 197-8)

Catherine Morland's obstacles to using her sense of probability, and knowing her own heart and the hearts of others, are chiefly literary, but her problem doesn't stop with her novel. Jane Austen's presentation of character turns on the analysis of self-knowledge. Elizabeth Bennet and Emma Woodhouse also have to progress and mature by working through falsehood towards truth. Like Catherine's, their ensnaring falsehoods are both of their own and other people's making. Jane Austen constantly returns to the theme of the morally well-meaning person whose susceptibilities are easy game for less well-meaning storytellers. Isabella Thorpe enjoys the sham thrills of Gothic novels, and lives through sham thrills in real life. Catherine Morland, deluded by her friend's affectation, is taken in partly because because she hasn't yet learnt to spot the language and logic of truth, but she begins very early to pierce Isabella's inflations, exaggerations and inconsistencies with her own beautiful matter-of-factness and honesty:

> They met by appointment; and as Isabella had arrived nearly five minutes before her friend, her first address naturally was—'My dearest creature, what can have made you so late? I have been waiting for you at least this age!'
>
> 'Have you, indeed!—I am very sorry for it; but really I thought I was in very good time. It is but just one. I hope you have not been here long?'
>
> 'Oh! these ten ages at least. I am sure I have been here this half hour.'
>
> (*NA*, p. 39)

> Isabella, on hearing the particulars of the visit, gave a different explanation: 'It was all pride, pride, insufferable haughtiness and pride! She had long suspected the family to be very high, and this made it certain. Such insolence of behaviour as Miss Tilney's she had never heard of in her life! Not to do the honours of her house with common good-breeding!—To behave to her guest with such superciliousness!—Hardly even to speak to her!'
>
> 'But it was not so bad as that, Isabella; there was no superciliousness; she was very civil.'
>
> 'Oh! don't defend her! And then the brother, he, who had appeared so attached to you! Good heavens! well, some people's feelings are incomprehensible. And so he hardly looked once at you the whole day?'
>
> 'I do not say so; but he did not seem in good spirits.'
>
> 'How contemptible! Of all things in the world inconstancy is my

aversion. Let me entreat you never to think of him again, my dear Cather-
ine; indeed he is unworthy of you.'
   'Unworthy! I do not suppose he ever thinks of me.'
   'That is exactly what I say; he never thinks of you.—Such fickleness!'
                                                (*NA*, pp. 129-30)

She also begins very early to question John Thorpe's disorganized
boasts:

> 'What do you think of my gig, Miss Morland? a neat one, is it not?
> Well hung; town built; I have not had it a month. It was built for a Christ-
> church man, a friend of mine, a very good sort of fellow; he ran it a few
> weeks, till, I believe, it was convenient to have done with it. I happened
> just then to be looking out for some light thing of the kind, though I had
> pretty well determined on a curricle too; but I chanced to meet him on
> Magdalen Bridge, as he was driving into Oxford, last term: "Ah!
> Thorpe," said he, "do you happen to want such a little thing as this? it
> is a capital one of the kind, but I am cursed tired of it." "Oh! d——," said
> I, "I am your man; what do you ask?" And how much do you think he
> did, Miss Morland?'
>    'I am sure I cannot guess at all.' (*NA*, p. 46)

But she is also gulled for the best reasons, because she judges the world
by her own standards of honesty and fidelity. She takes General
Tilney for a murderer, but he is is only a false, cold and mercenary
man. He hasn't killed his wife but his presence in his family kills its
life. Catherine takes Isabella for someone like herself, candid,
affectionate and true, as Henry points out. But what she has to
discover, like Marianne Dashwood, is the unreliability of truths as
well as lies. To judge every one by oneself is not much safer than
judging by literature. Catherine's literal truthtelling has a moral
attraction, especially in a world of accomplished liars and foolish
rattles – 'I walk about here, and so I do there; – but here I see a variety
of people in every street, and there I can only go and call on Mrs
Allen' (*NA*, p. 79) – but she has to explore the human variety.
   The heroines all have to learn the right use of imaginative energy,
to direct it towards the self and towards the world. To be properly
imaginative is to learn the right use of reason, to generalize and to
compare and scrutinize language, form and character in the attempt
to make out self and others. Discovering the truth is all very well, but
it doesn't solve everything. The novels also insist on the difficulty of
telling the truth, once you think you know it. Elizabeth Bennet works
painfully and scrupulously through to the admission of past delusions

and prejudices, and the knowledge of present feeling. She comes to a sense of herself, past and present, and a sense of other people, especially Darcy. Jane Austen's view of such discoveries has its simplicities, no doubt. The relationships in her novels may seem implausibly steady and reliable, but granted this assumption, or fiction, of stability, it remains true that she shows the grave difficulty of telling the truth. It is very hard even for the candid and self-critical Elizabeth. Imagination is needed to know the truth, but is scarcely a guarantee.

In *Sense and Sensibility* too, Jane Austen is concerned with the distortions and illusions created by narrative imagination, encouraged by literary stereotype or personal fantasy. Jane Austen got over her pleasure in burlesques of sensibility in early adolescence and her novels are free to show subtle and realistic analyses of the illusions created by imagination, even in good minds. Marianne is infected by romantic stereotypes which tell the story of love and marriage along certain easy lines: love occurs once, and only once; marriage does not need wealth, but wealth is conveniently assumed in a reasonable 'competence'; the mind can be read in the graces of face and figure. Such fictions contrive to be flattering and self-flattering, conferring on the most unreasonable desires the appearance of a modest simplicity and virtue. These romantic versions of the good life are not only false but predatory and lazy. Marianne's intelligence and candour tell stories interestingly fashioned out of sense and nonsense, virtuous aspiration and greed, radical feeling and conventionality. Just as Cervantes criticizes the follies of anachronistic chivalry and at the same time condemns a world without chivalry, so Jane Austen sets Marianne's romantic selections and wish-fulfilments amongst the prevailing social fictions which have no ideal, no passion, no individuality, nothing but a destructive, careless and materialist conformity. Colonel Brandon draws attention to the ambivalence of the critique of romanticism when he advises Elinor not to wish away Marianne's 'romantic refinements', for they are 'frequently . . . succeeded by such opinions as are but too common, and too dangerous!' For the reader there is the larger presence of the social versions of 'the good life', which prevail in the novel's world, particularly as practised and preached by John Dashwood and his wife, and other imaginative and unimaginative spokesmen for prudence, and for materialism.

The imaginative stories people tell in *Sense and Sensibility* are illustrative of extremes of sense and sensibility. Marianne's impetuous version of the good life is, as Elinor points out, unchecked by other stories, even that so handy as her own father's second marriage. The most striking contrast to Marianne's storytelling is that of Lucy Steele. Lucy's is an abuse of imagination. She tells many stories, is a good hand at flattery, compliment and guile, but her central story, balancing the love-stories told of and told by Elinor and Marianne, is the story she tells about her secret engagement to Edward. As we have seen, it is an incisive image of total self-seeking and self-possession. Whereas Marianne gives away her limitations, her control, and her selectivity, exposing herself in many ways, Lucy is able to be totally on guard, quite alert in the worst way to the nature and the thoughts of her listeners. When she goads Elinor she is committing an attack through narrative, a marvellous aggressive move since its covertness means that she is able to display her velvet glove, while Elinor has to pretend that there is nothing hurtful beneath grace and smoothness. Lucy's story is a perfect instance of the imaginative corruption of narrative which many excellent narrative artists have liked to imagine: Virgil's Sinon, lying his way into Troy; Satan to Eve, lying his way into Eden; and Iago to Othello, lying his way to destruction. Lucy's style is noticeably less elegant than Sinon's, Satan's, or Iago's, but her technique is very like theirs. It relies on a sharp perception of her listener, a histrionic ability to act out lies and a delight in pitting an uninhibited rationality against the restrictions of honesty. The Trojans can't resist Sinon's self-accusations, and give him welcome and a hearing. Jane Austen's web of imaginative story-telling, good and bad, interweaves imaginative with unimaginative narratives. Lucy is contrasted, as a narrator, with her less adroit sister:

> 'Good gracious! (giggling as she spoke) I'd lay my life I know what my cousins will say, when they hear of it. They will tell me I should write to the Doctor, to get Edward the curacy of his new living. I know they will; but I am sure I would do not such a thing for all the world.—"La!" I shall say directly, "I wonder how you could think of such a thing. *I* write to the Doctor, indeed!"'( *SS*, p. 275)

It is the right nemesis for Lucy to be betrayed by Miss Steele's leaky-minded stupidity. It is also one of Jane Austen's most cunning strokes to marry her imaginative liar to the unimaginative rattle, Robert Ferrars, whose self-admiring stories stupidly solicit admiration:

... she did not find that the emptiness and conceit of the one, put her at all out of charity with the modesty and worth of the other. . . .

'Upon my soul,' he added, 'I believe it is nothing more; and so I often tell my mother, when she is grieving about it. "My dear Madam," I always say to her, "you must make yourself easy. The evil is now irremediable, and it has been entirely your own doing. Why would you be persuaded by my uncle, Sir Robert, against your own judgment, to place Edward under private tuition, at the most critical time of his life? If you had only sent him to Westminster as well as myself, instead of sending him to Mr. Pratt's, all this would have been prevented." This is the way in which I always consider the matter, and my mother is perfectly convinced of her error.' (*SS*, pp. 250-1)

Robert Ferrars is the perfect victim of Lucy's art.

Throughout these narrative contrasts and comparisons the novel's action is of course advanced, for the reader too is being informed and surprised, but the dialogues show the narrative artist's profound interest in the psychology of narrative imagination.

Like Elinor, Emma has to endure a painful, just and inactive silence, in which her imagination plays back her errors. This is exactly the right nemesis for her. It answers Mr Knightley's early wish to see her 'in love and doubtful of the outcome', but also silences the talker who has sinned against silence and wounded Miss Bates. Emma's is the imaginist's nemesis. There is an end to her zeal and speculation once she realizes that Harriet's story about Knightley may be true, that this minor character in her fantasy has an independent and threatening fantasy-life of her own, which she has unwittingly encouraged. Mr Knightley refuses to take up the cliché in which Mrs Weston invites him to 'imagine any thing nearer perfect beauty than Emma', and reads it literally: 'I do not know what I could imagine.' (*E*, p. 39) The literal-mindedness is typical and valuable. Emma never refuses such challenges, and indeed freely issues them to herself and others. She has indulged her energies in shaping experience, and also in the flattering sense of power and ability that goes along with the shaping. Jane Austen doesn't keep her in silent inactivity for long, but feelings of passive helpfulness and remorse are so unusual that their oppression is hateful. Like Catherine, Marianne and Elizabeth, Emma has to learn that the intelligent and imaginative mind, in spite of insight, wit and invention, can make mistakes. Each learns a different lesson because each of them is distinct in moral nature, personality and mind.

*Mansfield Park* weighs the growth of imagination against a mere accumulation of facts:

> 'How long ago it is, aunt, since we used to repeat the chronological order
> of the kings of England, with the dates of their accession, and most of the
> principal events of their reigns!'
>     'Yes,' added the other; 'and of the Roman emperors as low as Severus;
> besides a great deal of the Heathen Mythology, and all the Metals, Semi-
> Metals, Planets, and distinguished philosophers.' (*MP*, pp. 18-19)

As Fanny develops her stories show an unobtrusive growth in confidence. From the very beginning she has, like Catherine Morland, the
strength of sincerity. Apart from Edmund she is the best-informed
person in the novel and her information is personally shaped and
assimilated. Unlike her accomplished and shallowly educated cousins,
whose problems are not so much unaided by other people's ideas, as
totally unformulated and ungeneralized, Fanny is properly educated.
She learns to use fact and idea for the purposes of self-understanding
and a sense of the world. Her versions of experience have certainty,
form and life. Unlike Mary Crawford, whose wit shows some accomplishment and reading, though her liveliness often dresses up thread-
bare and commonplace opinions, Fanny steadies her wishes and
demands by knowledge and reason – 'That weather is all from the
South'. Fanny combines a firm sense of where she is with a clear
enough sense that the world is large and unknown. She must begin,
though not stay, at home, and she comes to know that her home is in
Mansfield Park.

Fanny learns the lessons of imagination by listening – to voices in
books, drawing-rooms, on staircases, in shrubberies, wildernesses and
great houses. She listens intently to Mrs Rushworth:

> . . . Mrs. Rushworth, who had been at great pains to learn all that the
> housekeeper could teach, . . . was now almost equally well qualified to
> shew the house. On the present occasion, she addressed herself chiefly to
> Miss Crawford and Fanny, but there was no comparison in the willingness
> of their attention, for Miss Crawford, who had seen scores of great houses,
> and cared for none of them, had only the appearance of civilly listening,
> while Fanny, to whom every thing was almost as interesting as it was new,
> attended with unaffected earnestness to all that Mrs. Rushworth could
> relate of the family in former times, its rise and grandeur, regal visits and
> loyal efforts, delighted to connect any thing with history already known,
> or warm her imagination with scenes of the past. (*MP*, p. 85)

In Edmund's presence she has confidence, even early on, and can speak out and explain when she disagrees. Even her hesitations show sense and delicacy, and her reasoning is careful and steady:

> 'No,' replied Fanny, 'but we need not give up his profession for all that; because, whatever profession Dr. Grant had chosen, he would have taken a —— not a good temper into it; and as he must either in the navy or army have had a great many more people under his command than he has now, I think more would have been made unhappy by him as a sailor or soldier than as a clergyman. Besides, I cannot but suppose that whatever there may be to wish otherwise in Dr. Grant, would have been in a greater danger of becoming worse in a more active and worldly profession, where he would have had less time and obligation—where he might have escaped that knowledge of himself, the *frequency*, at least, of that knowledge which it is impossible he should escape as he is now.'
>
> (*MP*, pp. 111-12)

Her attention to 'that knowledge of himself' is significant, but even more significant is her use of imaginative conjecture. As a child, she thought she would go to Ireland via the Isle of Wight, the only island she knew, and called 'the Island'.[1] As a young woman, she knows more, and her imaginative excursions are founded on knowledge, to generate more inquiry. It is Fanny, not the proficient Bertram girls, who asks Sir Thomas about the slave-trade. Her imagination begins at home, but travels beyond. For a long time, Fanny is too little of a teller, too much of a listener. As a fearful child and a stranger in Mansfield Park, she is shy and diffident, as we all are on arriving in foreign parts. She is also put down by the clever talkativeness of her cousins and the daunting harangues of Mrs Norris, which encourage her timidity. But she can open her heart to Edmund, until he is drawn away to listen, charmed if doubtful, to Mary Crawford's wit and humour. Fanny has to learn to do many things in order to make her entrance into the world, to give as well as take, provide as well as accept provision, teach as well as learn, tell as well as listen. She boldly refuses to agree, when Henry Crawford assumes that she shares his nostalgia for the good times of the Mansfield theatre, and amazes her listener. An even greater advance is marked when she tells her sister Susan the story of Mansfield Park, in their chilly bedroom in Portsmouth, thus establishing both her own ability and her favourite theme:

> Susan was growing very fond of her, and though without any of the early delight in books, which had been so strong in Fanny, with a

---

[1] So did her author. See *Letters*, passim.

disposition much less inclined to sedentary pursuits, or to information for information's sake, she had so strong a desire of not *appearing* ignorant, as with a good clear understanding, made her a most attentive, profitable, thankful pupil. Fanny was her oracle. Fanny's explanations and remarks were a most important addition to every essay, or every chapter of history. What Fanny told her of former times, dwelt more on her mind than the pages of Goldsmith; and she paid her sister the compliment of preferring her style to that of any printed author. The early habit of reading was wanting.

Their conversations, however, were not always on subjects so high as history or morals. Others had their hour; and of lesser matters, none returned so often, or remained so long between them, as Mansfield Park, a description of the people, the manners, the amusements, the ways of Mansfield Park. (*MP*, pp. 418-9)

Edmund needs her listening, 'Let me talk to you a little. You are a kind, kind listener', and she says: 'If you only want me as a listener, cousin, I will be as useful as I can. . . .' (*MP*, pp. 268-9) And at the end he comes to want her for much more than a listener, because he is 'always with her, and always talking confidentially.' (*MP*, p. 470)

The abuses of imagination are best represented in this novel by Mrs Norris. When she is rebuked by Sir Thomas for her part in the Mansfield theatricals, she hastily moves away from uncomfortable memories to brag of the marriage she has arranged. Self-indulgence and self-love are reflected in every step of her style and her story. Although she uses the forms of flattery and denigration, these are only branches of her main medium, which is the boast. Her author knows that boastful narrators diffuse their self-praise over all details, their very language wheedling a favourable response from the listener. She tries to placate the disapproving and exhausted Sir Thomas through a far from unimaginative story :

'My dear Sir Thomas, if you had seen the state of the roads *that* day! I thought we should never have got through them, though we had the four horses of course; and poor old coachman would attend us, out of his great love and kindness, though he was hardly able to sit the box on account of the rheumatism which I had been doctoring him for, ever since Michaelmas. I cured him at last; but he was very bad all the winter— and this was such a day, I could not help going to him up in his room before we set off to advise him not to venture: he was putting on his wig— so I said, "Coachman, you had much better not go, your Lady and I shall be very safe; you know how steady Stephen is, and Charles has been upon the leaders so often now, that I am sure there is no fear." But, however, I soon found it would not do; he was bent upon going, and as I hate to be worrying and officious, I said no more; but my heart quite ached for him at every jolt, and when we got into the rough lanes about Stoke, where what with frost and snow upon beds of stones, it was worse than anything you can imagine, I was quite in an agony about him. And then the poor horses too!—To see them straining away! You know how I always feel for the horses. And when we got to the bottom of Sandcroft Hill, what do you think I did? You will laugh at me—but I got out and walked up. I did indeed. It might not be saving them much, but it was something, and I could not bear to sit at my ease, and be dragged up at the expense of those noble animals. I caught a dreadful cold, but *that* I did not regard. My object was accomplished in the visit.' (*MP*, pp. 189-90)

*Persuasion* begins with the closed imagination of Sir Walter Elliot as he reads his own story in the Baronetage, his favourite book. One long conversation in the novel perfectly illustrates the chain of characteristic narrative. Sir Walter shows off and solicits admiration, while Mr Shepherd and Mrs Clay listen and then tell in flattering silences, smiles and stories. The obsequious but manipulative agent and his daughter are differently and deviously ingratiating listeners. Jane Austen can create the simple-minded and egotistical rattle, like John Thorpe in *Northanger Abbey* and Robert Ferrars in *Sense and Sensibility*, but she also knows that any subject can do for self-display. Anecdotes about other people can sound detached and impersonal, but be aggressively self-assertive, as in Sir Walter Elliot's views on the effects of naval service on good looks. It is a perfect piece of imaginative projection:

'A man is in greater danger in the navy of being insulted by the rise of one whose father, his father might have disdained to speak to, and of becoming prematurely an object of disgust himself, than in any other line. One day last spring in town, I was in company with two men, striking instances of what I am talking of, Lord St. Ives, whose father we all know to have been a country curate, without bread to eat; I was to give place to Lord St. Ives, and a certain Admiral Baldwin, the most deplorable looking personage you can imagine, his face the colour of mahogany, rough and rugged to the last degree, all lines and wrinkles, nine grey hairs of a side, and nothing but a dab of powder at top.—"In the name of heaven, who is that old fellow?" said I, to a friend of mine who was standing near, (Sir Basil Morley.) "Old fellow!" cried Sir Basil, "it is Admiral Baldwin. What do you take his age to be?" "Sixty," said I, "or perhaps sixty-two." "Forty," replied Sir Basil, "forty, and no more."' (*P*, pp. 19-20)

Mrs Clay's rejoinder recognizes both the abstract level of talk, and its deeper drift. Her momentary hesitation about the clergyman shows the hard work of an impromptu narrative artist, labouring in the medium of masked flattery, which poses its own problems. Her words are going a little too fast for her thoughts:

'Nay, Sir Walter,' cried Mrs. Clay, 'this is being severe indeed. Have a little mercy on the poor men. We are not all born to be handsome. The sea is no beautifier, certainly; sailors do grow old betimes; I have often observed it; they soon lose the look of youth. But then, is not it the same with many other professions, perhaps most other? Soldiers, in active service, are not at all better off: and even in the quieter professions, there is a toil and a labour of the mind, if not of the body, which seldom leaves a man's looks to the natural effect of time. The lawyer plods, quite care-worn; the physician is up at all hours, and travelling in all weather; and even the clergyman—' she stopt a moment to consider what might do for the clergyman;—'and even the clergyman, you know, is obliged to go into infected rooms, and expose his health and looks to all the injury of a poisonous atmosphere. In fact, as I have long been convinced, though every profession is necessary and honourable in its turn, it is only the lot of those who are not obliged to follow any, who can live in a regular way, in the country, choosing their own hours, following their own pursuits, and living on their own property, without the torment of trying for more; it is only *their* lot, I say, to hold the blessings of health and a good appearance to the utmost: I know no other set of men but what lose something of their personableness when they cease to be quite young.' (*P*, pp. 20-1)

The minor characters whose telling and listening form the narrative web of *Persuasion* define Anne Elliot's search for understanding by their negative example. Her imaginative search is made after she has listened too long and too deferentially to other people's story of the ways of the world, and her reappraisal involves the unsentimental criticism of herself, and of her wise and foolish mentors. *Persuasion* has the most insistently narrative theme of all the novels, except *Emma*. It perfectly follows, balances, and supplements the theme of *Emma* in its analysis of passive listening and silent narrative. Anne Elliot has the painful experience of being an involuntary eavesdropper on the conversation between Louisa and Captain Wentworth in the hedgerow, when she hears a version of her own story and hears herself spoken of as one still easily persuaded. There comes a time, however, when she can listen more hopefully, and even make her own enquiries. The last piece of startling news, told by Mrs Smith about her cousin's intentions, and his past, is news that she can take. The final turn in her fortunes shows Captain Wentworth as listener, in a role-reversal of great significance in this novel. Like Fanny, Anne uses a lyrical mode to express intense and earnest love, and to preserve a still essential reticence. Taking Anne for the good listener she is, as most people do, Harville tells the sad story about Benwick's portrait, which was painted for one woman, but is now to be framed for another. This provokes the discussion on man's and woman's constancy. The covert story is told in Anne's style, intelligent, reasonable, and emotionally high-pitched. She has been talking playfully, but humour gets left behind:

'Your feelings may be the strongest,' replied Anne, 'but the same spirit of analogy will authorise me to assert that ours are the most tender. Man is more robust than woman, but he is not longer-lived; which exactly explains my view of the nature of their attachments. Nay, it would be too hard upon you, if it were otherwise. You have difficulties, and privations, and dangers enough to struggle with. You are always labouring and toiling, exposed to every risk and hardship. Your home, country, friends, all quitted. Neither time, nor health, nor life, to be called your own. It would be too hard indeed' (with a faltering voice) 'if woman's feelings were to be added to all this.' (*P*, p. 233)

'God forbid that I should undervalue the warm and faithful feelings of any of my fellow-creatures. I should deserve utter contempt if I dared to suppose that true attachment and constancy were known only by woman. No, I believe you equal to every important exertion, and to every domestic forbearance, so long as—if I may be allowed the expression, so long as you have an object. I mean, while the woman you love lives, and lives for you. All the privilege I claim for my own sex (it is not a very enviable one, you need not covet it) is that of loving longest, when existence or when hope is gone.' (*P*, p. 235)

The listening is crucial, and Captain Wentworth at last tells his story. Jane Austen's chain goes on to the end. In her world, as in ours, telling and listening take many shapes. Anne's imaginative reasoning moves quickly ahead to conjecture. But it is firmly grounded in memory.

Memory is as important a mode of storytelling as imagination, and not always separate from it. Jane Austen's people look before and after, telling stories, more or less complete, more or less explicit, about the past as well as the future. Sometimes they do not tell. Just as all novelists have to show fantasy, hope, desire, plans or projection, so all novelists have to show regret, nostalgia and revision. Characters in novels join memory with expectation, since they have pasts as well as futures. Though a sense of historical time was only just beginning to get into fiction when Jane Austen was writing, a sense of personal time is inseparable from everything we think of as novelistic, from the Bible to Beckett. Even Odysseus's dog has a memory.

Novelists deal differently with the stories we tell as we look back and forward. Jane Austen is particularly interested in the controls which we exercise over our nostalgia and regret. All her novels bring up the question of the need to use reason and to put memories in their proper place. Marianne Dashwood has come to terms with past hope and desire without being overwhelmed either by sourness or nostalgia. As she recovers from her passion for Willoughby, her problem with the past is not only that of putting feelings behind her. She has the unpleasant experience of seeing the past destroyed, as memory recalls mere illusion, and unreality is horridly duplicated. What is remembered was never as it was imagined; Marianne 'felt the loss of Willoughby's character yet more heavily than she had felt the loss of his heart'. She is relieved when his confession to Elinor is told again to her, and explains how it really was. The story of his story fills in the hollow places of her speculation about the past events, causes and contingencies. His story creates a substance for reader and character, different, but different sides of the same coin: Marianne asks, rationally enough, for some sense of past actuality. Her imagination hopes, though cautiously:

> 'As for regret,' said Marianne, 'I have done with that, as far as *he* is concerned. I do not mean to talk to you of what my feelings have been for him, but what they are *now*.—At present, if I could be satisfied on one point, if I could be allowed to think that he was not *always* acting a part, not *always* deceiving me;—but above all, if I could be assured that he never was so *very* wicked as my fears have sometimes fancied him, since the story of that unfortunate girl'—
> She stopt.—Elinor joyfully treasured her words as she answered,
> 'If you could be assured of that, you think you should be easy.'
> (*SS*, p. 344)

Even though Marianne's imagination has learnt caution, Jane Austen is stern and doesn't allow her to retrieve much of the past:

> In the evening, when they were all three together, Marianne began voluntarily to speak of him again;—but that it was not without an effort, the restless, unquiet thoughtfulness in which she had been for some time previously sitting—her rising colour, as she spoke—and her unsteady voice, plainly shewed.
> 'I wish to assure you both,' said she, 'that I see every thing—as you can

desire me to do.'

Mrs. Dashwood would have interrupted her instantly with soothing tenderness, had not Elinor, who really wished to hear her sister's unbiassed opinion, by an eager sign, engaged her silence. Marianne slowly continued—

'It is a great relief to me—what Elinor told me this morning—I have now heard exactly what I wished to hear.'—For some moments her voice was lost; but recovering herself, she added, and with greater calmness than before—'I am now perfectly satisfied, I wish for no change. I never could have been happy with him, after knowing, as sooner or later I must have known, all this.—I should have had no confidence, no esteem. Nothing could have done it away to my feelings.'

'I know it—I know it,' cried her mother. 'Happy with a man of libertine practices!—With one who had so injured the peace of the dearest of our friends, and the best of men!—No—my Marianne has not a heart to be made happy with such a man!—Her conscience, her sensitive conscience, would have felt all that the conscience of her husband ought to have felt.'

Marianne sighed, and repeated—'I wish for no change.'

(*SS*, pp. 349-50)

Jane Austen creates this scene with her unerring sense of the psychology of narrative discourse. She knows how difficult it is for Marianne to tell, and registers the physical tension and effort. She knows also that no two listeners are alike. Elinor has to hold back Mrs Dashwood's impetuous tenderness, in order to hear the story as coolly as possible. She herself retells it coolly, after Marianne's sigh has shown the pain of listening to her mother's version. Her story is imaginative and thoroughly rational:

'The whole of his behaviour,' replied Elinor, 'from the beginning to the end of the affair, has been grounded on selfishness. It was selfishness which first made him sport with your affections; which afterwards, when his own were engaged, made him delay the confession of it, and which finally carried him from Barton. His own enjoyment, or his own ease, was, in every particular, his ruling principle.'

'It is very true. *My* happiness never was his object.'

'At present,' continued Elinor, 'he regrets what he has done. And why does he regret it?—Because he finds it has not answered towards himself. It has not made him happy. His circumstances are now unembarrassed—he suffers from no evil of that kind; and he thinks only that he has married a woman of a less amiable temper than yourself. But does it thence follow that had he married you, he would have been happy?—The inconveniencies would have been different. He would then have suffered under the pecuniary distresses which, because they are removed, he now reckons as nothing.' (*SS*, p. 351)

Elinor's rigorous imagination uses memory unnostalgically. She refuses to cut off the past from the future it might have led to. It is an aspect of the hardness of the novel that she should make the refusal for Marianne. Jane Austen does not show the revisions of memory taking place in Marianne's mind, though they are implicit in the brief summary which tells us that 'in time' Marianne came to love her husband as much as she had loved Willoughby. The novels coming after *Sense and Sensibility* fill in this gap.

Elizabeth Bennet looks back imaginatively, vividly, fully, and with feeling. She feels chagrin at the past blindness of her imagination, its easy susceptibility and its determined misreadings. Emma looks back with shame at her elations, her interpretations and her fantasies, all grounded in selective and self-flattering speculations. Like Elizabeth, she looks back at the stories she has told herself. Once admitted, the acknowledgement of her love for Mr Knightley illumines a past in which she has been only half-awake, in spite of her pride in perception and plan:

> This was the conclusion of the first series of reflection. This was the knowledge of herself, on the first question of inquiry, which she reached; and without being long in reaching it.—She was most sorrowfully indignant; ashamed of every sensation but the one revealed to her—her affection for Mr. Knightley.—Every other part of her mind was disgusting.
> With insufferable vanity had she believed herself in the secret of everybody's feelings; with unpardonable arrogance proposed to arrange everybody's destiny. She was proved to have been universally mistaken; and she had not quite done nothing—for she had done mischief.
>
> (*E*, pp. 412-3)

Anne Elliot takes the whole novel to remember. Jane Austen shows her energetic, useful, unself-pitying. Her memory moves away from isolated nostalgia to review the past, to understand, and to make imaginative revisions of value. It is a part of Anne's imaginative strength that she can accept the past without violent blame and remorse. She can accept it as a part of herself. In her imaginative memory she is very like Fanny Price. Anne describes her strengths of memory to Captain Wentworth, and misleads him by her assurance and warmth as she looks back to Lyme Regis:

> 'The last few hours were certainly very painful,' replied Anne: 'but when pain is over, the remembrance of it often becomes a pleasure. One

does not love a place the less for having suffered in it, unless it has been all suffering, nothing but suffering—which was by no means the case at Lyme. We were only in anxiety and distress during the last two hours; and, previously, there had been a great deal of enjoyment. So much novelty and beauty! I have travelled so little, that every fresh place would be interesting to me—but there is real beauty at Lyme: and in short' (with a faint blush at some recollections) 'altogether my impressions of the place are very agreeable.' (*P*, pp. 183-4)

As Jane Austen merges the everyday narratives of common life with the larger and more crucial enterprises of imagination and memory, she comes to show a strength of mind which reveals itself through storytelling, public and private. As we move through our lives, we are all engaged in making up an informal autobiography which we form and which forms us. Jane Austen's last three novels, through their distinct and different heroines, show the ability to tell that personal story with all its variety and its errors, in its whole truth. Fanny Price and Emma long to speak candidly to Edmund and Mr Knightley, as they have been able to speak candidly to themselves. They are contrasted with other intelligent people who cannot so faithfully or so toughly accept the story of the self – Sir Thomas Bertram or Jane Fairfax. Anne Elliot is able to speak at last, after so much listening. What she speaks about is crucial. It is in no spirit of moral pedantry that she goes back to the past and tells Captain Wentworth that she stands by her past persuadability. Fanny accepts the whole past, including folly and fantasy. Anne accepts the whole past, which has given her eight years of pain, and destroyed the sense of a future. She takes it, without erasing anything. That final story which Jane Austen's most rational and passionate lovers tell is more than a declaration, it is the endorsement of the personal life. Unlike those great chroniclers of memory and imagination, Wordsworth, Thackeray and Beckett, who suggest the dangers of recalling the past, Jane Austen raises no problems about the authenticity of memory. She is all too clearly alive to the temptations of blotting out, revising or hating the past, and the heroines of her mature fiction stand by their entire story.

What the critic laboriously analyses, the novelist knows. When William Price tells his tales of adventure in the Mediterranean and the West Indies, we see everyone's response. Fanny's 'deep interest' and 'absorbed attention' solicit Henry Crawford's admiration for her ardour and sensibility, but he also feels chagrin and respect, 'he wished he had been a William Price'. Mrs Norris never listens to other people's stories, and fidgets 'about the room', disturbing everybody 'in quest of two needlefulls of thread or a second hand shirt button in the midst of her nephew's account of a shipwreck or an engagement'. Even Lady Bertram occasionally looks up from her work: 'Dear me! how disagreeable. – I wonder any body can ever go to sea.' Not the least interesting listener is Sir Thomas, who finds the recitals 'amusing in themselves' but whose 'chief object in seeking them, was to understand the recitor, to know the young man by his histories'. Jane Austen thoroughly understood how we come to know each other in our telling and our listening. Her novels show a full and thorough use of this knowledge.

# V

# Social Groups

If Jane Austen, like Thackeray,[1] had observed that she had no head above her eyes, instead of making her modest jokes about working on a two-inch square of ivory, and finding three or four families in a country village the very thing to work on,[2] her powers of social analysis might have commanded more respect. Thackeray's remark need not be applied too literally either to his own work or to Jane Austen's, but it may draw our attention to the power of her social drama. Where Thackeray's descriptions of social groups are full and lengthy, hers are spare and slight, often compressed by incisive summary or sketch. Like him, she delineates her society but usually avoids direct criticism, analysis and argument. She offers no far-reaching generalizations about class, wealth, or manners, and her dramatized spokeswomen and spokesmen make few overt attempts to criticize society. Commentary is subordinated to drama and chronicle, but it is neither invisible nor absent. Her sharp and profound insight into social structures, relationships and roles creates a series of critical scenes. Generalization emerges, quietly, but accumulating power. Her social scenes make comparisons of interplay which have the disarming yet provocative air of illustrating without defining. Her light, bright, and sparkling comedy criticizes while it diverts.

Among those critics who seem restricted by her own images of limit is Richard Simpson, who damns with faint praise the small scale on which her imagination seems to work:

> She defined her own sphere when she said that three or four families in a country village were the thing for a novelist to work upon. Each of these 'little social commonwealths' became a distinct entity to her

---

[1] Said in a conversation with George William Curtis, and quoted by Gordon Ray, *Thackeray: The Age of Wisdom* (1945-6), p. 119.

[2] *Letters*, p. 401.

imagination, with its own range of ideas, its own subjects of discourse, its own public opinion on all social matters. Indeed there is nothing in her novels to prove that she had any conception of society itself, but only of the coterie of three or four families mixing together, with differences of intellect, wealth, or character, but without any grave social inequalities.

(*Critical Heritage*, No. 44, p. 250)

Bemused by the famous and fatal formula of a few families in a village, he fails to see the expanding context in which her little commonwealths are set. He makes an even more damaging mistake in not perceiving that the analysis of a coterie can unfold that total social view which he misses in her novels:

Of organized society she manifests no idea. She had no interest in the great political and social problems which were being debated with so much blood in her day. The social combinations which taxed the calculating powers of Adam Smith or Jeremy Bentham were above her powers. She had no knowledge how to keep up the semblance of personality in the representation of society reckoned by averages, and no method of impersonating the people or any section of the people in the average man. (loc. cit.)

Mary Bennet could scarcely better this absurdly irrelevant demand on the novelist's imagination. Jane Austen, like all literary artists, is no more concerned with the abstractions and calculations of economists and sociologists, than she is interested in that impersonation of social particulars which makes fiction interesting to the common reader and valuable to the historian. No one expects Adam Smith and Jeremy Bentham to imagine the individual life of social groups. Calculations, averages and sections of society do not form Jane Austen's materials but her social groups are imagined models and microcosms of social structure and organization. Her treatment of those differences of 'intellect, wealth, and character', may not solve or even formulate political problems of class and economic difference, but her small-scale drama generates ideas about groups. Because 'each of these "little social commonwealths" became a distinct personal entity to her imagination', it does not follow that her social insights remain artlessly, innocently, and superficially directed to small particulars. She imagines variations of social behaviour, which recur, with different *dramatis personae*, to reflect and imply social insight.

Simpson is not the only critic who leans heavily on the '3 or 4 families'. The anonymous writer of a review in *St. Paul's Magazine* (*Critical Heritage*, No. 43, p. 232) also insists on the limitations of her scope and scale, though he attributes them to social realism in portraying a genuinely sequestered, contracted, and immobile village life:

> But this is probably a true picture of village life in England half-a-century ago, and perhaps even now, though the feminine sphere of thought and action has greatly enlarged with the progress of education, something of the same kind of small gossip, and small agitation, and mean rivalry, and base detraction, might go on wherever there existed a contracted circle. . . .

Even today, we can find the similar imputations of a lack of interest in larger political issues.[3] She has been accused of a lack of interest in feminism, for instance, because she makes no reference to Mary Wollstonecraft.[4] But her comic portrayals of feminine company and feminine conversation are eloquent of limitation. Within her social groups, Jane Austen frequently shows a serious restlessness, critical and even subversive, which looks beyond social limits. Marianne Dashwood rudely refuses to join in empty prattle or mercenary assumptions. Elinor Dashwood makes a courteous but qualified contribution to social games of competition and aggression. Henry Tilney and Elizabeth Bennet mock and mime routines and rituals of fashionable coteries. Fanny Price wants to know about the slave-trade, though rebuked by the silence of the other ladies. Anne Elliot feels too proud to approve coteries which pride themselves on class but not cultivation.

Jane Austen does not speak only through those characters who can represent something of her own insight. The comic presentation of society includes but does not rely exclusively on such superiorities. But before we look at the satirical self-analysis of the life of groups, it seems essential to insist on the breadth and mobility of Jane Austen's social imagination. While attacking Jane Austen for a lack of calculating power, her critics sometimes fail to take proper count of her families and villages. She never limits herself to three or four families in a village. The novels may use them as a starting-point, which is a different matter. If the novel begins with one family – and most novels have to start from some single point – there is invariably some immediate precipitation of social change. *Northanger Abbey* begins

[3] A striking exception is Avrom Fleishman, op. cit.
[4] See Patricia Beer, *Reader, I Married Him* (London, 1974).

by taking its heroine from a small and uneventful village to a stirring town. *Sense and Sensibility* begins with changes brought about in two branches of a family by deaths and inheritances. *Pride and Prejudice* introduces strangers in its third sentence. *Mansfield Park* summarizes the scattered fortunes of three sisters, and then conveys its heroine from poverty in Portsmouth to the comforts of Mansfield. *Emma* is the most socially restricted of the major novels, but begins with a contraction and change in family life which is to bring expansion and renewal. *Persuasion* begins with disruption and removals caused by economic change and peace after a war.

There are limitations in Jane Austen's studies of social life. As everyone knows, her chronicles exclude exclusively male company, but there are conversations which imply some knowledge of men's behaviour, like the off-stage manoeuvres of John Thorpe and General Tilney, the on-stage discourse of the Knightley brothers, and Mr Knightley's reports of men talking to men.

The society of women is wholly leisured. Except in *Sanditon*, where there are several interesting exceptions, women are never shown doing any work which is paid, and seldom any which is useful. Women at work are shadowy; the most solid shadows are those cast by the housekeeper at Sotherton (whose routine as a guide to the great house has instructed her employer, Mrs Rushworth, and whose cream cheese and pheasants' eggs are 'spunged' by Mrs Norris) and Hannah, daughter of James the coachman at Hartfield (who is observed approvingly by Mr Woodhouse when she turns the locks the right way and never bangs the doors). Mrs Weston has been Emma's governess, but is promoted to a prosperous marital state immediately before the novel begins; Jane Fairfax is preserved from the governess-trade, as she calls it, just before the novel ends. This professional limitation reflects the restriction to middle-class and gentry, with the two aristocratic infusions, from Lady Catherine de Bourgh in *Pride and Prejudice*, and Lady Dalrymple and Miss Carteret in *Persuasion*. There are also glimpses of people in trade, like the Philipses and the Gardiners in *Pride and Prejudice*, and the Cole family in *Emma*. The aristocrats are heavily satirized, the people in trade treated sympathetically, harsh satire being reserved for their snobbish or hypocritical connections, like Mrs Elton and Miss Bingley.

Jane Austen's societies are restricted in their class composition, though the vague fringe suggests mobility, upwards and downwards. The societies portrayed are neither small, nor enclosed, nor static.

Jane Austen's imagination could not have been confined to a few families in a village, but demands the material of social changes and renewals. Her conversations generally exclude politics, as in the famous scene where the talk of Catherine Morland with Henry and Catherine Tilney turns from nature, via enclosures, to politics, from which it was 'an easy step to silence'. When we are brought up against the not uncommon subjects of enclosures, war, or the slave-trade, the conversation invariably turns back. Jane Austen's social imagination strikes noticeably against its limits.

The bounds of her coteries and groups are constantly broken, and their closeness challenged, by fresh arrivals and departures. Her inhabitants are constantly on the move, entering new coteries. To refuse to see the social intrusions and erosions in the novel is to ally ourselves with Mrs Bennet in her quarrel with Darcy. He proposes that the country cannot supply enough subjects for the study of character, 'in a country neighbourhood you move in a very confined and unvarying society'; Mrs Bennet replies that there is just as much alteration of people 'going on in the country as the town', and Elizabeth, 'blushing for her mother', explains that Darcy is referring to the relative absence of variety. Of course Darcy himself ignores the comings and goings in which he participates, and even Mrs Bennet cannot confine herself to the prescription of three or four families: 'I know we dine with four and twenty families'.

Jane Austen's novels make do with fewer than four and twenty named families, though a habit of cleverly casual name-dropping[5] conveys an air of social density beyond the novel's focus. She chooses to vary and enlarge her company. Each novel devises the action for an expanded social experience, which tests and instructs the central characters. *Northanger Abbey* ranges from the small village of Fullerton in Wiltshire, to Bath, then to Northanger Abbey in Gloucestershire, and back home to Fullerton. *Sense and Sensibility* moves from Norland Park in Sussex, to Barton Cottage, near Barton Park in Devonshire, then to London, and back home by way of Cleveland in Somerset. *Pride and Prejudice* begins in the village of Longbourn, near the small town of Meryton in Hertfordshire, then to London, on the way to Hunsford near Westerham in Kent, back to Longbourn, because of events taking place in Brighton and London, then to Derbyshire and home again. In *Mansfield Park* the main action takes

[5] An excellent example is Miss Bates's arrival at the ball in *Emma* (p. 323).

place in Mansfield, during important voyages to and from Antigua, in the West Indies, but also moves to Portsmouth, London, Twickenham, Richmond, then back to Mansfield Park. *Emma*, most static of the novels, brings people to Highbury from London, and the north of England, and Bristol, and takes some of its permanent residents away on short journeys. In *Persuasion* the action takes place in Kellynch, Uppercross, Lyme Regis, and Bath.

Such moves simply describe the chief places of the action, whether performed or reported, but beyond this map is a larger one. Before settling in Norland, as the beginning of the novel describes, Mrs Dashwood, with her husband and children have come from Stanhill, as we are casually informed (*SS*, pp. 13, 30), and Colonel Brandon has a sister in Avignon. Elizabeth Bennet has hoped to go on holiday to the Lakes, to forget the trials of human nature amongst rocks and mountains, and the novel's ending moves her and Jane away from home and shows the Wickhams on the move, 'from place to place in quest of a cheap situation'. In *Mansfield Park*, William Price goes and comes from his voyages, even stirring Henry Tilney's discontent with his sailor's tales. Henry and Mary Crawford are a restless pair, constantly on the move, like Willoughby in *Sense and Sensibility*. The confinement of Emma, who has never seen the sea, is the more marked for the busy comings and goings of other characters, some of whom have been to Weymouth, Southend, but not Cromer or Ireland, and several of whom go to London on business, to visit the barber and the dentist,[6] to see friends and family, and on gallant adventures to buy a piano and get a picture framed. It is perfectly fitting, though quietly recounted, that Emma's wedding journey should take her at last to the sea. *Persuasion* is played against a background of naval adventures which we are not allowed to forget even at the end, and Mrs Croft has shared many of her husband's voyages, crossed the Atlantic four times, and naturally overestimates Mrs Musgrove's knowledge of geography.

Although the scale of Jane Austen's map is noticeably different from our own, in spite of Atlantic and Mediterranean voyages, short distances take us over a varying society. When Anne Elliot moves a short distance from the village of Kellynch to the village of Uppercross, she observes the separateness and exclusiveness to be found even in neighbouring communities. Anne's insight into a change of place reflects her author's. Even a movement from one house to another is

---

[6] Jane Austen gives a harrowing account of three visits with her nieces to a London dentist, *Letters*, pp. 322, 327-8.

carefully observed as productive of variety and contrast.[7] Small maps record large tracts of imaginative distance. Our attention is drawn to distance and movement by the characters themselves, as they complain of confinement, like Catherine Morland, Mary Crawford, or Emma, in their sharply distinct ways, or prefer to stay at home, like Fanny Price. Some are sophisticatedly aware of environment, like Darcy, Mary Crawford, Mrs Grant, Anne Elliot; Sir Thomas Bertram goes so far as to conduct an experiment in environmental change, with results which teach him as well as Fanny, and more than he anticipates. The novels may appear still, but the stillness is often interrupted by a bustle of journeys. Jane Austen reverses the procedures of picaresque novels, for though her characters are often on the road, travelling by private or public transport, their adventures never occur during the journeys, but at home or during their visits. Journeys are recounted briefly and quickly, through glimpses of meals, inns, payments, changes of vehicle,[8] weather, wayside sights, departures and arrivals. People move about for reasons of business, marriage, health, visits, and holidays. Connections are lost and kept. Departures are voluntary and enforced, happy and distressed. Journeys end in lovers' meetings and family reunions. Societies change to suggest that society changes. We see change through the dispersal, contraction, expansion, and removal of families and neighbourhoods. There is a constant change of population, for the population of small societies is seen to alter as much as human nature. The three, four, or more families do not stay in one place, but move house, welcome, or do not welcome, old acquaintances and strangers, and lose their sons and daughters to professional or married life. Jane Austen's novels turn on the discovery of new places, of new people, and of oneself.

Some of the half-kept secrets of her personal life, like the legendary meeting with the 'unnamed gentleman' at a seaside place,[9] or the acceptance and quick rejection of a proposal of marriage from Harris Bigg-Wither,[10] are associated with holidays and visits. Her surviving letters are practical proofs of the many journeys, visits and removals which were so important in her own life. We know how vital place and

---

[7] The *Letters* are full of such observations.

[8] The *Letters* also contain sharp and amusing comments on travel and transport.

[9] *Memoir*, op. cit., Chap. ii, and R. W. Chapman, *Jane Austen: Facts and Problems* (Oxford, 1948), pp. 63-9.

[10] *Memoir*, op. cit., ibid., and Chapman, op. cit., pp. 61-63.

change were for her, as a woman and as an artist, how she apparently stopped writing after the family moved from Steventon to Bath and Southampton in 1801, how she was deeply distressed by the move, how she began to write again in 1809 when she went to settle in Chawton, with her mother and sister.[11] The letters are full of the problems of Jane Austen's journeys, since the ladies of her family never travelled any distance alone, as the unfortunate Catherine Morland was forced to do. But even the confinements of family life were open to a wider world; as Brian Southam insists: 'The family group was constantly changing and constantly supplied with news.'[12] Her scene-changes, however, are not simply reflections of personal experience, but traditional moves in epic and novel. The writings of Homer, Virgil, Cervantes, Dante, Swift, Voltaire, Plutarch, Samuel Johnson, Fielding, Sterne, Fanny Burney, Henry James, James Joyce and D. H. Lawrence tell their stories of imaginary journeys. Novels need strange places and strange meetings.

Jane Austen's novels rely on such meetings. Groups of mixed acquaintance show up the forms of social rules and rituals. The facade of public propriety is mocked, criticized and used as a screen or a barrier. The public occasion gives Jane Austen an opportunity to begin, retard, and confuse the development of love, to satirize social manners and morals, and to analyse the interactions of group roles and relationships. She seems to balance an interest in depth and surface, manners and character, or structure and ethics, so evenly that it is hard to say which concern is primary. The novelist only shows social groups through the individuality of event and characters, but such individual life establishes general social truths. Jane Austen's constant request that her characters should know their own feelings makes plain her preoccupation with the human heart. But she also directs her people to look into their social behaviour. There are characters like the mocking Henry Tilney and the didactic Mr Knightley to be explicit within the novel about its social forms.

Festive occasions bring together social and psychological tensions, and provide the additional treat of mingled pain and pleasure. Her heroes and heroines have to be introduced into new societies and groups, since the world cannot conveniently be peopled from three or four families in a country village. Inbreeding is bad for society, character, and plots. Parties of pleasure are arranged by society to

[11] Chapman, op. cit., Chaps. iv, v, vi.
[12] B. C. Southam, *Jane Austen's Literary Manuscripts* (London, 1964), p. 5.

bring the sexes together, and the gatherings are productive and even instructive. Only two of the heroines, Fanny Price and Emma, marry within their own community. Proximity's dullness is stirred by the competition and provocation of attractive strangers like Mary Crawford and Frank Churchill. Social life is even encouraged by a Mr Collins and a Mrs Elton, the one intent on courtship and the other on bridal celebration. The neighbourhood needs to entertain its visitors, and the air of Jane Austen's most elegant or domestic parties and picnics can become heady and even aphrodisiac. Love, courtship, a knowledge of the heart and of the wide world develop best outside Jane Austen's family circles.

Most of the heroines have to travel further than Fanny and Emma in search of a husband, and finally leave home when they find one. There is nobody for Catherine Morland to marry in Fullerton, so Mrs Allen, languid chaperone though she is, has to bring her to Bath, which teems with promise. Elinor and Marianne Dashwood meet Edward Ferrars, Colonel Brandon, and Willoughby, through visits and accident. Bingley and Darcy are marked down by Longbourn and Meryton in two chapters, though victory has to wait till the end of the story. Anne Elliot's reunion with Captain Wentworth has the special excitement of strange familiarity after absence. All these meetings rely on the entertainments of public life, in large mixed parties or smaller domestic groups.

The stories turn on social limit and social change, so the groups which carry on the business of introductions and interchanges reflect intimacy and novelty. Rituals often seem to be designed or developed in order to combine the two. It is in public that Jane Austen's men and women have to get to know each other, and have to endure the hazards and inconveniences of social encounters. Public life is rough and smooth, rude and polite. It may be too polite for intimacy to flourish quickly, as Charlotte Lucas points out in one of those individually voiced opinions which can both hide and discover the author's judgement. In her prudent, matter-of-fact and expert manner, she points out the need for women to snatch every opportunity offered by dinner-parties, balls, round-games, or cards:

'But though Bingley and Jane meet tolerably often, it is never for many hours together; and as they always see each other in large mixed parties, it is impossible that every moment should be employed in conversing together. Jane should therefore make the most of every half hour in which she can command his attention.' (*PP*, p. 22)

Festive occasions are often clandestine. Time and privacy are in short supply, and decorum or hypocrisy require that sexual attentions and intentions of all sorts should be disguised. So Jane Austen's men and women pretend to be intent on dancing, eating, exploring, paying calls, planning improvements, rehearsing theatricals, being nice to their parents, being polite to their acquaintance, and playing games of all kinds. Meanwhile they make the most of all these activities and rites to solicit, pursue and compete. As Tom Bertram watches an impromptu dance in Mansfield Park, he says carelessly to Fanny, his knowingness reminding us that this is Regency England: 'They are so many couple of lovers – all but Yates and Mrs Grant – and, between ourselves, she, poor woman, must want a lover as much as any of them !' (*MP*, p. 119) Lydia and Catherine Bennet chase boisterously and openly, all the way to Meryton, and far beyond to Brighton. Their aunt gives nice little hot suppers, with conveniently noisy games of lottery tickets, after the officers have been well-dined. Mrs Bennet gives substantial dinners, with good soup, haunches of venison roasted to a turn, partridges which please even the pampered palate of Mr Darcy, and offers the additional pleasures of Mr Bennet's covert, when Bingley and Darcy have killed all their own birds. Each pursuit has its own style. Miss Bingley pursues Darcy through the letters he writes and the books he reads. Isabella Thorpe is as expert as Fanny Burney's Miss Larolles, in *Cecilia*, at placing herself modestly in conspicuous positions. In almost every party the young ladies play, sing, and exhibit their painting and embroidery, resting only when they are married. The heroines convey through their genuine ability their author's contempt for the predatory education in feminine accomplishment. They attract naturally, and without effort, by their beauty, wit, liveliness, ardour, modesty, sincerity, and intelligence. Jane Austen's heroes are intelligent men who don't make the common mistakes of Mr Allen, Mr Bennet, and Sir Thomas Bertram, but are captivated by the real thing. They and their less honourable fellows pursue and solicit with presents, carriage-rides, dances, Shakespearian readings, good works on their estate, wit and instruction. And almost all these necessary offerings and solicitations of men and women, bent on marriage or seduction, love or an establishment, are made in public. Theatricals, improvements, games, dances, and music were all deliberately noted by the novelist as emblems of such dual purpose, long before her critics applied themselves to the study of her symbols.

All novelists love parties, for their drama, their interplay, their competitiveness, and their erotic opportunities. Each novelist chooses his parties according to his age and his taste. Jane Austen's polite chronicles of flirtation are less sensuous, less vicious and less gorgeous than Thackeray's, Dickens's or Scott Fitzgerald's. But a conversation in the Assembly Rooms at Bath, in a crowded set, with chaperones lining the walls, offers as much opportunity for stealthy seduction and betrayal as Lord Steyn's expensive entertainments in *Vanity Fair*, the artificial rites of the Veneering banquets in *Our Mutual Friend*, or the magnificent sleaziness of Gatsby's parties, with jazz, flappers and champagne. Jane Austen anticipates Henry James – who so under-estimated her craft – in a liking for conversational exchange, some-times astonishingly direct, sometimes highly cryptic, with space for the revealing gesture and time for the unspoken word. But she seems to go beyond Thackeray, Dickens, James, and Scott Fitzgerald in her special interest in the structures of social organisms. She may scarcely ever mention government, and show no concern for Parliament, but her small groups have a carefully structured organization. The structure is the effect of sharp vision, as well as dramatic art. She likes to observe the changing behaviour of a group, to show what holds it together, and what pulls it apart, to see how the group is led, and how domination can shift. Of course she is a novelist, not a social psycholo-gist,[13] and her dramatic scenes of group life are joined to the total conception of character and feeling, as they must be in all good novels. But although social roles and dynamics are related to the larger private lives, through distinctions of function and a sense of causality, she is conspicuous amongst English novelists for her understanding of the psychology of groups. Her moral analysis of character is also con-ducted in her group-dramas.

In *Emma* rites and decorum are recorded, strains and responses registered, in the exploring party in Donwell Abbey. Mr Knightley insists on being host, having politely and effectively declined the services of Mrs Elton, the kind of woman who presses her services on mere unmarried men in a combination of matrimonial patronage and residual predatoriness. Jane Austen follows the strawberry party with the even more discordant and clandestine picnic on Box Hill, and exacerbates public and private strains until ceremony collapses. The quarrel of Jane Fairfax and Frank Churchill begins in the heat of one party, and continues in the next. Jane Austen amuses herself with the

[13] I have avoided the use of obviously applicable modern terminology in describing her social groups.

sober record of the ordeals of two parties with the same people, coming one after the other. The summer heat is bad for the spirits and energies of hosts and guests, and we are made to feel its uninterrupted oppression. More than the weather an unusual social effort is responsible for the failures of ceremony and pleasure. The secret engagement of Frank Churchill and Jane Fairfax is causing unendurable strains, which are felt by the innocent host, Mr Weston, and his innocent guests who don't know what is going on, as an undercurrent of obscure but infectious disturbance. There are other strains too, dividing the party in spite of the gregarious host's attempts to bring people together, to look at 'the prospects', and to enjoy the cold collation. The beauties of Box Hill and all the pleasures of the picnic are wasted. There is division instead of unity: Jane Fairfax avoids Frank Churchill, and takes away her aunt with her, to find refuge in the Eltons' company. The Eltons continue their malicious slighting of Harriet and Emma. Mr Knightley misinterprets both Frank's flirtatiousness and Emma's response, as well he may. Frank Churchill finds refuge, relief, and revenge in a game of flirtation. It allows him to speak in double meanings, which Emma will receive playfully, and which Jane will understand only too seriously – 'I am comfortable today' and 'I can have no self-command without a motive'. Emma's response fluctuates. She feels mild pleasure at being entertained and flattered, and relief after awkwardness and silence. She is aware of her underlying detachment, certain that she doesn't care for him, but she also feels a vague disappointment: 'Not that Emma was gay and thoughtless from any real felicity; it was rather because she felt less happy than she had expected.'

The others feel less happy than they expected. Jane Austen anticipates Thackeray in reminding us that there is nothing so dismal as a party that turns sour or cold, to impose strains on the rituals of polite propriety, and to frustrate the festive purpose. Frank's flirtatiousness gets more febrile and more impudent. Emma recognizes the game, joins in, grows uneasy, tries to cool the heat, and when he says amorously, 'You are always with me', she replies coolly, 'Dating from three o'clock yesterday'.

Jane Austen's letters record her own playful, amused, and perhaps exaggerated chronicles of flirtation. 'They do not know how *to be particular*', she writes to Cassandra about a couple at the Harwoods' ball, who may 'profit by the three successive lessons which I have given them'.[14] She describes her behaviour with Tom Lefroy, who was

14 *Letters*, p. 1.

'excessively laughed at' about her, – he remembered her in his old age as the girl for whom he'd had 'a boyish love' [15] – and tells Cassandra that their behaviour at a ball was 'everything most profligate and shocking in the way of dancing and sitting down together'.[16] As a novelist, she expertly records the difficulty of a public flirtation which becomes too conspicuous and intense. Emma thinks it is only a game on her side, but is wrong, as usual: 'Your gallantry is really unanswerable. But (lowering her voice) – nobody speaks except ourselves, and it is rather too much to be talking nonsense for the entertainment of seven silent people.' Frank Churchill's voice rises, 'Let my accents swell to Mickleham on one side, and Dorking on the other', and his hyperbole and wit rise also. He is 'the genius and flirt' [17] of the occasion. The seven silent people begin to get restive. Their social genius is rebuked. Mrs Elton can't tolerate the description of Emma 'who, wherever she is, presides'; her vivacious telegraphese begins to sound nervously rattled, '*I* never was in any circle – exploring parties – young ladies – married women –', and is scarcely to be reassured by her 'caro sposo's' familiar 'Exactly so' and his thinly disguised hostility, 'but some ladies say any thing'. She is later to show her dignity by the feat of patronizing four people in one solecistic sentence: 'Pass Mr Elton, Knightley, Jane and myself.'

Emma is indeed to say 'any thing'. She nervously affects carelessness when Mr Knightley shows that he too can play the game of innuendo, inquiring grimly: 'Is Miss Woodhouse sure that she would like to hear what we are all thinking of?' Frank Churchill's punishing exhibitionism decides to 'attack them with more address' and introduces a new game. It is the irresistible competition in dullness in which Emma loses her head and does what Frank Churchill himself has once said no one would wish to do to Miss Bates – slights her. As Mr Knightley is to point out, when he reproaches her at the end of the picnic, it is a public insult made in front of her niece, and fully comprehended. Miss Bates is wounded, and behaves with restraint and decorum. Emma's precarious and undeserved eminence collapses. But there is to be another wound, less publicly inflicted. Frank Churchill miserably and desperately drops the unsuccessful games and attacks Jane Fairfax through innuendo. 'Very lucky', he observes as the Eltons walk off,

[15] Chapman, op. cit., Chap. v.

[16] *Letters*, p. 2.

[17] *Letters*, p. 43, where she describes a young man as 'altogether rather the genius and flirt of the evening'.

Mr Elton recording his inability to entertain young ladies, and Mrs Elton muttering about the fatigue of exploring so long on one spot, 'Very lucky – marrying as they did, upon an acquaintance formed only in a public place !' Jane Fairfax hears out the double-tongued speech, and replies in the same covert style, breaking her silence and their secret engagement, with appropriate stealth. After the covert dialogue which no one else can understand, he resorts more furiously and furtively to flirtation with Emma, 'I shall come to you for my wife', to signal acceptance of Jane's decision, and return Emma to her incorrigible match-making.

The occasion is totally public, but privacy is preserved. There is no single person who has understood all the games and *double-entendres*. Harriet and Mr Weston are the most innocent, as usual. Mr Knightley misunderstands Emma's feelings, she misunderstands Frank Churchill's. Jane Fairfax understands and misunderstands both, and Miss Bates takes to herself the most cruelly legible stroke of wit, the most aggressive turn in the game, and the gravest breach of decorum. The Eltons understand nothing, except their own jealousy. There has been no genius of the occasion, and the rites of hospitality have been violently reversed.

Through ritual, structure, and character, the Box Hill picnic is attached to the novel's past, which has been intent on the festivities and games played in groups. We have seen Emma preside, and her dominance has sometimes been approved, sometimes disapproved. It has always been related to those social pressures which visibly shape her elated sense of power and proficiency. We first see her at her best as hostess, though there is something daunting about one so young being so good at social manipulation even in a dinner-party in her own home. On this occasion she is cool, not excited, and in command. Like the Box Hill party, the occasion is a characteristic model of harmony and disharmony. It is the family party at Highfield, when John Knightley and Isabella come to stay, and is composed of two groups, of kinship, interest, and mind. Mr Woodhouse is among friends, and the host gives way to the fond father. Emma, slightly apart, is the hostess who must not relax, alert to prevent or heal rifts. She is not alone in the responsibility, but has the help of Mr Knightley's sense and sensibility:

> ... John Knightley made his appearance, and 'How d'ye do, George?' and 'John, how are you?' succeeded in the true English style, burying under a

calmness that seemed all but indifference, the real attachment which would have led either of them, if requisite, to do every thing for the good of the other.

The evening was quiet and conversible, as Mr. Woodhouse declined cards entirely for the sake of comfortable talk with his dear Isabella, and the little party made two natural divisions; on one side he and his daughter; on the other the two Mr. Knightleys; their subjects totally distinct, or very rarely mixing—and Emma only occasionally joining in one or the other.

The brothers talked of their own concerns and pursuits, but principally of those of the elder, whose temper was by much the most communicative, and who was always the greater talker. As a magistrate, he had generally some point of law to consult John about, or, at least, some curious anecdote to give; and as a farmer, as keeping in hand the home-farm at Donwell, he had to tell what every field was to bear next year, and to give all such local information as could not fail of being interesting to a brother whose home it had equally been the longest part of his life, and whose attachments were strong. The plan of a drain, the change of a fence, the felling of a tree, and the destination of every acre for wheat, turnips, or spring corn, was entered into with as much equality of interest by John, as his cooler manners rendered possible; and if his willing brother ever left him any thing to inquire about, his inquiries even approached a tone of eagerness.

While they were thus comfortably occupied, Mr. Woodhouse was enjoying a full flow of happy regrets and fearful affection with his daughter.

'My poor dear Isabella,' said he, fondly taking her hand, and interrupting, for a few moments, her busy labours for some one of her five children —'How long it is, how terribly long since you were here! And how tired you must be after your journey!' (*E*, pp. 99-100)

Style and subject are clearly marked, but the characters reveal more than their distinctive qualities of intellect and character. Their social and personal relationships emerge through the hidden hostilities of family conversation. Emma watches for discord, and hastily changes the subject from the Southend journey to herself, dexterously pretending to find the subject painful: 'I must beg you not to talk of the sea.' A later collision is avoided by the diversionary subject of Mrs and Miss Bates: 'I have not heard one inquiry after them.' In a last effort of hospitable subject-changing, she asks her brother-in-law about his friend Mr Graham's bailiff from Scotland: 'But will it answer?' Despite the energies of tactful, ingenious, or hypocritical hostess-skills, a dangerous point is reached in Mr Woodhouse's vicarious arguments about health, in which he unconsciously attributes 'many of his own feelings and expressions' to Mr Perry, and provokes his son-in-law to respond in a 'voice of very strong displeasure'. The party is not over yet, and Mr John Knightley's outburst is deflected by his brother, who introduces the subject, appropriately enough, of a diverted path. Mr Woodhouse's agitation is calmed: 'The soothing attentions of his daughters gradually removed the present evil, and the immediate alertness of one brother, and better recollections of the other, prevented any renewal of it.'

A clear and amusing record of a family party, it displays the tact and tactlessness, the social sensibility and insensibility, of guests and hosts. But the ritual roles do not coincide with the actual perform-ances. They depend rather on the social sense and energy of each character. Between the awareness and the imagination of Mr Knight-ley and Emma, who act as host and hostess, and the innocence of Mr Woodhouse and Isabella, is Mr John Knightley, touchy son-in-law and guest. The scene brackets family resemblances and social affinities in the congeniality of two couples (Mr Woodhouse and Isabella, Mr Knightley and Emma), and the complementary union of the married couple. The group's shape is composed of several kinds of relationship, its drama created by what the characters bring to the group in their abilities, roles and associations. Mr Woodhouse is innocent but un-consciously aggressive, as he plays the parental game of trying to get his daughter back, observed by Jane Austen with shrewdness and sympathy. Mr John Knightley plays the role of the possessive husband, who resents his father-in-law's interference, but knows in his heart, fitfully, that there is no sense in protesting against the gentle selfishness or the hypochondria that father and elder daughter enjoy in common. Emma and Mr Knightley lead, manipulate, anticipate and divert, but they do not have the wayward group entirely in their control. Sensitive soothing helps as well as the clever change of sub-ject. She makes her characters aware of the weaknesses, dangers and remedies, provides them with some art and energy, but creates the social comedy from harmony and discord. The comedy shows her sense of a balance, loss and recovery of power, dependent on kinship, marriage, congeniality, complicity, intelligence and imagination. Personal powers are exhibited in personal relations and in public life.

She frequently shows groups which are controlled or dominated by leaders. The leaders sometimes lead by intelligence and tact, but some-times by a brute energy. Mrs Elton is a great dominator, neither sensi-tive nor intelligent, but intent on establishing a central role for herself as the new bride. Far from attempting to create harmony and make everyone happy, or at least not openly hostile, she wants only the pleasure of domination, which she usually achieves at the expense of the other members of the group. Her total lack of social sensibility helps her to push people about, ignore them or rush patronizingly into intimacy. Her modes of address reflect not only her vulgarity, but make claims to familiarity with new acquaintances, in 'Jane Fairfax', 'Knightley', her 'old beau' Mr Woodhouse, and her 'caro sposo'. Jane Austen takes great care to characterize Mrs Elton's style. It is not vulgar in a stereotyped fashion, but blindly over-intimate, boastful, self-flattering, and domineering:

> In this style she ran on; never thoroughly stopped by any thing till Mr. Woodhouse came into the room; her vanity had then a change of object, and Emma heard her saying in the same half-whisper to Jane,
> 'Here comes this dear old beau of mine, I protest!—Only think of his gallantry in coming away before the other men!—what a dear creature he is;—I assure you I like him excessively. I admire all that quaint, old-fashioned politeness; it is much more to my taste than modern ease; modern ease often disgusts me. But this good old Mr. Woodhouse, I wish you had heard his gallant speeches to me at dinner. Oh! I assure you I began to think my caro sposa [*sic*] would be absolutely jealous. I fancy I am rather a favourite; he took notice of my gown. How do you like it?— Selina's choice—handsome, I think, but I do not know whether it is not over-trimmed; I have the greatest dislike to the idea of being over-trimmed—quite a horror of finery. I must put on a few ornaments *now*, because it is expected of me.' (*E*, p. 302)

When the gentlemen join the ladies in the drawing-room, Mr Weston walks in from his day of business in London and a late dinner at Randalls, and the display of idiosyncrasy becomes more complicated. The social mixture thickens. Mr Weston's gregarious and friendly domination takes over from Mrs Elton's harsher powers. His over-sociable humour is also set beside John Knightley's unsociability:

> John Knightley only was in mute astonishment.—That a man who might have spent his evening quietly at home after a day of business in London, should set off again, and walk half-a-mile to another man's house, for the sake of being in mixed company till bed-time, of finishing his day in the efforts of civility and the noise of numbers, was a circumstance to strike him deeply. A man who had been in motion since eight o'clock in the morning, and might now have been still, who had been long talking, and might have been silent, who had been in more than one crowd, and might have been alone!—Such a man, to quit the tranquillity and independence of his own fire-side, and on the evening of a cold sleety April day rush out again into the world!—Could he by a touch of his

finger have instantly taken back his wife, there would have been a motive; but his coming would probably prolong rather than break up the party.

(*E*, pp. 302-3)

Jane Austen gets comedy out of such complex play of contrasting attitudes. It is not a static play. She likes to show the mobility of social occasions, and Mr Weston joins the company 'with all the right of being principal talker, which a day spent any where from home confers'. She knows that roles and performances are products of situation, and not of fixed characteristics. Mr Weston shows his wife the letter from Frank, which she reads to Emma, and he then proceeds to look around for fresh listeners, moving to Mr Woodhouse and Mr Knightley. Taking their joy for granted, he does not notice their lack of enthusiasm, and Jane Austen's free indirect style gently observes: 'They were the first entitled, after Mrs Weston and Emma, to be made happy.' He moves on to share his good news with a more resistant listener, Mrs Elton, now ready to recover her temporarily lost dominance. Jane Austen devotes almost a whole chapter to the power-game played by Mr Weston and Mrs Elton, making a brilliant comic analysis of the manoeuvres of two egoists, jostling for the floor. Mrs Elton first gains by interpreting Mr Weston's conventional politeness, 'I hope I shall soon have the pleasure of introducing my son to you', as 'a particular compliment', and asserts her interests as patronizing hostess by offering an invitation to the expected arrival, then making an affected bridal joke about husbands opening their wives' letters, on behalf of 'married women'. Mr Weston replies pleasantly but briefly to the banter, before directing it firmly back again to Frank. She takes the subject back with a skilful move; Frank's home in Yorkshire, 190 miles from London, is 'Sixty-five miles farther than from Maple Grove to London'. When she makes one loud 'call for a compliment', he responds 'with a very good grace', then having 'done his duty' he can 'return to his son'. The structure of the dialogue is a tug-of-war between two interests, and we are pleased when the pleasanter, warmer, and more generous egoist wins. The father defeats the bride. Even his mode of triumphant exit is carefully noticed: 'Tea was carrying round, and Mr Weston, having said all he wanted, soon took the opportunity of walking away.' The party ends rather badly, with the four card-players leaving the others 'to their own powers'. But their powers are in abeyance:

. . . Emma doubted their getting on very well; for Mr. Knightley seemed little disposed for conversation; Mrs. Elton was wanting notice, which nobody had inclination to pay, and she was herself in a worry of spirits which would have made her prefer being silent. (*E*, p. 311)

Mr John Knightley, in a fairly genial mood, is alert to the increased sociability of Highbury, telling Emma 'Your neighbourhood is increasing, and you mix more with it', and Mr Knightley hastens to agree that it is Randalls that has made the difference, silently but jealously denying Frank Churchill's impact. Emma rejects her brother-in-law's suggestion, that she won't have time for the children, with an amused and amusing reference to 'uncle Knightley' at home, and the chapter returns to Mrs Elton, in a quiet, withering insult: 'Mr Knightley seemed to be trying not to smile, and succeeded without difficulty, upon Mrs Elton's beginning to talk to him.'

With the dexterity of an accomplished juggler, Jane Austen begins slowly, then increases the number of balls in the air. The social scene is analytic and comic. It sustains a constant attention to the private occupations that determine, interrupt, and underlie the social surface. Each character's social response registers personal preoccupations as well as social roles and functions. On this occasion, neither Mr Knightley nor Emma feels up to the role of good guest or tactful hostess. The private life casts its shadows on the social scene, and roles shift in obedience to personal preoccupations. Here is the art of the surface, but its roots go deep. In the previous scene where Mr Knightley and Emma led so proficiently, they were relaxed, unclouded by personal problems. The second scene shows how the novelist qualifies her sense of role and interaction according to time, place and feeling.

Throughout the course of *Emma*, which has a lavishly social action, relationships turn on precisely that increase in sociability which Mr John Knightley observes. Strangers come in to alter the balance of groups and families. There are signs of larger changes too, like the Coles' dinner-party, which heralds a new era in their social life. Yet Jane Austen is less interested in shifts of class, however firmly she registers them, than in pressures of personality. The two are not always separable, so the gain to the student of the inner life need not be a loss to the analyst of groups. Mrs Elton's snobbishness, boastfulness and gorgeousness are all socially significant of class, wealth, and aspirations. But there are controls and correctives in the evaluation of social mobility. The Coles are polite, modest, and considerate. Even their deferential treatment of Mr Woodhouse and his daughter is not so much the ingratiation of humility as a courteous attention to health and habits.

In *Sense and Sensibility*, the portrait of the Steele sisters, whose mode is crude and sly flattery, shows a balance of social type and profounder psychology. The elder Miss Steele is a comic humour simple enough to have come out of the world of Fanny Burney's *Cecilia*, like 'the inimitable Miss Larolles' comically recalled by Anne Elliot as she observes her own jockeying for position in the concert. Miss Steele's broader humour does not obtrude, but is kept firmly in its place, as a crude foil for her more subtle sister, and a significant repetition of a social type. When this pair of flatterers appear in a social group, their role is unvaryingly performed in concert as they wheedle and toady their way into favour. They are provided with a pair of social superiors to flatter and are no more disapproved than those who hungrily lap up the compliments and services, and offer hospitality to get more. Jane Austen's dinner-parties at Hartfield show her interest in the centrifugal strains of a group whose individual members and sub-groups are held together with great effort, but she also turns her attention to the more homogenous groups. She loves to create dramatic structures with a centripetal action, organized around some central subject. In Volume Two, Chapter Twelve, of *Sense and Sensibility* she displays such a group in a condensed social drama composed of three brief scenes. The first scene takes place at the dinner-table in the Dashwoods' 'very good house' in Harley Street, and is quickly followed by two other scenes in the drawing-room, first when the ladies are alone, and then after they are joined by the gentlemen.

Jane Austen links her scenes smoothly and tensely. The social implications are many. The Miss Steeles are strangers but are preferred to kin because they are so good at flattery and appear to offer no threatening aspiration. Elinor observes the aggression of the polite assembly as the hostess, Fanny Dashwood, and the guest of honour, Mrs Ferrars, pointedly slight her and behave graciously to Lucy. Like Jane Austen's, her contempt and amusement are evenly divided between the flattered and the flatterer. The comedy of manners creates a neatly effective model of complementary and interdependent levels of inferiority and superiority, and also fully exploits the comic effect of self-deception. The foolishly flattered ladies pin their faith on the deceiving flatterer, who in her turn is blind to the true reasons for her success, as she takes the response to flattery for an encouragement to aspiration, whereas its tolerance depends entirely on the assumption that she will stay in her place. Jane Austen registers differences of intellect as well as differences of class in her analysis of unstable hierarchy, and she doesn't fail to register the consequences of prevailing stupidity. The grandeur of the dinner is matched by a poverty of conversation:

> . . . no poverty of any kind, except of conversation, appeared—but there, the deficiency was considerable. John Dashwood had not much to say for himself that was worth hearing, and his wife had still less. But there was no peculiar disgrace in this, for it was very much the case with the chief of their visitors, who almost all laboured under one or other of these dis-qalifications for being agreeable—Want of sense, either natural or improved—want of elegance—want of spirits—or want of temper.
> (*SS*, p. 233)

In the party at Hartfield, Mr Weston and Mrs Elton were pressing the ever-interesting topics of paternity and marriage, but the total lack of any subject for conversation in the very good house in Harley Street is even more marked when the ladies are alone in the drawing-room:

> . . . for the gentlemen *had* supplied the discourse with some variety—the variety of politics, inclosing land, and breaking horses—but then it was all over; and one subject only engaged the ladies till coffee came in, which was the comparative heights of Harry Dashwood, and Lady Middleton's second son William, who were nearly of the same age. (*Ibid.*)

All there is to talk about is the height of the two little boys, William not being present to obstruct conversational conjecture. The stupid-ities and hostilities of the dinner-party continue in the round-game of flattery:

> Had both the children been there, the affair might have been deter-mined too easily by measuring them at once; but as Harry only was present, it was all conjectural assertion on both sides, and every body had a right to be equally positive in their opinion, and to repeat it over and over again as often as they liked.
> The parties stood thus:
> The two mothers, though each really convinced that her own son was the tallest, politely decided in favour of the other.
> The two grandmothers, with no less partiality, but more sincerity, were equally earnest in support of their own descendant.
> Lucy, who was hardly less anxious to please one parent than the other,

thought the boys were both remarkably tall for their age, and could not conceive that there could be the smallest difference in the world between them; and Miss Steele, with yet greater address gave it, as fast as she could, in favour of each.

Elinor, having once delivered her opinion on William's side, by which she offended Mrs. Ferrars and Fanny still more, did not see the necessity of enforcing it by any farther assertion; and Marianne, when called on for her's, offended them all, by declaring that she had no opinion to give, as she had never thought about it. (*SS*, pp. 233-4)

Straight-faced comedy and elegant form are eloquent. Polite conversation, hospitality, rank, leisure and ladies are all censured in the rapid, matter-of-fact summary which mocks polite nonsense in its symmetry, and nails the social type in its duplication. (Its extreme brevity and gracefulness put it at a great distance from Fanny Burney's loud and lengthy scenes of conflicting humours.) The very curtness proposes its offhand brevity as the right medium for the absurd elaboration of polite nothings. In spite of brevity, character is kept up. Lucy's flattery is intelligent enough to hover in compromise, while her sister oscillates meaninglessly; Elinor is polite and honest enough to speak her opinion; Marianne refuses to play. The social strains of the evening mount, as Elinor compounds her unpopularity by being sincere on the wrong side, and Marianne offends everyone by having no opinion at all. The pattern is then repeated, with a variation, as the gentlemen return from the dining-room, to improve neither conversations nor tempers. A new and unfortunate subject for group discourse is discovered in Elinor's screens. Once more everyone except Elinor, Marianne and Colonel Brandon behaves according to type (insincerity) and ruling passion (acquisitiveness). The false ceremony ends in open attack, tenderness and tears. The breakdown of nerve and politeness is the right climax to a drama in which high and low are paraded in the vicious circle of flattery. The mercenary society pretends it has a heart, then exposes its heartlessness to provoke Marianne's hysterical loyalties. Miss Morton's landscape is praised instead of Elinor's screens: 'Do you not think they are something in Miss Morton's style of painting, ma'am? – *She does* paint most delightfully! – How beautifully her last landscape is done!' Subtlety goes beyond the social criticism which lies on the surface. Mrs Ferrars answers Marianne's question most lucidly, with 'Miss Morton is Lord Morton's daughter'; but Jane Austen forces us to see all the implications of the breakdown of decorum, and of decorum itself, which has

at least had the merit of saving Elinor's face. As soon as we start align-
ing our sympathy it is made hard for us to continue to do so. John
Dashwood has precipitated the conflict, because he mistakenly uses
the screens to flatter Elinor and solicit Colonel Brandon's attention.
The party ends with his misplaced ingratiating words to Colonel
Brandon as he disparages Marianne in the attempt to promote the
interests of Elinor:

> 'She has not such good health as her sister,—she is very nervous,—she has
> not Elinor's constitution;—and one must allow that there is something
> very trying to a young woman who *has been* a beauty, in the loss of her
> personal attractions. You would not think it perhaps, but Marianne *was*
> remarkably handsome a few months ago; quite as handsome as Elinor.—
> Now you see it is all gone.' (*SS*, p. 237)

Jane Austen's criticism is levelled at the social structure where
flattery is endemic. The flattered become the flatterers, and gross mis-
calculations are made by the calculating.

Jane Austen's satire on vulgarity and mercenariness is not restricted
to the social climbers. The have-nots may be greedy, but the haves
behave as if they were have-nots. The aristocrats are criticized
strongly, both in the dullness of the Dalrymples in *Persuasion* and the
offensiveness of Lady Catherine de Bourgh in *Pride and Prejudice*.
Darcy's disdain has to be turned against his own aunt, as well as
against Elizabeth's mother, as she too shows off, flatters and domin-
eers. Lady Catherine's loudness is beautifully audible in the drawing-
room at Rosings, where it is encouraged by her sycophants. Decorum
is fragile and easily broken. The hearts and minds of the characters are
implicitly shown in the broad comedy of manners, and the serious
characters are involved in a complex social response, which the
novelist does not explicitly analyse. As Elizabeth is enjoying herself in
conversation with Colonel Fitzwilliam, who is talking so agreeably 'of
Kent and Hertfordshire, of travelling and staying at home, of new
books and music' that she is better entertained than she has ever been
'in that room before', her hostess is jealous and curious of the unusual
'spirit and flow'. So is Darcy. He just looks curious, but his aunt does
'not scruple to call out' with aristocratic bullying brashness:

> 'What is that you are saying, Fitzwilliam? What is it you are talking
> of? What are you telling Miss Bennet? Let me hear what it is.'
> 'We are speaking of music, Madam,' said he, when no longer able to
> avoid a reply.

'Of music! Then pray speak aloud. It is of all subjects my delight. I must have my share in the conversation, if you are speaking of music. There are few people in England, I suppose, who have more true enjoyment of music than myself, or a better natural taste. If I had ever learnt, I should have been a great proficient. And so would Anne, if her health had allowed her to apply. I am confident that she would have performed delightfully.' (*PP*, p. 173)

The social collision continues, with Lady Catherine snubbing Elizabeth:

'I have told Miss Bennet several times, that she will never play really well, unless she practises more; and though Mrs. Collins has no instrument, she is very welcome, as I have often told her, to come to Rosings every day, and play on the piano forte in Mrs. Jenkinson's room. She would be in nobody's way, you know, in that part of the house.'

Mr. Darcy looked a little ashamed of his aunt's ill breeding, and made no answer. (*Ibid.*)

Mind and sensibility are discriminated, and social leadership comically displayed. Elizabeth and Darcy talk about musical diffidence as an emblem of social diffidence, to be interrupted by the rude demands and commands of the hostess, which Elizabeth neatly foils by returning to the piano. Lady Catherine repeats her inane flattery of Anne, who 'would have been a delightful performer, had her health allowed her to learn', Darcy neither replies nor shows any response, and Elizabeth receives the unqualified 'instructions on execution and taste' with 'all the forbearance of civility'. The clash of manners and minds is carefully patterned. Once more the group is given a central subject, that of music. This time we have no rise into unbearable conflict, because only one person is behaving badly, and the courtesy of the others makes its own quiet rebuke and preserves the polite surface of the evening. Not until Lady Catherine actually enters Longbourn, to offend as a guest just as she has offended as a host, and threatens Elizabeth's personal life, does it become necessary to breach decorum and make the elementary intellectual effort to defeat her. The release of this later conflict in the shrubbery owes something to the tension and control of the earlier scenes at Rosings. The local scenes make it clear that decorum and courtesy are expensively bought, and we are not surprised when the novel comes to show that the payments cannot be kept up.

Domination and submission, flattery and condescension, rudeness and decorum give symmetry to many groups. The comic criticism of class and rank is crossed and controlled by a sense of character. If we are in danger of supposing that Mrs Bennet's bad manners are accounted for by her low origin, we see Lady Catherine's even greater offensiveness. If we are in danger of feeling too sharply Elizabeth's social shame at her parents' behaviour, we see Darcy put through the same experience. If we come to criticize Darcy's diffidence, we see its advantage over his aunt's assertiveness. In a novel where pride is a conspicuous theme, the social groups frequently illustrate its forms and functions.

There are some forms of social domination, however, which are shown to be acceptable and even desirable. Jane Austen frequently tolerates the domination of intelligence and experience. Henry Tilney enthusiastically instructs Catherine Morland. It is a delicate relationship, since Catherine is weaker in personality and mind than the energetic and self-confident Emma, who does not easily admit Mr Knightley's claim to have the right of experience in criticizing her. The tutorial exchanges between Henry and Catherine are leavened by her sincerity and his teasing, but Jane Austen is aware that there is danger in asserting such consistent intellectual victories. Catherine is charmed by his intelligence and his attractiveness, which are shown through his 'spirit and flow', in its delicate flirtatiousness, personal address and light exaggeration. He is charmed, too, by her malleability, impressionability, good looks and sincerity. The laughter which often bursts out at her expense can be silenced as he is taken aback by her fresh feelings. Her honesty is so unusual that her truths have at times the weight of wit. When she tells him that all she has to do at home in Fullerton is to go and call on Mrs Allen, 'Mr Tilney was very much amused. "Only go and call on Mrs Allen!" he repeated. "What a picture of intellectual poverty!"' When naïve openness neatly arrives at the declaration, 'I cannot speak well enough to be unintelligible', he applauds her excellent unconscious 'satire on modern language'. But the balance of power is still in danger of tipping over too much towards Henry's masterful experience, tutorial instructiveness and satire, so Jane Austen makes adroit use of his sister, Eleanor Tilney. She mediates between him and Catherine, good-humouredly criticizing the critic, 'You are more nice than wise', changing the subject as cleverly as Emma, and to a similarly tactful end: 'Come, Miss Morland, let us leave him to meditate over our faults in the utmost propriety of diction, while we praise Udolpho in whatever terms we like best. It is a most interesting work. You are fond of that kind of reading?' The dialogue is enlarged to include a valuable third party. The disarming presence of a sisterly qualification valuably preserves Catherine and the reader from a sense of Henry's unrelieved superiority. But Eleanor's touch is gentle, her tone permissive: 'We shall get nothing more serious from him now, Miss Morland. He is not in a sober mood. But I do assure you that he must be entirely misunderstood, if he can ever appear to say an unjust thing of any woman at all, or an unkind one of me.' Henry's niceties are at once placed and permitted. The slightly unbalanced duet has been replaced by a trio, which redresses the balance, through Eleanor Tilney's not too sedate politeness, information, taste, and humour. Moreover, the edge is taken off Jane Austen's stridently ironic comments on 'the advantages of natural folly in a beautiful girl'. Eleanor and Henry are more intelligent and experienced than Catherine, but the reliability of his admiration for Catherine's fresh and sincere feeling is reinforced by his sister's recognition. When he speaks satirically of Isabella Thorpe's qualities as a sister-in-law, 'Open, candid, artless, guileless, with affections strong but simple, forming no pretensions, and knowing no disguise', Eleanor responds with an innuendo that she knows will not be picked up by Catherine's modesty and simplicity: 'Such a sister-in-law, Henry, I should delight in.' The danger of dominance passes, and a genuinely friendly group is created. Such groups are not all that easy to find in Jane Austen's novels.

Jane Austen's heroines are intelligent women, who have to live in the restricted families and neighbourhoods with which the novels begin. This limited society is usually enlarged to bring in some new life, more entertaining, experienced and intelligent. Jane Austen likes to begin with a dearth of good company. (The only exception is *Sense and Sensibility*.) In *Northanger Abbey* Catherine finds good company in Bath. In *Sense and Sensibility* the Dashwood household is cultivated and even studious, certainly more self-sufficient than most of the families in which the heroines are born and brought up, but the additions of Willoughby and Colonel Brandon expand its experience. In *Pride and Prejudice*, the effects of intellectual isolation leave their marks on Mr Bennet, and through him on his daughters, and perhaps his wife. Darcy and Bingley are valuable additions, and even before Elizabeth sheds her prejudice against his pride, we can enjoy the conversation of Darcy, Bingley and Elizabeth.

Intellectual isolation is Emma's problem. She has dominated her governess, and her father, then loses Miss Taylor's rational, if over-tolerant, companionship. Emma and Anne Elliot draw our attention to this form of loneliness which probably did not oppress Jane Austen herself, living as she did among clever, cultivated, reading and writing people. But she was not protected from the company of uncongenial people, as her letters make plain in their many chronicles of unequal company. This one is characteristically sharp but good tempered:

> I am to take the Miss Moores back on Saturday, & when I return I shall hope to find your pleasant, little, flowing scrawl on the Table.—It will be a releif to me after playing at Ma'ams—for though I like Miss H. M. as much as one can at my time of Life after a day's acquaintance, it is uphill work to be talking to those whom one knows so little. Only *one* comes back with me tomorrow, probably Miss Eliza, & I rather dread it. We shall not have two Ideas in common. She is young, pretty, chattering, & thinking chcifly (I presume) of Dress, Company, & Admiration.—Mr. Sanford is to join us at dinner, which will be a comfort, and in the even'g while your Uncle and Miss Eliza play chess, he shall tell me comical things & I will laugh at them, which will be a pleasure to both.
>
> (*Letters*, p. 419)

Like Emma, she found nothing too small to occupy her mind, the novelist's mind to which nothing human can be alien. On the occasion when she marks Emma's imagination idling happily on the doorstep of the draper's shop, she perhaps forgets momentarily that her heroine often finds life tedious and boring. When we observe Emma at home, in the tedium of her family life, tactfully soothing her father with patient gentle words and backgammon, we are seeing something very important in the societies and society of Jane Austen's novels – the strength of family life.

Family life in Jane Austen's world is 'à la mortal, finely chequered'. Living with other people in close communities, even in large houses, has many problems. (Jane Austen knows that it is much more difficult in small houses. Fanny finds Portsmouth almost unbearable, and Mrs Collins has to take great pains to see little of her husband.) Family life is very difficult but family ties are very strong. No one lives alone. No one leaves home, except for the navy, adoption or marriage. There is one divorce, and a large number of incompatibilities. Jane Austen does not write novels which simply assume and describe such diffi-culties and such toleration. Her insight into individual character and social codes goes beyond assumptions and descriptions to suggest explanations. Since she presents individuals, not averages or sections, what may seem intolerably rigid in families and marriages, contemplated in the gross, is imagined and so elucidated.

The restless motion of the novels makes plain the satisfactions and restrictions of repose. Life is difficult for Elizabeth Bennet, Emma, and Anne Elliot, who are all daughters afflicted by the difficulty of living with mothers or fathers. (Jane Austen attends sufficiently to heredity to describe one parent of intelligent heroines as gifted: Mr Bennet, Emma's dead mother, and Anne's dead mother.) Jane Austen told her family that Mr Woodhouse died two years after Emma's marriage to Mr Knightley, but the release happened only in that pleasant limbo beyond the novel with which Jane Austen gratified her friends' yearnings for a fictional afterlife. Within the novel, Emma has no choice. Elizabeth and Anne are able to leave home when they marry, but till then they must stay with parents as uncongenial as Mrs Bennet and Sir Walter Elliot. To generalize Jane Austen's social situations is to neglect her particularities. Emma's father, though able to provide neither rational nor playful companionship – no wonder she needs to make matches – is affectionate and sweet-tempered. Emma feels no distaste for his paternal fussing. He calls her 'a fairy' and gives her the memorable advice to warm herself thoroughly before going to bed. It seems an anachronistic error to see him, as Ronald Blythe does,[18] as 'a menace'. He has had his own way, as Mr Blythe says, but only in little things. Even his weaker daughter has managed not only to get married, but to prefer her strong husband to her feeble father. Emma is never in any real danger of giving up Mr Knightley. On the whole, the parents in these novels are unpredatory, unpossessive, even pre-Oedipal, and it is probably Mr Woodhouse's affectionate fussiness and hypochondria which make it tempting to exaggerate his threat to procreation.

General Tilney, Mrs Bennet, and Sir Walter Elliot are tolerated by their children. Eleanor and Henry Tilney are patient and compliant, but kept so well under as to make Henry's resistance almost incredible. Elizabeth Bennet is able to relieve her feelings and maintain decorum because her mother doesn't understand her sometimes impatient wit. Mrs Bennet commends Jane's charms by referring to the gentleman who wrote some pretty verses 'on her': ' "And so ended his affection," said Elizabeth impatiently. "There has been many a one, I fancy, overcome in the same way, I wonder who first discovered the efficacy

---

[18] See his introduction to the Penguin edition of *Emma* (Harmondsworth, 1966), p. 15.

of poetry in driving away love",' a remark which silences her mother, and interests Darcy, who replies with a quotation from *Twelfth Night* suitably adapted and assimilated. Elizabeth trembles when her mother speaks, and again when she is silent, since she may speak again, and wit isn't always available to cover embarrassment and silence. Like Emma and Knightley, Elizabeth Bennet is socially proficient, but not always in the mood or spirits to handle testing situations. Her relationship with her father, like Emma's with Mr Woodhouse, or Elinor Dashwood's with her mother, shows Jane Austen's cool and realistic anticipation of the grotesque parent-child reversals in Dickens's *Little Dorrit* and *Our Mutual Friend*.

Within the drama of the social group, good talk is more common than congenial company. Mr Elliot admits that Anne has a right to be 'nice' about the company she keeps, but protests against her high standards when she admits to being too proud to defer to the grand and dull Dalrymples. Her definition of a precise social ideal is answered by his defence of the second-best, well expressed in an interesting mixture of sincerity, compliment, pragmatic worldliness and insight:

> 'My idea of good company, Mr. Elliot, is the company of clever, well-informed people, who have a great deal of conversation; that is what I call good company.'
>
> 'You are mistaken,' said he gently, 'that is not good company, that is the best. Good company requires only birth, education and manners, and with regard to education is not very nice. Birth and good manners are essential; but a little learning is by no means a dangerous thing in good company, on the contrary, it will do very well.' (*P*, p. 150)

Most of the company in the novels of Jane Austen is merely good company. At times it sinks below Mr Elliot's standard. But each novel ends with a movement out of old company into new, in the best company of congenial married lovers, and this conclusion is not a facile inflation. It depends on the foretaste of good company within the novels. We end with a sense of renewed community, which supports and strengthens the hope for the good marriage and the next generation. Fiction's happy endings may be inflated, as they often are in Dickens, or invoke compromises of fable and likelihood, as in Thackeray's *The Newcomes*, or hesitate on the verge of optimism as in *Middlemarch*. It is not Jane Austen's way to expand the novel's horizons at its end, like some of her Victorian successors, with bigger and bolder statements of vision. Her endings, however, while resting on the invocation of the best we have seen within the novel, do stress hope and a new order. Each ending, therefore, does do a little more than make an end of this story. It also suggests a beginning.

*Northanger Abbey* ends with a joke about the reader's anticipation 'that we are all hastening to felicity together' and another about Eleanor Tilney's husband having been earlier introduced through his washing-bills. There is a little seriousness in each joke. Jane Austen does not end with single instances of married felicity. And she does like to base her hopes on truly glimpsed possibility, personal and social. The happy couple are seen off in company. We have already seen the good company of Eleanor, Henry and Catherine, and it is now joined, not just by a shadowy young, rich, and noble bridegroom who facilitates the happy ending for Catherine and Henry, but with another marriage to help on the sense of good neighbourhood. 'Everybody smiled,' says the author, and the anonymous everyone can include not only the stable, ordinary contentedness of Catherine's parents, but the contemporary joys of her own generation.

At the end of *Sense and Sensibility*, the sisters' happy marriages are united, as their misfortunes have always been. But Jane Austen gently underlines the sense of community:

> Between Barton and Delaford, there was that constant communication which strong family affection would naturally dictate;—and among the merits and the happiness of Elinor and Marianne, let it not be ranked as the least considerable, that though sisters, and living almost within sight of each other, they could live without disagreement between themselves, or producing coolness between their husbands. (*SS*, p. 380)

It calmly glances back to a scene of action where most of the marriages have been unhappy, tolerable, or disgracefully congenial, like the union of John and Fanny Dashwood. Though its tones are the typically caustic tones of the most sardonic narrator of all the novels, the cool irony is invoked in the interests of affirming harmony. The happy ending has a stronger foundation than that of a single couple. But it is not simply the duplicated coupling of 'an old play'. It has been laid down in our experience of the grave and playful conversations of the two couples.[19]

[19] In *Jane Austen's Literary Manuscripts*, op. cit., p. 56, Brian Southam has suggested that the reference to the conversation Elinor missed when she regrets Norland may be a loose end left over in revision since it is explained by nothing in the novel. But it surely refers to Edward Ferrars. We don't hear this conversation, but we hear about it.

These two socially hopeful endings may reflect no more than Jane Austen's own experience of an actively congenial family life. But the sense of social renewal and expansion grows unmistakably as her fiction matures. Hers is not a darkening vision, even though the three later heroines steadily contemplate solitude before they are fortunately allowed to deserve love. *Pride and Prejudice* ends with good-tempered tolerance and reconciliation. Jane Austen expressly disclaims revolutions and conversions. Things are a little improved in the Bennet household, Mr Bennet is drawn to Pemberley, informally, 'when he was least expected', Catherine and Mary improve, for convincingly practical reasons. The characters of Wickham and Lydia 'suffer no revolution', remain within the orbit of the Darcy and Bingley aid, generally at a convenient distance. We can imagine the unmiraculous reconciliations with Miss Bingley, paying off 'every arrear of civility to Elizabeth' and being 'almost' as attentive to Darcy as before, and Lady Catherine de Bourgh descending to test the conduct of Mrs Darcy and inspect the pollution of Pemberley. Threats are banished, and when Bingley buys an estate within thirty miles of Pemberley, there is stability and civilization in a small company of friends. Jane Austen's last sentence quietens any discomfort at the admission of Lady Catherine, the banishment of the Wickhams, and the apparent neglect of Mrs Bennet. This harmony is nice but not proud : 'With the Gardiners, they were always on the most intimate terms. Darcy, as well as Elizabeth, really loved them; and they were both ever sensible of the warmest gratitude towards the persons who, by bringing her into Derbyshire, had been the means of uniting them.' (*PP*, p. 388) The novels end with a deliberated and impartial gesture to social tact.

The last three novels give similar support to the happy ending. *Mansfield Park* cannot quite dispel the guilt and misery which other pens are left to dwell on, but which Jane Austen's pen needs to mention. The last pages include the marvellous detail of Sir Thomas's relief at casting off Mrs Norris, who had begun to seem to him 'like a part of himself, that must be borne for ever'. If we feel the ruthlessness of Mansfield's dismissals it is not because they have not been most thoroughly imagined. Intransigent elements are banished, but the ending is more than just a fairy-tale. The community which Fanny has grown to value, and love, uncritically, has been improved. Its adoption of the little girl from Portsmouth had been condescending and unrealistic, because Sir Thomas and Mrs Norris hoped to let her make no difference, while herself feeling different. Rank is not allowed to keep its circles closed, and the novel's conclusion once more celebrates a refreshed and strengthened community. It owes improvement to the heroine, and gives her the home and the good company she deserves.

*Emma's* comic ending calmly permits Mr Elton to join the hands of Mr Knightley and Emma, in an unfussed recognition of his clerical function. Like the other weddings in the novels, and the weddings of Jane Austen's own society, this one is so quiet that Mrs Elton has to have the finery 'detailed by her husband'. The last quavering choric notes of the Eltons and the never-seen Selina are overpowered by 'the wishes, the hopes, the confidence, the predictions of the small band of true friends who witnessed the ceremony'.

Friends surround Captain Wentworth and Anne Elliot at the end of eight years of waiting. Brian Southam [20] points out that in altering the last page of *Persuasion* Jane Austen added a paragraph which 'extends the reference to Mrs Smith and links her more closely to the fortunes of Anne and Wentworth'. His suggestion that Jane Austen felt 'some uneasiness about Mrs Smith's place in the story' may be right, but the extended reference is perfectly in character with her usual sense of an ending. Here too she uses and emphasizes the sense of community and friendship which is more strongly present in this novel than in any other. It is felt by Anne in the happy household and marriage of the Harvilles, in their warm and informal style of hospitality, and in the signs of a group of affectionate, congenial, and helpful people, regretted earlier by Anne, for 'these would have been her friends'. At the end, they are to be her friends. She feels wryly that her contribution to the new community is unequal, consisting only of Mrs Smith and Lady Russell. Jane Austen liked to link two communities, joining the best of the old in support and renewal. The end of the novel reaches out most imaginatively to a future. In the penultimate chapter, the lovers have their first private talk in the novel, and look ahead and back. Jane Austen creates an elaborate, ambitious and moving setting for the happy couple, who are seen together amongst the usual crowd. Their isolation and its business set them apart, as an ideal pair standing for universal hopes of love, yet place them as real inhabitants of the hubbub of the town. It is a quieter anticipation of the ending of Dickens's *Little Dorrit*, which may have unconsciously

[20] Op. cit., p. 97. Mary Lascelles earlier discussed the development of Mrs Smith, op. cit., pp. 192-4.

recollected this modest precedent. Jane Austen does not attempt the sublime, but records happiness:

> There they exchanged again those feelings and those promises which had once before seemed to secure every thing, but which had been followed by so many, many years of division and estrangement. There they returned again into the past, more exquisitely happy, perhaps, in their re-union, than when it had been first projected; more tender, more tried, more fixed in a knowledge of each other's character, truth, and attachment; more equal to act, more justified in acting. And there, as they slowly paced the gradual ascent, heedless of every group around them, seeing neither sauntering politicians, bustling house-keepers, flirting girls, nor nursery-maids and children, they could indulge in those retrospections and acknowledgements, and especially in those explanations of what had directly preceded the present moment, which were so poignant and so ceaseless in interest. All the little variations of the last week were gone through; and of yesterday and to-day there could scarcely be an end.   ,
> (*P*, pp. 240-1)

Had Jane Austen been versed in the final resonances of Victorian novel-endings, she might have placed this triumph at the end as a valediction to the reader. The actual ending typically provides a firmer, more specific sense of the good society. As Anne finds her best company at last, the conclusion of the novel invokes a real community, and places love and marriage, uncomplacently, in the real world:

> His profession was all that could ever make her friends wish that tenderness less; the dread of a future war all that could dim her sunshine. She gloried in being a sailor's wife, but she must pay the tax of quick alarm for belonging to that profession which is, if possible, more distinguished in its domestic virtue than in its national importance. (*P*, p. 252)

# VI

# Properties and Possessions

Ever since Fielding designed an appropriate dwelling for Mr All-worthy in *Tom Jones*, the houses in fiction have been carefully planned and furnished. Allworthy's house is the best of Gothic, and can rival the Grecian style. Its situation is sufficiently low to be sheltered from the north-east by an oak grove, sufficiently elevated to yield fine prospects. Its lawns and tree-clumps are landscaped by man; its cascades, lake and meandering river by nature. The rooms in the front enjoy views of the park, waters, ruined abbey, villages, animals and a cloud-topped ridge of high mountains. Its river reaches a sea, its mountains are lost in sky. Extensive without, it is commodious within. House and environs possess unity and variety, look out on civilization and nature, are products of both but owe more to nature than to art. The view was drawn, with a fine balance of sobriety and wit, from Glastonbury Tor, near Fielding's birthplace, and the house probably draws on features of Ralph Allen's house at Prior Park, near Bath, and Sharpham Park, near Glastonbury, combined and varied by the novelist's natural powers and artifice.

Jane Austen must have remembered[1] these eloquent advantages when accommodating Darcy at Pemberley, and Fielding's principles of ironic symbolism may also have determined the choice of North-

---

[1] The sympathetic habitat begins, amusingly, in the fragment of burlesque, *Evelyn, Volume the Third, MW*, ed. R. W. Chapman (Oxford, 1954). The Webbs' residence in the idyllic village of Evelyn is described with geo-metrical accuracy, as being geometrically exact in its order:

It was in the exact centre of a small circular paddock, which was enclosed by a regular paling, & bordered with a plantation of Lombardy poplars, & Spruce firs alternatively placed in three rows. A gravel walk ran through this beautiful Shrubbery, and as the remainder of the paddock was unincumbered with any other Timber, the surface of it perfectly even & smooth, and grazed by four white Cows which were disposed at equal distances from each other, the whole appearance was uncommonly striking. (p. 181)

anger Abbey for General Tilney, Rosings for Lady Catherine de Bourgh, Mansfield Park for the Bertrams and Sotherton for Mrs Rushworth. Fielding's comic irony held Allworthy's great house and prospects at arm's length from the reader's judgement, dangerously grand, suspiciously eloquent, an ideal environment for an ideal or idealizing human occupant. Jane Austen's comic imagination founded her sympathetic habitats more firmly, more craftily, and yet more naturally in her fictions, by using her characters as architects and builders. It is their insight and projection which make the houses so sympathetic. The pathetic fallacy is extended and civilized. Her symbolic houses are conspicuous instances in an art inclined always to merge symbol in surface, but their symbolism is an aspect of her characters. It may well have been her assimilations and variations of Fielding which consolidated the symbolic environment as a tradition in the novel. Fielding's design is passed on through Jane Austen to the architects of Thrushcross Grange, Wuthering Heights, Gateshead, Thornfield Manor, Ferndean, Lowood, the House of Usher, Lowick, Gardencourt, Poynton and Castle de Stancy. Throughout the nineteenth century houses grew more like their owners, in style and contents.

Jane Austen placed the sympathetic habitat within the minds of her characters but its existence is not wholly subjective. She invented the suitably malleable material which made the house the right kind of shell for its occupant. She saw environment as a case both forming and formed by people. Her houses are animated, or fail to be animated, by the life led within their walls and beneath their roofs. They are restored, improved, or left unimproved, by likely people. Households, as well as owners, partake of this life of houses. The houses accommodate guests as well as hosts. Homes are significantly commodious or restricted, old or modern, elegant or heavy, big or small. They are good shelters, hives with isolated cells, prisons or protections. They stifle or facilitate life, welcome or fail to welcome the visitor. Roofs and walls allow for growth or enclose life. Houses are beautiful or ugly, but their beauty is more than skin-deep. In Jane Austen gardens are the woods where destinies are found and lost, in small evergreen shrubberies, ordered wildernesses, by dangerous ha-has and gates, in damp grounds and old temples, by rich lawns and fertile waters.

Houses and grounds begin to be fully animated in *Northanger Abbey*. It may have been the demands of a plot requiring a Gothic abbey with an unGothic atmosphere which developed Jane Austen's imaginative architecture. We see Northanger through Catherine Morland's eyes and imagination. At first sight Northanger is a disappointment to her, her 'passion for ruins', second only to her 'passion for Henry Tilney', having formed great expectations from Mrs Radcliffe's castles in Italy. (She has already been disappointed by not going to Blaize Castle.) Her first impressions are obscure:

As they drew near the end of their journey, her impatience for a sight of the abbey—for some time suspended by his conversation on subjects very different—returned in full force, and every bend in the road was expected with solemn awe to afford a glimpse of its massy walls of grey stone, rising amidst a grove of ancient oaks, with the last beams of the sun playing in beautiful splendour on its high Gothic windows. But so low did the building stand, that she found herself passing through the great gates of the lodge into the very grounds of Northanger, without having discerned even an antique chimney.

She knew not that she had any right to be surprized, but there was a something in this mode of approach which she certainly had not expected. To pass between lodges of a modern appearance, to find herself with such ease in the very precincts of the abbey, and driven so rapidly along a smooth, level road of fine gravel, without obstacle, alarm or solemnity of any kind, struck her as odd and inconsistent. She was not long at leisure however for such considerations. A sudden scud of rain driving full in her face, made it impossible for her to observe any thing further, and fixed all her thoughts on the welfare of her new straw bonnet:—and she was actually under the Abbey walls, was springing, with Henry's assistance, from the carriage, was beneath the shelter of the old porch, and had even passed on to the hall, where her friend and the General were waiting to welcome her, without feeling one aweful foreboding of future misery to herself, or one moment's suspicion of any past scenes of horror being acted within the solemn edifice. The breeze had not seemed to waft the sighs of the murdered to her; it had wafted nothing worse than a thick mizzling rain; and having given a good shake to her habit, she was ready to be shewn into the common drawing-room, and capable of considering where she was.

An abbey!—yes, it was delightful to be really in an abbey!—but she doubted, as she looked round the room, whether any thing within her observation, would have given her the consciousness. The furniture was in all the profusion and elegance of modern taste. The fire-place, where she had expected the ample width and ponderous carving of former times, was contracted to a Rumford, with slabs of plain though handsome marble, and ornaments over it of the prettiest English china. The windows, to which she looked with peculiar dependence, from having heard the General talk of his preserving them in their Gothic form with reverential care, were yet less what her fancy had portrayed. To be sure, the pointed arch was preserved—the form of them was Gothic—they might be even casements—but every pane was so large, so clear, so light! To an imagination which had hoped for the smallest divisions, and the heaviest stone-work, for painted glass, dirt and cobwebs, the difference was very distressing. (*NA*, pp. 161-2)

When she finds herself inside, the furniture is too modern, the light too bright, the walls too clean, even the authentic windows disturbingly clear. She later finds the restorations too effective, and the servants' quarters too convenient. As an abbey it is lacking in mystery, insufficiently sinister. But Catherine's passion works hard on its possibilities, aided by her real insight which has already detected something wrong in her host and his family's life. Northanger turns out after all to be the right kind of dwelling for Jane Austen's version of Montoni, whose modern tyrannies are every bit as bad and potent as those imagined by Mrs Radcliffe in *The Mysteries of Udolpho,* and who does bring 'misery' to the heroine. Host and guest are set at cross-purposes in a place designed to mislead them both. What General Tilney offers is as obscure to his guest as her expectations – in all senses – are unknown to him. He is the owner of the Abbey, his autocracy ordering his household, demanding its prompt attendance in the elegant dining-room on the stroke of five, keeping a good table, ingratiatingly belittling his possessions but demanding admiration for contrivance and property, and evicting his guest the minute he discovers her unsuitability for his purposes. Hospitality can be no more effectively and thoroughly breached, even in the Gothic novels where the heroines were lodged in a solitary and gloomy room. The ironic symbolism of Jane Austen's house is a comic but bitter account of a family and its life, a host and his predatory entertainments.

The symbolism of the house depends on its contents as well as its structure. Northanger Abbey first provides objects for Catherine's literary imagination to embellish. Houses are shells, but not empty shells, and Jane Austen provides an inner coating of things which joins people with building. She goes beyond Fielding to create a house filled with expressive objects. The things in Northanger Abbey are set in action as dramatic properties, but are so thoroughly imagined in relation to the people who own and use them that they invoke a variety of human responses, answering to human imagination, needs, appetites and wishes. Almost everything in the Abbey carries the imprint of the improving hand, but Jane Austen's solid sense of likelihood prevents her from making merely melodramatic furniture and fittings. The improving hand isn't only the grasping hand of General

Tilney, but the neutrally recorded hand of his father. Some part is played by the sensible housekeeping of Eleanor, who decided to keep the old chest in Catherine's room as a useful container for 'hats and bonnets'. But General Tilney's guardianship and responsibility are emphasized. He shows Catherine the disappointing rooms and their contents. Having hoped 'for the smallest divisions, and the heaviest stone-work, for painted glass, dirt and cobwebs', she finds the unstained window-panes, despite their arches, too large. Her self-deprecating host thinks she is looking for more opulence, not more antiquity, and his promise of fine gilding elsewhere is interrupted only by his passion for punctuality at meals. As Catherine gets ready for dinner in her room, she is disappointed by the papered walls, anticipating the future fictional occasion when her fastidious descendant, Henry James's Mrs Gereth, is kept awake by the wallpaper of Waterbath, having been accustomed to the walls of Poynton, unsullied by any scrap of pasted paper.

Jane Austen dramatizes her heroine's attentiveness to the first object that catches her attention, the 'immense heavy chest' which looks so antique:

> She advanced and examined it closely: it was of cedar, curiously inlaid with some darker wood, and raised, about a foot from the ground, on a carved stand of the same. The lock was silver, though tarnished from age; at each end were the imperfect remains of handles also of silver, broken perhaps prematurely by some strange violence; and, on the centre of the lid, was a mysterious cypher, in the same metal. Catherine bent over it intently, but without being able to distinguish any thing with certainty. She could not, in whatever direction she took it, believe the last letter to be a *T*; and yet that it should be anything else in that house was a circumstance to raise no common degree of astonishment. If not originally their's, by what strange events could it have fallen into the Tilney family?
> (*NA*, pp. 163-4)

This is the first of Catherine's necessary object-lessons. The heavy old chest is eloquent of ordinary life and ordinary likelihood: it opens, after her strenuous efforts, to reveal the most innocent linen, 'a white cotton counterpane, properly folded, reposing at one end of the chest in undisputed possession'. The object seems to flout her by its very blandness. In creating this sly suggestiveness, Jane Austen draws on a mild comic animism which is found less often in the novels than in her letters, where the play of comic imagination is free to make the nonsensical jokes that intimacy will tolerate and even enjoy:

The Tables are come, & give general contentment. I had not expected that they would so perfectly suit the fancy of us all three, or that we should so well agree in the disposition of them; but nothing except their own surface can have been smoother;—The two ends put together form our constant Table for everything, & the centre peice stands exceedingly well under the glass; holds a great deal most commodiously, without looking awkwardly.—They are both covered with green baize & send their best Love.—The Pembroke has got its destination by the sideboard, & my mother has great delight in keeping her money & papers locked up.— The little Table which used to stand there, has most conveniently taken itself off into the best bed-room. . . . (*Letters*, pp. 82-3)

In *Northanger Abbey* Jane Austen seems to remember Don Quixote, archetypal mis-imaginer. She makes Catherine follow up 'the adventure of the chest' with the second adventure of the 'high, old-fashioned black cabinet'. It impresses her as having been strangely lying in wait, unobserved in its alcove during her first inspection of the room. It also seems mysteriously reminiscent of the ebony cabinet in Henry Tilney's Gothic parody. It does not fit the object in Henry's tale exactly, as Catherine's candour has to admit: 'It was not absolutely ebony and gold; but it was Japan, black and yellow Japan of the handsomest kind; and as she held her candle, the yellow had very much the effect of gold.' She is observant, as well as honest, and this object is also described minutely, as she examines it minutely. So also are the all-too-clearly discriminated contents of its drawers, discovered with chagrin in the light of day to be bills listing 'Shirts, stockings, cravats and waistcoats', items of expenditure on 'letters, hair-powder, shoe-string and breeches-ball', together with the larger paper enclosing the rest, the farrier's bill for poulticing a chestnut mare. The inventory of everyday life joins with the natural contents of the chest to chasten the heroine's imagination. Catherine feels rebuked as a corner of the chest 'catches her eye', in another mildly animistic stroke of comic play. But a third trial by objects awaits her in the furniture of the deceased mother's room. Instead of the Radcliffean objects of her book-lined imagination (like the black veil which has arrested her earlier in the novel) what shocks her is a large well-dusted room with 'a bright Bath stove, mahogany wardrobes and neatly-painted chairs, on which the warm beams of a western sun gaily poured through two sash windows'.

The irony makes a neat reversal, for the objects are indeed startling. Most of the things in the Abbey are sinister too in their modern fashion. The decaying part of the quadrangle has been pulled down to make room for new offices without any thought of 'uniformity of architecture'. The subdued emblem of restoration looks ahead to George Eliot's *Daniel Deronda* and to Thomas Hardy's symbolism of aesthetic unity in *A Laodicean*, his Victorian version of *Northanger Abbey*, complete with sympathetic habitat and romantic heroine. 'The General's improving hand' has made some of those changes which cause Catherine 'almost' to 'rave'. The objects in his house are the instruments of display and solicitation. He offers the breakfast set:

> He was enchanted by her approbation of his taste, confessed it to be neat and simple, thought it right to encourage the manufacture of his country; and for his part, to his uncritical palate, the tea was as well flavoured from the clay of Staffordshire, as from that of Dresden or Sêve. But this was quite an old set, purchased two years ago. The manufacture was much improved since that time; he had seen some beautiful specimens when last in town, and had he not been perfectly without vanity of that kind, he might have been tempted to order a new set. He trusted, however, that an opportunity might ere long occur of selecting one—though not for him-self. (*NA*, p. 175)

Every single word of the General's humble and pastoral apology is false. In his own house, and in Henry's interestingly incomplete Parsonage, he uses things and places to flatter himself and the hoped-for heiress. If the heroine is wrong about her host, he is equally wrong about his guest. Neither of them is, however, completely mistaken. He is a villain, and she is the heroine. If he is proffering and praising things for the purpose of his imaginative desires, so is she. And she is not entirely wrong about the objects in the story. The portrait of Mrs Tilney which hangs significantly in Eleanor's room, and not in the drawing-room, is scarcely conspicuous on its first appearance, but that 'mild and pensive countenance' is highly expressive in retrospect. It is unlike the mysterious painting in Henry's parody, but its echo is not simply dissonant. The twists and turns of burlesque and bathos, parody and surprise, are perfectly matched in the complex behaviour of the objects.

It seems significant that the single object in the Abbey which is in no way associated with General Tilney is a hyacinth, the only sign of spring and natural growth at Northanger Abbey. One of those small indexes of the advancing year which Jane Austen places so discreetly into the action, it is mentioned briefly but is not visually present. The hyacinth is part of Catherine's aesthetic advance in appreciation, and is associated with Eleanor Tilney's nature. It is brought into the breakfast conversation by Catherine's desire to change the subject:

'What beautiful hyacinths!—I have just learnt to love a hyacinth.'
'And how might you learn?—By accident or argument?'
'Your sister taught me; I cannot tell how. Mrs. Allen used to take pains, year after year, to make me like them; but I never could, till I saw them the other day in Milsom-street; I am naturally indifferent about flowers.'
'But now you love a hyacinth. So much the better. You have gained a new source of enjoyment, and it is well to have as many holds upon happiness as possible. Besides, a taste for flowers is always desirable in your sex, as a means of getting you out of doors, and tempting you to more frequent exercise than you would otherwise take. And though the love of a hyacinth may be rather domestic, who can tell, the sentiment once raised, but you may in time come to love a rose?' (*NA*, p. 174)

The object is embedded in the natural flow of talk. So also is the other innocent object in Catherine's adventures with things, the fine netting cotton to be matched by Isabella which she hopes to hear of in her friend's letter, only to be disappointed by a grimmer tale of prices and values.

Northanger Abbey was a splendid environment for Jane Austen's object-making imagination. In *Sense and Sensibility* she continues to play with the device of appropriate .things in appropriate places, always locating description in the mind of her characters. Places and objects are animated as they become prominent to people, and are proportioned by individual viewpoint. The novel begins with Norland, so it is never described; its objects are invoked only as they become subjects of conversation, as objects of individual response. In the second chapter, the abstract nature of John and Fanny Dashwood's mean acquisitiveness is made plain through their duet about money. There is a penultimate diminution as we move from the smallest sum to 'some little present of furniture' which is made even less by being unspecified. Even this is transformed into a minus quantity, as Fanny reminds John that Mrs Dashwood will be taking off 'all the china, plate, and linen' of Stanhill, her former home:

'Her house will therefore be almost completely fitted up as soon as she takes it.'
'That is a material consideration undoubtedly. A valuable legacy indeed! And yet some of the plate would have been a very pleasant addition to our own stock here.'

'Yes; and the set of breakfast china is twice as handsome, in my opinion, for any place *they* can ever afford to live in.' (*SS*, p. 13)

Jane Austen's wit is never quieter in its damage than in the line 'That is a material consideration undoubtedly.' The theme of material considerations permeates the society of the novel. It is an environment in which sense and sensibility are formed, tested, falsified, or improved.

In Marianne's enthusiastic nostalgia, Norland is curiously unspecific, invoked through its 'dead leaves', and is as vague in her raptures as in Elinor's refusal to be moved by them. Compared with the colours and motions of Shelley's autumnal rapture,[2] the leaves are imprecisely felt, small indexes of Marianne's unobservant and stereotyped feeling for nature:

'Oh!' cried Marianne, 'with what transporting sensations have I formerly seen them fall! How have I delighted, as I walked, to see them driven in showers about me by the wind! What feelings have they, the season, the air altogether inspired! Now there is no one to regard them. They are seen only as a nuisance, swept hastily off, and driven as much as possible from the sight.'
'It is not every one,' said Elinor, 'who has your passion for dead leaves.'
(*SS*, pp. 87-8)

Marianne's response to nature lacks both the precision and the openness of the more rational romanticism of Fanny Price and Anne Elliot. But vague though it is, Marianne's sensibility rebukes the insensibilities of John and Fanny Dashwood. When John boasts about the plans for Fanny's new greenhouse and flower-garden which are to replace the 'old thorns' and 'old walnut trees', Elinor prudently decides not to tell her sister. The relative lack of possessiveness and materialism in Mrs Dashwood and her daughters is shown in the impetuous choice of Barton Cottage. They decide to move before they have seen their new home, sending their possessions round by sea – another small detail which deprives John Dashwood of any opportunity to help, and shows Jane Austen's thoroughness of imagination. No object is too small for the author's providential care as author. When the family arrives in Barton, there is a minutely detailed description, from which one could draw a plan:

A small green court was the whole of its demesne in front; and a neat wicket gate admitted them into it.

---

[2] 'The Ode to the West Wind' was published in 1820.

As a house, Barton Cottage, though small, was comfortable and com-pact; but as a cottage it was defective, for the building was regular, the roof was tiled, the window shutters were not painted green, nor were the walls covered with honeysuckles. A narrow passage led directly through the house into the garden behind. On each side of the entrance was a sitting room, about sixteen feet square; and beyond them were the offices and the stairs. Four bed-rooms and two garrets formed the rest of the house. It had not been built many years and was in good repair. In com-parison of Norland, it was poor and small indeed!—but the tears which recollection called forth as they entered the house were soon dried away.

(*SS*, p. 28)

The environment is important as it is received by the individual experience. The smallness of the house invokes various responses: Mrs Dashwood's impractical plans for improvement, Elinor's controlled rejection of the need for a new grate in the spare bed-chamber, Mr Palmer's rude criticism of the low-pitched roof and Willoughby's speech about the cottage which protests a romantic disregard of great possessions, and is typical of him in its glib and superficial reaction. He means what he says, but his sensibility is quite as unreliable as insin-cerity:

'You would rob it of its simplicity by imaginary improvement! and this dear parlour, in which our acquaintance first began, and in which so many happy hours have been since spent by us together, you would degrade to the condition of a common entrance, and every body would be eager to pass through the room which has hitherto contained within itself, more real accommodation and comfort than any other apartment of the hand-somest dimensions in the world could possibly afford.' (*SS*, pp. 73-4)

Even Robert Ferrars, the essential fool of the novel, makes his contri-bution:

'For my own part,' said he, 'I am excessively fond of a cottage; there is always so much comfort, so much elegance about them. And I protest, if I had any money to spare, I should buy a little land and build one myself, within a short distance of London, where I might drive myself down at any time, and collect a few friends about me and be happy. I advise every body who is going to build, to build a cottage. My friend Lord Courtland came to me the other day on purpose to ask my advice, and laid before me three different plans of Bonomi's. I was to decide on the best of them. "My dear Courtland," said I, immediately throwing them all into the fire, "do not adopt either of them, but by all means build a cottage." And that, I fancy, will be the end of it.

'Some people imagine that there can be no accommodations, no space in a cottage; but this is all a mistake. I was last month at my friend Elliott's near Dartford. Lady Elliott wished to give a dance. "But how can it be done?" said she; "my dear Ferrars, do tell me how it is to be managed. There is not a room in this cottage that will hold ten couple, and where can the supper be?" *I* immediately saw that there could be no difficulty in it, so I said, "My dear Lady Elliott, do not be uneasy. The dining parlour will admit eighteen couple with ease; card-tables may be placed in the drawing-room; the library may be open for tea and other refreshments; and let the supper be set out in the saloon." Lady Elliott was delighted with the thought. We measured the dining-room, and found it would hold exactly eighteen couple, and the affair was arranged precisely after my plan. So that, in fact, you see, if people do but know how to set about it, every comfort may be as well enjoyed in a cottage as in the most spacious dwelling.' (*SS*, pp. 251-2)

The variants of materialism are largely demonstrated through things of price and value. Marianne's protested disregard of wealth is tested by Elinor's quotation of real prices and incomes, as she compares her smaller 'wealth' with Marianne's larger 'competence'. There is a crucial side-scene in the jeweller's shop, Gray's, in Sackville Street. As we are carefully told, Elinor is there to negotiate 'the exchange of a few old-fashioned jewels of her mother' and John Dashwood 'to bespeak Fanny a seal'. Robert Ferrars flourishes his self-regarding and trivial materialism in his nonsensical dallyings with toothpick-cases, chronicled by Jane Austen in appropriate pomp and circumstance:

> At last the affair was decided. The ivory, the gold, and the pearls, all received their appointment, and the gentleman having named the last day on which his existence could be continued without the possession of the tooth-pick case, drew on his gloves with leisurely care. . . . (*SS*, p. 221)

Miss Steele's attentiveness to objects is silly, but she is more concerned than Robert Ferrars with the world outside. Her trivial-mindedness is curious, and takes stock of Marianne's price and value. 'Minute observation and minute curiosity' are chronicled through their inventory of dress, number of gowns, cost of washing, annual allowance, value and make of gown, 'the colour of her shoes, and the arrangement of her hair'. Jane Austen does not just present and criticize sartorial passion, as George Eliot is inclined to do in *Middlemarch*, where to care about clothes is nearly always immoral. Jane Austen is more tolerant and more precise. She discriminates between feelings for dress. Miss Steele joins her crude commercial interest in the price-tags to the smart stylishness of Willoughby's choice, Miss

Grey, the elegant propriety of Lady Middleton, and the dandyism of Robert Ferrars. In *Northanger Abbey* the undemanding but total sartorial energies of Mrs Allen are balanced against the acceptable and natural vanities of Catherine Morland, and the flaunting of Isabella Thorpe, who shares a taste for coquelicot ribbons with her author.[3] In *Mansfield Park*, the complacent self-regard of Lady Bertram is roused to lend her maid to Fanny, though characteristically too late. Fanny's own doubtful pleasure in the gown Sir Thomas gives her for Maria's wedding, worn for that first dinner at the Parsonage and admired by Edmund with a precise eye for its 'glossy spot' because Miss Crawford has one 'something the same' (*MP*, p. 222), is beautifully placed.

Jane Austen's letters to Cassandra show a constant but constantly self-amused preoccupation with dress, and this aspect of the human concern with things is dramatically varied and frequently tolerated. We are made to feel that Jane Austen knows everything about her characters. It is more than frivolous when she says she always suspected that Mrs Darcy's favourite colour was yellow, Mrs Bingley's green.[4]

Her knowledge of her characters' attitudes to houses, clothes and accessories extends to other creature comforts. Mrs Jennings's harmless indulgences of the flesh show the largeness of her nature. She is facile, generous, kind, compassionate and likes to enjoy life. She presses old Constantia wine and dried cherries on Marianne's disappointed heart, to be astonished when they don't work. She is eager to help other people to the pleasures of the world, and her 'ample jointure' is described in the perfect adjective. She describes to Elinor the joys of Colonel Brandon's place in the country with appropriate gusto:

> 'Delaford is a nice place, I can tell you; exactly what I call a nice old fashioned place, full of comforts and conveniences; quite shut in with great garden walls that are covered with the best fruit-trees in the country: and such a mulberry tree in one corner! Lord! how Charlotte and I did stuff the only time we were there! Then, there is a dove-cote, some delightful stewponds, and a very pretty canal; and every thing, in short, that one could wish for: and, moreover, it is close to the church, and only a quarter of a mile from the turnpike-road, so 'tis never dull, for if you

---

[3] 'I . . . shall put in the Coquelicot one, as being smarter;—& besides Coquelicot is to be all the fashion this winter.' (*Letters*, pp. 37-8)

[4] *Letters*, p. 310.

only go and sit up in an old yew arbour behind the house, you may see all the carriages that pass along. Oh! 'tis a nice place! A butcher hard by in the village, and the parsonage-house within a stone's throw. To my fancy, a thousand times prettier than Barton Park, where they are forced to send three miles for their meat, and have not a neighbour nearer than your mother.' (*SS*, pp. 196-7)

Unlike the Dashwoods and the Steele sisters, Mrs Jennings is a materialist with nothing mean about her – she is a Wife of Bath whose pleasures are of the table rather than the bed, though Jane Austen may mean more than she finds it decorous to say. Her language is crammed with appreciations, her very proverbs appetitive: 'One shoulder of mutton, you know, drives another down.' The phrase may be on the gross side, but her author comes to a not dissimilar, if more elegantly expressed, conclusion. There is no doubt about Jane Austen's sense of her quality as well as her limitations. She is a tolerant character, and her fleshliness is thoroughly understood and tolerated by her author.

When Margaret Dashwood puts in a bid for memorability by imagining that they have all been left a fortune apiece, everyone, as Edward Ferrars says, chooses appropriate objects. It is the individuality of her people's needs and desires which shapes Jane Austen's object-world. Like the elaborately detailed fiction of Thackeray, Henry James, Arnold Bennett and Scott Fitzgerald, her novels establish a sense of social surfaces and manners. We can date and describe clothes, houses, furniture, food, drink and means of transport through the information in the novels. But in the novels of Thackeray, James, Bennett and Scott Fitzgerald information is dispersed through generalized and complete descriptions. Whenever there is a room, or a person, we see its furniture and its clothing. This does not mean that there is no discrimination or that objects and places are not dramatically expressive. The kitchen and the factory in Bennett's *Anna of the Five Towns* play an essential role in the affective life of the characters, and Gatsby's shirts are part of his style and his imagination. But all the rooms and clothes in these novels are solidly specified. Mrs Lowder's plutocratically hideous drawing-room in *The Wings of a Dove* and Maggie's dress in *The Golden Bowl* are eloquent of their possessors in many ways, but James is visibly the describing source. The food, drink, furniture, ornaments and service in *Vanity Fair*, *The Newcomes* and *The Virginians* tell us a great deal about class, income, households, characters and countries, but it is Thackeray who sets and specifies the scene. Jane Austen keeps very strictly to what appears to be her self-created rule of characteristic description. If someone in the novel is not registering the appearance, cost or savour of things, they are kept out. There is enough variety of materialism in all the novels to give a full social range, but it is not her habit to describe every house, every meal, everyone's clothes, all the furniture. Objects come in as they strike the characters, sometimes vaguely, sometimes clearly, sometimes lovingly, sometimes obsessionally, sometimes stupidly. There is never a routine description of things.

We not only know what Willoughby cared for, but see how his dress and accessories are part of his charm for Marianne. Jane Austen's brilliant and solid chronicle of social objects goes beyond a psychological record, which fills the world with things in order to dramatize individual attitudes and appetites. She needs to make her discriminations for the purpose of a moral argument. Her presentation anticipates Henry James's more explicit insistence, made through Madame Merle's materialistic lecture to the romantic Isabel Archer, on the subject of expressive things:

> 'There's no such thing as an isolated man or woman; we're each of us made up of some cluster of appurtenances. What shall we call our "self"? Where does it begin? where does it end? It overflows into everything that belongs to us—and then it flows back again. I know a large part of myself is in the clothes I choose to wear. I've a great respect for *things*! One's self—for other people—is one's expression of one's self; and one's house, one's furniture, one's garments, the books one reads, the company one keeps—these things are all expressive.'
>
> (*The Portrait of a Lady*, Vol. I, Chap. xix)

Jane Austen shows the unpleasant possibilities of becoming too attached to things. She also knows that life in her society is inevitably lived with and through things. The people in her novels become restricted and even reified by living too much in the company of objects. She shows how the object-stuff can flow back into the self or spirit through the things people care about and demand. Perhaps it is the moderated materialism of Mrs Jennings that allows her to put the matter in a nut-shell. She describes Miss Grey's price and Willoughby's values:

> 'Fifty thousand pounds, my dear. Did you ever see her? a smart, stilish girl they say, but not handsome. I remember her aunt very well, Biddy Henshawe; she married a very wealthy man. But the family are all rich

together. Fifty thousand pounds! and by all accounts it wo'nt come before it's wanted; for they say he is all to pieces. No wonder! dashing about with his curricle and hunters! Well, it don't signify talking, but when a young man, be he who he will, comes and makes love to a pretty girl, and promises marriage, he has no business to fly off from his word only because he grows poor, and a richer girl is ready to have him. Why don't he, in such a case, sell his horses, let his house, turn off his servants, and make a thorough reform at once?' (*SS*, p. 194)

Jane Austen's knowledge and imagination go even beyond the assimilation of people to their properties. She shows how we relate to people through their accessories, how we can assimilate not only both object and person, but may attach ourselves to other people's property and properties. Marianne pretends to make romantically low demands, but actually wants a great deal. Her conventional and fashionable materialism is easily compatible with a self-centred and vague enthusiasm. Her demands pick up Willoughby's demands – as demands will. She starts wanting 'a carriage, perhaps two, and hunters' as well as music and books. Food for the mind mingles with food for the fancy, and some of her desires are merely glamorous. Jane Austen makes silly Mrs Bennet say that she still has a soft spot for a red coat, but she knows that is is not only fools who respond to each other in full social panoply. An eye for sexual colour and shape, for instance, tends to take in the aids to colour and shape, and so the reifications of love proceed. Marianne starts to fall in love with Willoughby:

His manly beauty and more than common gracefulness were instantly the theme of general admiration, and the laugh which his gallantry raised against Marianne, received particular spirit from his exterior attractions. —Marianne herself had seen less of his person than the rest, for the confusion which crimsoned over her face, on his lifting her up, had robbed her of the power of regarding him after their entering the house. But she had seen enough of him to join in all the admiration of the others, and with an energy which always adorned her praise. His person and air were equal to what her fancy had ever drawn for the hero of a favourite story. . . . His name was good, his residence was in their favourite village, and she soon found out that of all manly dresses a shooting-jacket was the most becoming. (*SS*, p. 43)

Willoughby's shooting-jacket is the becoming aid which helps to create his dashing 'manly' image. Like advertisers who blur the appeal of objects in the appeals of nature, Jane Austen knows how to create the conventional social and sexual stimulus for the weak, romantic susceptibility. After the shooting-jacket, Colonel Brandon's flannel waistcoat is naturally less appealing, in a society accustomed to correlate sex with health, sport and youth. Jane Austen's sense of the social determinations of our affective life seizes on the irresistible blend in an image approved by society and literature. Far from being tactless in dwelling on Colonel Brandon's twinges of rheumatism, she is strongly attacking the cosmetic element in sexual attraction. It might be an exaggeration to suggest that she anticipates Beckett's geriatric love-stories: she is scarcely marrying off Marianne to an old and impotent husband, as we may infer from her concluding comments on Brandon's recovery of tone, and the information that 'in time' Marianne came to love him as much as she had once loved Willoughby. 'In time' is a candid and searching phrase – it has taken Marianne time to lose the romantic image of appearance in the reality of experience. The romantic image itself thrives on instant response. In *Northanger Abbey* there is an analysis of materialism in which Catherine is redeemed, but where people tend to show either a harmless or a harmful attitude to the object-world, and hence to each other. *Sense and Sensibility* begins to recognize a more complex interaction of things and people. This interaction develops in *Pride and Prejudice,* where a heroine more intelligent than Marianne and more fallible than Elinor shows how wit and imagination can be entangled in appearances. In this novel Jane Austen seems to feel freer to admit that appearances may not always be irrelevant. Elinor and Marianne were matched with husbands of sterling quality, designed to defeat or outlive the dangers of charm and good looks. In *Pride and Prejudice* Jane Austen relaxes her rigour, admitting that outside and inside are at times appropriately matched. Elizabeth's liveliness and Darcy's elegance are charms which reflect mind and body. But there is enough rigour present to keep hero and heroine apart until they come to understand the nature of what they love. Darcy comes to admire Elizabeth, after first feeling no attraction. He is drawn by her fine eyes and also by her figure. But he cannot be allowed to possess her without understanding that love is not possession, and that her outside has not revealed her whole mind. But if he misreads, so does she. There is more to each than meets the eye. She first admires him – as she half-seriously tells Jane – in his image, which she first gazes at unabashed by physical presence, on the visit to Pemberley. His image is there in more ways than one.

Pemberley echoes the worthiness of Squire Allworthy's seat. Its beauties and prospects are seen through Elizabeth's eyes. The houses in *Pride and Prejudice* are nearly all taken for granted by the author because they are taken for granted by the characters, though environment is given some character by objects and habits.

As soon as the characters visit a new place, it is put before the reader. Elizabeth visits Charlotte Collins's new house and is immediately shown round. Mr Collins is a minute guide, self-gratified by possessions, liking to show Elizabeth what she has missed, fishing for praise, and inclined to unselective enumeration:

> After sitting long enough to admire every article of furniture in the room, from the sideboard to the fender, to give an account of their journey and of all that had happened in London, Mr. Collins invited them to take a stroll in the garden, which was large and well laid out, and to the cultivation of which he attended himself. To work in his garden was one of his most respectable pleasures; and Elizabeth admired the command of countenance with which Charlotte talked of the healthfulness of the exercise, and owned she encouraged it as much as possible. Here, leading the way through every walk and cross walk, and scarcely allowing them an interval to utter the praises he asked for, every view was pointed out with a minuteness which left beauty entirely behind. He could number the fields in every direction, and could tell how many trees there were in the most distant clump. (*PP*, p. 156)

He is the perfect cicerone for the visit to Rosings, and sense is submerged in his anxiety to put the other guests at their ease: 'I would advise you merely to put on whatever of your clothes is superior to the rest, there is no occasion for any thing more.' His way with things reflects Lady Catherine's more rational superiority: 'Lady Catherine will not think the worse of you for being simply dressed. She likes to have the distinction of rank preserved.' Rosings is introduced and described through Mr Collins's eyes, voice and values, enumerating 'the windows in front of the house' and relating 'what the glazing altogether had originally cost Sir Lewis De Bourgh'. The owner of Rosings resembles General Tilney in her appreciation of her guest's appreciation. She patronizes through servants, plate and food, especially delighted 'when any dish on the table proved a novelty'. Every object in the drama of Lady Catherine's hospitality, including the fish used in the game of casino and the piano which she offers for Elizabeth's use, is a comic counter in the game of demand-and-supply which she plays so happily, best of all with Mr Collins, who is just the guest the hostess requires.

When Elizabeth comes to Pemberley, we not only see it through her eyes, but against the background of the visit to Rosings. Jane Austen manipulates those contrasts and parallels which form all fictions through the characters' sensibility. The plentiful and refreshing luncheon, elegantly presented, 'beautiful pyramids of grapes, nectarines, and peaches', and even the diffident and shy hospitality of Georgiana Darcy, are contrasted with the ostentation of Rosings. The handsome house is a sympathetic habitat in every way. Its saloon has a northern aspect which is cool in summer – Jane Austen is always attentive to temperature – and the sense of space is neither intimidating nor lofty. Like Allworthy's house, it partakes of the handsomeness and honesty of its owner:

> It was a large, handsome, stone building, standing well on rising ground, and backed by a ridge of high woody hills;—and in front, a stream of some natural importance was swelled into greater, but without any artificial appearance. Its banks were neither formal, nor falsely adorned. Elizabeth was delighted. She had never seen a place for which nature had done more, or where natural beauty had been so little counteracted by an awkward taste. (*PP*, p. 245)

Jane Austen makes her heroine appreciate the quality of the furnishings too, as 'suitable to the fortune of their proprietor' and his taste, 'neither gaudy nor uselessly fine', as she makes the contrast with Rosings. But Jane Austen does not make Elizabeth aware only of Darcy's property and taste. She responds also to a less definable quality in the atmosphere of the house, suggested by the variety and spaciousness. As Elizabeth goes over Pemberley, there is a sense of movement and exhilaration:

> Every disposition of the ground was good; and she looked on the whole scene, the river, the trees scattered on its banks, and the winding of the valley, as far as she could trace it, with delight. As they passed into other rooms, these objects were taking different positions; but from every window there were beauties to be seen. (*PP*, p. 246)

The vivid account of moving through a sequence of large rooms with large windows extending over wide vistas also conveys the heroine's elation. Outside and inside, Pemberley extends her acquaintance with Darcy, and in tangible or intangible ways it offers her a charm and a guarantee. Jane Austen is creating the spirit of a place.

Mansfield Park,[5] like Northanger Abbey, resembles its owner. It is grand, large and daunting, and does not make Fanny feel at home: 'The grandeur of the house astonished, but could not console her. The rooms were too large for her to move in with ease; whatever she touched she expected to injure, and she crept about in constant terror of something or other.' (*MP*, p. 14) Unlike Northanger, Mansfield is a neutral ground, which can be re-occupied and changed. In this novel, Jane Austen moves away from the simple equation of possessor and possessions to examine the home as a communal place.

As a home, Mansfield is imperfect. It does not put any of its children entirely at ease; its father is too remote and repressive, its mother too languid, letting responsibility pass into the mean and greedy hands of Mrs Norris, too indulgent and too harsh. (Indulgence and harshness are two sides of the same coin: Mrs Norris acts only for herself.) It is she who proposes the adoption of Fanny, her method being to work through the hospitality and generosity of others. She maintains an image at very little expense. It is she who organizes the keeping-down of Fanny, whose unlit fire is warm enough for her until Sir Thomas comes to give her the warmth he has not known was lacking. Maria and Julia give her unwanted sashes and toys, her cousin Tom teases her and showers on her a profusion of workboxes, her cousin Edmund gives her what she needs – until Mary Crawford comes to engross the new mare and more. Fanny, called 'creepmouse' by Tom, steals artlessly into a room of her own, and it becomes the only 'nest of comforts' in Mansfield Park. It is a room with a view, for the outward look of Fanny looks ahead to George Eliot's Dorothea Brooke and E. M. Forster's Lucy Honeychurch. Fanny looks beyond the indoor world of the drawing-room to the evening sky to gaze at those stars that are visible from the window, and longs to see those out of sight. We see the light infiltrating more indirectly into the East room, through 'a gleam of sunshine' and in the air she thinks of giving to her geraniums, while also inhaling 'a breeze of mental strength herself'. She collects the cast-off objects that can be cherished only by loving memory, and the room becomes the archive of Mansfield Park:

> The aspect was so favourable, that even without a fire it was habitable in many an early spring, and late autumn morning, to such a willing mind

---

[5] The following discussion of *Mansfield Park* draws at points upon my essay entitled 'The Objects in *Mansfield Park*' in John Halperin (ed.), *Jane Austen: Bicentenary Essays* (New York, 1975).

as Fanny's, and while there was a gleam of sunshine, she hoped not to be driven from it entirely, even when winter came. The comfort of it in her hours of leisure was extreme. She could go there after any thing unpleasant below, and find immediate consolation in some pursuit, or some train of thought at hand.—Her plants, her books—of which she had been a collector, from the first hour of her commanding a shilling—her writing desk, and her works of charity and ingenuity, were all within reach;—or if indisposed for employment, if nothing but musing would do, she could scarcely see an object in that room which had not an interesting remembrance connected with it.—Every thing was a friend, or bore her thoughts to a friend; and though there had been sometimes much of suffering to her—though her motives had been often misunderstood, her feelings disregarded, and her comprehension under-valued; though she had known the pains of tyranny, or ridicule, and neglect, yet almost every recurrence of either had led to something consolatory; her aunt Bertram had spoken for her, or Miss Lee had been encouraging, or what was yet more frequent or more dear—Edmund had been her champion and her friend;—he had supported her cause, or explained her meaning, he had told her not to cry, or had given her some proof of affection which made her tears delightful—and the whole was now so blended together, so harmonized by distance, that every former affliction had its charm. The room was most dear to her, and she would not have changed its furniture for the handsomest in the house, though what had been originally plain, had suffered all the ill-usage of children—and its greatest elegancies and ornaments were a faded footstool of Julia's work, too ill done for the drawing-room, three transparencies, made in a rage for transparencies, for the three lower panes of one window, where Tintern Abbey held its station between a cave in Italy, and a moonlight lake in Cumberland; a collection of family profiles thought unworthy of being anywhere else, over the mantle-piece, and by their side and pinned against the wall, a small sketch of a ship sent four years ago from the Mediterranean by William, with H.M.S. Antwerp at the bottom, in letters as tall as the main-mast.

To this nest of comforts Fanny now walked down to try its influence on an agitated, doubting spirit—to see if by looking at Edmund's profile she could catch any of his counsel, of by giving air to her geraniums she might inhale a breeze of mental strength herself. (*MP*, pp. 151-2)

Every aspect of the room responds to the values of its occupant and her occupation. Unlike the drawing-room, which Mary Crawford's wit accurately describes as 'too hot', its low temperature rears a fragile life and makes it strong. The things in the room are harmonized by Fanny's capacity for love and acceptance, 'the whole . . . so blended together, so harmonized by distance, that every former affliction had its charm'. The ability to use memory and imagination to include, and not exclude, is implicit in Fanny and Anne Elliot. It is an aspect of the self-knowledge which distinguishes the rational passions of Fanny and Anne from the dissociated feelings of the Bertrams, the Crawfords and the Elliots. Fanny's life comes to have wholeness. Her nest of comforts also joins together the family things, creates a small warm space for herself at the heart of the house. Edmund's praise of her 'little establishment' is less playful and more promising than he knows.

For Mansfield Park lacks a heart and a centre. But it is not a static habitat, and its adopted child changes its shape and its atmosphere. It has, after all, taken her in. The spirit of the place is more susceptible to improvement than Sotherton, and the novelist dwells on the emblem of Sotherton to show the greater mobility of Mansfield. We see Mansfield largely through Fanny's eyes, but we first hear the details of Sotherton from Edmund, who describes it to Mary Crawford when he sits next to her at dinner, as an Elizabethan house, 'a large, regular, brick building – heavy, but respectable looking. . . . It is ill-placed. It stands in one of the lowest spots of the park; in that respect, unfavourable for improvement. But the woods are fine. . . .' (*MP*, p. 56) Mary realizes that Edmund is making 'the best of it'. What he says next applies to much more than his attitude to a house: '. . . had I a place to new fashion, I should not put myself into the hands of an improver. I would rather have an inferior degree of beauty, of my own choice, and acquired progressively.'

On the 'improving' visit to Sotherton every aspect of house and grounds is suggestive and the significances emerge and expand through the viewpoints of the characters. The heavy opulence is all too expressive of Mr Rushworth. Maria Bertram chooses him for his property, and house and owner are almost interchangeable in their inertness. On the visit to Sotherton Maria's elation is carefully evaluated as 'a pleasure to increase with their approach to the capital free-hold mansion, and ancient manorial residence of the family, with all its rights of Court-Leet and Court-Baron'. (*MP*, p. 82) The cottages are 'a disgrace' but the church is fortunately 'not so close to the Great House as often happens in old places' where 'the annoyance of the bells must be terrible'. Like its owner, 'it is heavy, but respectable looking'. 'The situation of the house excluded the possibility of much prospect from any of the rooms' and every 'room on the west front looked across a lawn to the beginning of the avenue immediately beyond tall iron palisades and gates.' Its chapel is elegant, but no longer used, and makes a good set for *double-entendres*. The pictures are abundant, 'and some few good, but the larger part were family portraits, no longer any thing to any body but Mrs Rushworth'. The family profiles in Fanny's room were thought of being unworthy to be anywhere but in her room: Mansfield has a better curator than Sotherton.

When the members of the Mansfield party leave the house to go over the grounds, Jane Austen goes beyond the symbolism of place to make a theatre for many different responses and acts. The desire to improve Sotherton is a specious excuse, the merest of alibis. Instead of discussing improvements, they wander after each other to suffer what Jane Austen calls 'cross accidents'. Henry Crawford sees 'walks of great promise'. Fanny is left alone on her bench in the wilderness, while Mary and Edmund find their way to the avenue she has longed to see. Maria squeezes dangerously through the gate with Henry Crawford, unwilling to wait for Mr Rushworth, who has forgotten to bring the key. She risks tearing her gown and falling into the ha-ha, as warned by Fanny. Julia follows them, escaping and pursuing. As Fanny sees Maria and Henry go off together, 'taking a circuitous, and as it appeared to her, very unreasonable direction to the knoll, they were soon beyond her eye', it is conspicuous as the single occasion when Henry and Maria move out of sight of character and reader.

The house and grounds are designed for appropriate action, though it is expressive rather than crucial. It is typical of Jane Austen's matter-of-factness in symbolism, her merging of symbol in surface. To call the Sotherton scene proleptic would be a tautology. What is done in Sotherton is typically done, and the small-scale action anticipates the later crisis and climax, because these too are totally in character.

The only happy person on the expedition is Mrs Norris, who characteristically carries off the booty she has 'spunged', the cream cheese, beautiful little heath, and the pheasant's eggs which she is going to get hatched by one of the maids at Mansfield (like Fanny). The things Mrs Norris takes away are not hospitably presented but acquired by her scrounging flatteries from the gardener and the housekeeper. The things are part of the place, though they tell us about the guests as well as the host and hostess. Every superficial detail of the Sotherton visit, including the journey there and back, contributes to a realistic account of a family visit, is deeply founded in character, and therefore forms an organic part of the total structure.

Other places and things develop in significance. Hospitality is warmer at the Parsonage whose large round dining-table covered in

dishes is seen through the jealous disapproval of Mrs Norris. Its
hospitality is expressive of the childless Mrs Grant's spoiling of her
husband, whose good table eventually kills him. It is also, of course,
eloquent of his own indulgence, and the geese, turkeys and pheasants
play an important role in establishing character. But Mrs Grant, like
Fanny, does grow things and the evergreens in her shrubbery will last.
Fanny rhapsodizes on them, and Mary Crawford carelessly admits
that they do very well for a village parsonage.

The Parsonage contains its visitors, Mary and Henry Crawford,
and its elegance and hospitality are pressed into symbolic service as
Edmund becomes charmed by Mary:

> A young woman, pretty, lively, with a harp as elegant as herself; and
> both placed near a window, cut down to the ground, and opening on a
> little lawn, surrounded by rich shrubs in the rich foliage of summer, was
> enough to catch any man's heart. The season, the scene, the air, were all
> favourable to tenderness and sentiment. Mrs. Grant and her tambour
> frame were not without their use; it was all in harmony; and as every
> thing will turn to account when love is once set going, even the sandwich
> tray, and Dr. Grant doing the honours of it, were worth looking at.
>
> (*MP*, p. 65)

There is a quiet but definite approximation of the woman to place and
object, appropriate to Mary's assimilation to a surface of richness and
ease, and to Edmund's response to appearances. As General Tilney
is assimilated to his possessions by putting too much vital energy into
them, and using them to manipulate other people until they begin to
be an inseparable aspect of self, so Mary's genuine vitality and intelligence are endangered. She struggles against the assimilation by her
environment, but it has been going on for too long, and she cannot
escape. Edmund progresses to 'acquire' his 'inferior beauty', who is
superior in many ways.

Hospitality and donation become more prominent in *Mansfield
Park*. If Fanny brings warmth and strength to Mansfield Park, she
has also drawn warmth and strength from its hospitality, and from its
presents which she treasures as sacred objects. She has been taught
by Edmund, who first gave her the things that human beings need for
love and growth: writing materials to write to her brother, the new
mare for healthy exercise, books for the mind, wine for her aching
head, a chain for her cross. She has to learn to give as well as to
receive, and a step in her education is marked when she heals a family

wound by making Betsy a present of a silver knife. Sir Thomas is capable of good giving too (a home, a fire and a gown), and even Lady Bertram tries to lend her maid and offers a prospective puppy. Mrs Norris does not give a present to her god-child, Betsy. She gives one present, the mysterious 'something considerable' to William, which the reader knows from internal evidence is less than the ten pounds given him by Lady Bertram, and the exact amount of which was revealed by Jane Austen to her family. She was as aware as Henry James of the occasional need for not specifying things.

Mansfield Park contains enough good things given to Fanny, to be animated by memory and love, and returned in her gratitude and growth. For Mansfield Park does nourish its adopted child. She in her turn adopts the East room for her own. The major act of hospitality brings in an outsider to strengthen and sweeten the community. Jane Austen makes it clear, however, that the good giving and good taking are dependent on considerable purchasing-power. Fanny and Edmund are not materialists, but they are fully provided with material comforts.

In *Mansfield Park*, the sympathetic habitat is most developed, but also most open. It is as if the simpler moral associations of places were there most thoroughly expressed, and a limit reached. Sotherton and Portsmouth are simple habitats. The rooms, food, words and gardens of Mansfield Park, and even the exterior and interior of Mansfield Parsonage – which is, after all, to be inherited by Fanny and Edmund – are dramatized more variously to embody hopes for harmony and for change. After *Mansfield Park* it is not surprising that Jane Austen moves away from the houses to the significance of smaller and more shifting things.

In *Emma* hospitality and donation become prominent themes. Everyone is a guest, some are hosts and guests. Everyone either gives or takes, some do both. Jane Austen's implicit analysis of social relationships depends on objects as on groups. Human beings create for themselves a social case or cover composed of things, and relate to each other through more movable objects. The prominent hosts in the novel are Mr Woodhouse, Mr Weston and Mr Knightley. Mr Woodhouse is generous within the bounds of his own narrow imagination, egocentrically fastidious and hypochondriacal. Mr Weston's generosity is harmlessly over-hospitable, and his good wine does no more than precipitate Mr Elton's proposal to Emma. Mr Knightley's sense of propriety is entirely approved by his author, but he makes it plain to Mrs Elton that the hospitality of Donwell Abbey cannot be delegated.

Hospitality is a form of giving and taking, and blends with the theme of donation. Benefactors benefit themselves and the people to whom they give. Emma and her father give generously to Miss Bates and Mrs Bates – 'I sent them the whole hind-quarter' – but it is easier to give things than a proper attention. It serves Emma right when Jane Fairfax sends back her arrowroot. Jane has had to accept too many benefactions and it is good that she rebels. She is beset by treacherous objects, like Frank's piano and his letters, Mr Perry's carriage and the alphabet game. The carefully named 'Frank' has better luck with Mrs Bates's broken spectacles, and having fastened the rivet 'was very warmly thanked both by mother and daughter'. Emma is a clever manipulator of objects too, and uses charades, her picture, and a broken shoe-lace, to help on her match-making for Harriet and Mr Elton. Mr Knightley's things are like him. The last of the best baking apples and his strawberries are good and generously given. Miss Bates is good at accepting presents, unlike Mrs Elton who tires of strawberries in one half hour's talk:

—'The best fruit in England—every body's favourite—always whole-some.—These the finest beds and finest sorts.—Delightful to gather for one's self—the only way of really enjoying them.—Morning decidedly the best time—never tired—every good sort—hautboy infinitely superior—no comparison—the others hardly eatable—hautboys very scarce—Chili preferred—white wood finest flavour of all—price of strawberries in London—abundance about Bristol—Maple Grove—cultivation—beds when to be renewed—gardeners thinking exactly different—no general rule—gardeners never to be put out of their way—delicious fruit—only too rich to be eaten much of—inferior to cherries—currants more refresh-ing—only objection to gathering strawberries the stooping—glaring sun—tired to death—could bear it no longer—must go and sit in the shade.'

(*E*, pp. 358-9)

The ordinary world animates things through people, and people through things. Things take a hand in human destiny. Donation is only one form of communicating feeling through objects. Mr Weston's good wine raises Mr Elton's ardour and a secluded carriage on a snowy night perfects the scene. Emma's reading-lists are more admir-able than her reading, and Mr Knightley's preservation of one of them should alert us to his feelings. Mr Woodhouse's story about his grandson asking for a bit of string and his distress over the open air in Harriet's portrait – despite her shawl, – are endearing indexes of his triviality. Robert Martin's parlour, with the singing shepherd, promises well for Harriet's marriage, as do the walnuts he picks and the books he reads for her sake. His mother's present of the very fine goose to Mrs Goddard adds substance to her prospects. Mrs Elton's finery and Jane Fairfax's neat elegance are appropriate shells, the one fussy, the other restrained. These people need their survival kits, resembling other people inside and outside novels in needing or wanting to enlarge their powers, good or bad, with the aid of things.

In *Northanger Abbey, Sense and Sensibility,* and *Pride and Prejudice* there is a prevailing possessiveness. People clutch, hoard and acquire. In *Persuasion* the men and women are remembered through their possessions, but there is less emphasis on property. Dramatic properties are vital: Sir Walter Elliot has his Baronetage, his Gowland, and his room full of mirrors. (Admiral Croft turns most of them out.) The great parlour at Uppercross has the modern pianoforte (presumably replacing a harpsichord), and a disarray of little tables imported by the new generation, Louisa and Henrietta:

> To the Great House accordingly they went, to sit the full half hour in the old-fashioned square parlour, with a small carpet and shining floor, to which the present daughters of the house were gradually giving the proper air of confusion by a grand piano forte and a harp, flower-stands and little tables placed in every direction. Oh! could the originals of the portraits against the wainscot, could the gentlemen in brown velvet and the ladies in blue satin have seen what was going on, have been conscious of such an overthrow of all order and neatness! The portraits themselves seemed to be staring in astonishment.
>
> The Musgroves, like their houses, were in a state of alteration, perhaps of improvement. The father and mother were in the old English style, and the young people in the new. (*P,* p. 40)

Captain Wentworth has his ships, and talks about his first command, the *Asp,* with a fine sense of objects and audience when he compares it with an old pelisse for the benefit of the female listeners. We are told that Anne has loved his wit, and Jane Austen conveys this wit through his not too serious manipulations of simile and emblem. A wit which has been exhibitionist in Mary Crawford is given a certain solidity in Captain Wentworth through his not too portentous play with actual objects as sources for imagery. He has a sense of the object, but also a sense of the artifice of using emblems. He speaks with playful solemnity as he holds up the nut and uses it as an image for

Louisa's firmness. He is right not to sound too serious – it is an inaccurate symbol, because he says it is unlike its 'brethren' who 'have fallen, and been trodden underfoot'. Anne's objects are sacred ones, like Fanny's, but presented less conspicuously. She is willing to cut down on possessions, as her father and sister are not, finding it easier to leave their ancestral home than to retrench. When Mary asks Anne a resonant question which goes beyond its immediate occasion, 'Dear me ! What can *you* possibly have to do?', she gives a brief account of her management of things: making a duplicate of the catalogue of books and pictures, arranging the destination of Elizabeth's plants, and arranging her own 'little concerns, books and music'. The impedimenta of a cultivated human being are modestly but clearly brought in, as with Fanny's nest of comforts in *Mansfield Park*.

The course of true love is strewn with objects. In *Persuasion* they are unobtrusive but numerous. At Lyme Regis, Anne's perceptive eye registers character in the Harvilles' lodgings, 'so small as none but those who invite from the heart could think capable of accommodating so many. Anne had a moment's astonishment on the subject herself. . . .' She compares their hospitality 'from the heart' with 'the usual style of give-and-take invitations', depressed by the lost past: 'These would have been all my friends.' The rooms are small, but contain significant objects, which include 'the ingenious contrivances and nice arrangements of Captain Harville', who is one of the very few people in these novels who ever makes anything. Mrs Smith's charitable knick-knacks are also exceptional. Good food is made by servants, plants are occasionally grown, but most of the middle-class manufacture is amateur and utterly useless needlework, like Lady Bertram's carpetwork and endless fringe, or signs of accomplishment, like Charlotte Palmer's landscape in coloured silks, 'proof of her having spent seven years at a great school in town to some effect'. (*SS*, p. 160) Harville's craftsmanship is characteristic of the man – he is a sailor, ingenious and constructive, making the most of small spaces. The things are products of his industry, and also relics of his voyages – 'some few articles of a rare species of wood, excellently worked up, and with something curious and valuable from all the distant countries'.

Anne's imagination, like Fanny's, is far-ranging. She is granted a more sophisticated sense of environment than any earlier heroine, even participating in her author's interest in 'the effect of professional influence on personal habits'. Anne is also moved, not altogether pleasurably, by 'the picture of repose and domestic happiness', a vicarious enjoyment her author had sharply imagined. Jane Austen never shows love in a cottage, but this is the nearest we come to it. Anne's enjoyment of the riches in the Harvilles' small room in spite of the 'common necessaries provided by the owner, in the common indifferent light' is a counter-balance to Fanny's distaste for the small rooms, unkempt furniture, loud noise and indifferent food of her parents' home in Portsmouth. Fanny comes to appreciate the elegancies and proprieties of Mansfield even more than before, though not quite as her uncle intends when he contrives his experiment in environment. What she yearns for is all that may be understood by the sense of home, including its people, 'her uncle's woods and her aunt's gardens', and all its imperfections. It takes Portsmouth to make Mansfield a home. Anne too has a sense of home, and like Fanny's it is not proprietorial. Anne has to vacate her home too, and Jane Austen draws our attention to her detachment. She shows a moment's imaginative temptation when Lady Russell invokes the image of her being mistress of Kellynch. She comes to admit to herself that 'Kellynch Hall had passed into better hands than its owners'. But she has also glimpsed, in the Harvilles' lodgings, a life that has nothing to do with great estates or rich possessions.

The objects in the Harvilles' room summon up a thought of an alternative life, remote and desirable. But as her fortunes recover, and she comes to think that Captain Wentworth 'must love her', there are a few obstacles. On their first encounter in Bath, Captain Wentworth offers her the hospitality of his new umbrella, but she is pre-engaged to walk with her cousin, in her thick boots, thicker than Mrs Clay's. In the concert hall Mr Elliot interrupts a promising conversation with Captain Wentworth by interposing the concert bill and asking her 'to explain Italian again'. In the hotel rooms which are animated for us by Anne's sense of comings and goings – 'a quick-changing, un-settled scene. One five minutes brought a note, the next a parcel' – Elizabeth Elliot 'pointedly' gives Captain Wentworth the card for her evening party, 'Miss Elliot at home'. In the same bustle Captain Harville shows her Captain Benwick's picture, and the ensuing debate encourages Captain Wentworth to write his letter to Anne. The object-filled world is all about them as Captain Wentworth pretends to have forgotten his gloves in order to take out his letter 'from under the scattered paper' and place it before Anne. Her agitation makes Mrs Musgrove order a chair, but a chair will 'never do', since it will make her 'lose the possibility of meeting Captain Wentworth'. Her brother-in-law Charles, who has a sporting humour, sacrifices his 'engagement at a gunsmiths' to escort her home, but when they meet Captain Wentworth he asks him to take his place so that he can go off to see 'a capital gun' which the gunsmith is keeping unpacked 'to the last possible moment': 'By his description it is a good deal like the second hand double-barrel of mine which you shot with one day round Winthrop.' Separated by so many things, the lovers are finally brought together with the help of gloves and guns. Human beings have to make the best of the objects to hand. Jane Austen's world is full of small objects as well as symbols, and they are often arbitrary and accidental.

The objects in *Persuasion*, as in the other novels, serve plot, animate action, define characters and give a solid sense of the world. They also seem to be present in greater and freer abandon in this novel, lying around, as objects do,[6] in a casual clutter as part of the ordinary scenes and surfaces of life. Jane Austen occasionally uses objects as symbolic, like the ha-ha in *Mansfield Park*, or the autumn fields in *Persuasion*, but her touch with symbols is very delicate.

Accessory objects in *Persuasion* are often introduced with a fine carelessness, simply to give her people things to handle or look at while they think, feel or talk. On the occasion of the Elliot's evening party, which is 'but a card-party', the lovers, who don't play cards, meet, part, and meet again. They are relaxed and at ease together at last, even in the social scene. The environment seems stirred and brilliantly lit by Anne's radiance, but there is an absence of description and all the emphasis is placed within. As Anne and Captain Wentworth meet for one conversation, Jane Austen gives them 'a fine display of green-house plants' to admire. It is an occasion and a cover for the private exchange of memories. The object itself, though fine, green and natural, is wholly inert. When George Eliot brings Stephen Guest and Maggie Tulliver together in a conservatory, the colours and scents of the plants create an sensuous atmosphere and symbol. But Jane Austen, moved less by a symbolic urge than by a sense of appropriate-

---

6 Many of them seem to derive from actual objects, like the amber crosses, gold chains, and silver knife Chapman mentions in his notes to the *Letters*. Other conspicuous objects in the letters include good fires, sofas, a barouche, apricots, game, arrowroot, gooseberry pie, an embroidered stool, green baize, plants taken in from the frost, charades, whist, speculation, a round table, left-behind gloves, a new piano, pictures, well-proportioned rooms, and a shrubbery.

ness, simply chooses something which will give a sufficient sense of place and gesture for the conversation of love.

The author's dramatic self-effacement shows itself in her handling of things and places as much as in the handling of words. The novels [7] are full of encounters with objects, significant or casual. Objects may be present but are sparingly described. The hyacinths in *Northanger Abbey* are given neither a colour nor a space; the greenhouse plants are fine, but of no particular species. Objects may assert themselves, if people need them, as accessories, relics or personal emblems, but are sometimes kept in their place, as objects in a background. The reality of her social scenes, especially in *Persuasion*, depends strongly on the casual presences of objects.

Jane Austen's world is curiously lacking in a sense of an author's descriptive and symbolic manipulation of things, but it is at the same time a world where possessions and properties play a vivid part. Her human beings carry their outer casing with them, and it is made of clothes, ornaments, jewels, accessories, books, pictures, aids, furniture and houses. The inner self is not separate from the outer case which is slowly accreted like the encrustations on a sea-creature. The sense of a social world depends considerably on the shell. The intimate connection of things with their owners and donors is more personal in Jane Austen than in any other novelist before her, and perhaps after her too. People are what they possess, and carry objects with them like limbs. In Jane Austen's social and personal dramas, still-life plays a part.

---

[7] I have excluded *Sanditon*, as too brief a fragment for formal analysis, but it is of course crowded with places, houses, and objects. A typical instance is the 'blue shoe' which Mr Parker spots in the window of William Heeley, Shoemaker, as a sign of progress: 'There was no blue Shoe when we passed this way a month ago.—Glorious indeed!' (*MW*, p. 383)

# VII

# A Sense of the Author

Our sense of the author depends upon familiarity with all she has written and with as much biographical information and inference as can be mustered. But there is a more limited and concrete sense of the author which we gather from occasional or diffused pressures in the fictions.

*Northanger Abbey* follows the pastiche and burlesque of the juvenilia with anti-burlesque. It is a literary satire which depends on seriousness and realism. Its events and passions are not exaggerated but scrupulously contrasted with unreal literary example and expectation. Its method is critically comparative, depending on a clear sense of the reader within the novel and the reader outside. Jane Austen assembles five prominent characters who read novels. Catherine Morland has not read many, but admires *Sir Charles Grandison* and is introduced to *The Mysteries of Udolpho* and other 'horrid novels' by Isabella Thorpe, a devoted fan of Gothic fiction. Eleanor Tilney prefers history, but finds *The Mysteries of Udolpho* 'interesting'. John Thorpe is one of those vague readers who aren't sure what they have read, or by whom it was written, though he likes *Tom Jones* and *The Monk*. Henry Tilney, assured but not supercilious, is clever and experienced enough to know what he likes and why he likes it. Henry is granted his author's blend of satire and enthusiasm, not to mention her mimicry. He remonstrates with Catherine, and provides an amusing little fragment of burlesque. He has an essential instructive purpose within the novel, but it is the author's voice which introduces the form of literary comparison, sustains it discreetly but clearly, and brings it to a conclusion.

The author talks informally to the reader who is reading the novel, fully and briefly, soberly, ironically and playfully. She reveals that she is a woman[1] by referring to 'a sister-author'. (*NA*, p. 111) Her

[1] *Northanger Abbey*, a posthumous publication, was originally intended for anonymity.

address is very different from the genial confidences of Fielding, which may have helped to shape her running commentary. She confines herself strictly to technical guidance and discussion, creating our double awareness of her novel, and of the kind of novel she is not writing. The author's voice in *Tom Jones* speaks for the most fully human consciousness in the novel, but the author's voice in *Northanger Abbey* keeps within a small range of professional reference and feeling. Her longest digression, sometimes criticized as an uncontrolled intrusion, is part of a confidently established medium of cool, friendly and ironic commentary, with tones variously defiant, caustic and sober. It emerges easily out of the particularity of action, as she tells how Isabella and Catherine shut themselves up on rainy mornings to read novels:

> Yes, novels;—for I will not adopt that ungenerous and impolitic custom so common with novel writers, of degrading by their contemptuous censure the very performances, to the number of which they are themselves adding—joining with their greatest enemies in bestowing the harshest epithets on such works, and scarcely ever permitting them to be read by their own heroine, who, if she accidentally take up a novel, is sure to turn over its insipid pages with disgust. Alas! if the heroine of one novel be not patronized by the heroine of another, from whom can she expect protection and regard? I cannot approve of it. (*NA*, p. 37)

Hoping for support, not only from fellow-authors but also from the reader of the novel, she offers a brief dramatic sketch of a young lady putting down her book in shame because it is only a novel:

> 'Oh! it is only a novel!' replies the young lady; while she lays down her book with affected indifference, or momentary shame.—'It is only Cecilia, or Camilla, or Belinda;' or, in short, only some work in which the greatest powers of the mind are displayed, in which the most thorough knowledge of human nature, the happiest delineation of its varieties, the liveliest effusions of wit and humour are conveyed to the world in the best chosen language. (*NA*, p. 38)

It is an astonishingly bold defence for a young novelist. Her wit sobers down into serious judgement just as it is in danger of becoming too caustic, to make high claims which are neither playful nor ironic. She dares to introduce into her own novel an ambitious defence of the craft. Its passion is a reasonable pride, quiet but firm and confident. Its risk seems fully justified by the brilliant virtuosity of the novel. I cannot agree that the narrator and Henry Tilney get in each other's way.[2] One speaks to the reader within, the other to the reader without. The narrator speaks discreetly, and is often screened by the passive voice: 'It may be stated, for the reader's more certain information' and 'the maternal anxiety of Mrs Morland will be naturally supposed to be most severe. A thousand alarming presentiments of evil . . . must oppress her heart with sadness . . . and advice . . . must of course flow from her wise lips. . . . Cautions . . . must . . . relieve the fulness of her heart. Who would not think so?' (*NA*, p. 18) Sometimes the voice speaks even more quietly, interpolating a short aside like the comment on John Thorpe's critique of *Camilla*, 'the justness of which was unfortunately lost on poor Catherine'. (*NA*, p. 49)

An unusual use of the authorial address, probably peculiar to *Northanger Abbey*, is the brisk, businesslike commentary which unblushingly goes about its immediate technical functions of making transitions, introductions, or summaries:

> In addition to what has been already said of Catherine Morland's personal and mental endowments, when about to be launched into all the difficulties and dangers of a six weeks' residence in Bath, it may be stated, for the reader's more certain information, lest the following pages should otherwise fail of giving any idea of what her character is meant to be; that her heart was affectionate. (*NA*, p. 18)

> The following conversation, which took place between the two friends in the Pump-room one morning, after an acquaintance of eight or nine days, is given as a specimen of their very warm attachment, and of the delicacy, discretion, originality of thought, and literary taste which marked the reasonableness of that attachment. (*NA*, p. 39)

> The progress of Catherine's unhappiness from the events of the evening, was as follows. (*NA*, p. 60)

> Monday, Tuesday, Wednesday, Thursday, Friday and Saturday have now passed in review before the reader; the events of each day, its hopes and fears, mortifications and pleasures have been separately stated, and the pangs of Sunday only now remain to be described, and close the week. (*NA*, p. 97)

These neatly self-conscious sentences introduce chapters, but

---

[2] Walton Litz, op. cit., pp. 68-9. Mary Lascelles also suggests that Henry Tilney takes over the 'office of interpreter' but calls it 'a delightful piece of ingenuity', op. cit., pp. 61-2.

sometimes the same device is used to dismiss and conclude:

> And now I may dismiss my heroine to the sleepless couch, which is the true heroine's portion; to a pillow strewed with thorns and wet with tears. And lucky may she think herself, if she get another good night's rest in the course of the next three months. (*NA*, p. 90)

> The embraces, tears, and promises of the parting fair ones may be fancied. (*NA*, p. 153)

The cumulative effect is to keep us in touch with the author. The reminders are kept alive in the references to 'my heroine' and 'our heroine'. Jane Austen wants to sustain the sense of a narrator and the sense of a narrative. For her part she recognizes the existence of a reader who is following the story and actually turning the pages of a book. The sense of the book had of course been spiritedly alive in Sterne's *Tristram Shandy*, and more obliquely in Richardson, whose characters not only keep us aware of the acts and materials of writing but – like Pamela – may remark on their lives as good material for literature. Jane Austen keeps the matter-of-fact literary address alive in brief pressures until the sense of the book's physical presence bears in upon us strongly at the end. Even in the other novels where authorial address is more subdued, she tends to use the valedictory occasions for self-conscious address, perhaps inspired by the habit of epilogues in plays.

The concluding pages of *Northanger Abbey* carry her special mark. She unabashedly discusses the end of the story as the end of a book: 'The anxiety, which in this state of their attachment must be the portion of Henry and Catherine, and of all who loved either, as to its final event, can hardly extend, I fear, to the bosom of my readers, who will see in the tell-tale compression [3] of the pages before them, that we are all hastening together to perfect felicity.' (*NA*, p. 250) Feeling is interrupted, but the effect is not one of alienation. The comic technical observation is quickly followed by an unusually personal remark. The author claims – or seems to claim – acquaintance with the characters in the style favoured by Thackeray in *Vanity Fair* and George Eliot in *Scenes of Clerical Life*, who both abruptly admit that

[3] By an ironic turn in bibliographical destiny, the anticipated compression does not strike the reader who uses the first edition or the Chapman edition, which both include *Northanger Abbey* and *Persuasion* in one volume.

the authorial and professional voice has a personal stake in the story, a familiar knowledge of places and people:

> The marriage of Eleanor Tilney, her removal from all the evils of such a home as Northanger had been made by Henry's banishment, to the home of her choice and the man of her choice, is an event which I expect to give general satisfaction among all her acquaintance. My own joy on the occasion is very sincere. I know no one more entitled, by unpretending merit, or better prepared by habitual suffering, to receive and enjoy felicity. (*NA*, pp. 250-1)

Jane Austen's sense of words is beautifully present as she speaks of 'felicity' in these two very different sentences, moving from amusement to seriousness, recovering and savouring the word after lending it to irony. The feeling of her commentary curves sharply; warm congratulation is followed by the famous technical joke which neatly dovetails Eleanor's charming, rich, young peer and one of Catherine's 'most alarming adventures' in order to comply with the rules of composition. Then the last words of the novel leave a serious statement of the moral for a flippant joke: 'I leave it to be settled by whomsoever it may concern, whether the tendency of this work be altogether to recommend parental tyranny, or reward filial disobedience.'

The volatile but candid commentary often combines technical convenience and literary allusion:

> Her husband was really deserving of her; independent of his peerage, his wealth, and his attachment, being to a precision the most charming young man in the world. Any further definition of his merits must be unnecessary; the most charming young man in the world is instantly before the imagination of us all. Concerning the one in question therefore I have only to add—(aware that the rules of composition forbid the introduction of a character not connected with my fable)—that this was the very gentleman whose negligent servant left behind him that collection of washing-bills, resulting from a long visit at Northanger, by which my heroine was involved in one of her most alarming adventures.
>
> (*NA*, p. 251)

The barefaced admission of convenience is deceptively ironic. Beneath the declared function lies another. When she looks back to the origin of love it is in tones which mingle seriousness and comic irony:

> . . . I must confess that his affection originated in nothing better than gratitude, or, in other words, that a persuasion of her partiality for him

had been the only cause of giving her a serious thought. It is a new circumstance in romance, I acknowledge, and dreadfully derogatory of an
heroine's dignity; but if it be as new in common life, the credit of a wild
imagination will at least be all my own. (*NA*, p. 243)

A few paragraphs later, the author explains that a long narrative
passage was not conveyed to Catherine, the heroine, in the form in
which has just been communicated to us:

> I leave it to my reader's sagacity to determine how much of all this it
> was possible for Henry to communicate at this time to Catherine, how
> much of it he could have learnt from his father, in what points his own
> conjectures might assist him, and what portion must yet remain to be told
> in a letter from James. I have united for their ease what they must divide
> for mine. (*NA*, p. 247)

The irony of the last admission is typically two-faced, turning a
superficially convenient answer to a more important purpose. These
conspicuously authorial observations draw attention to a technical
device in order to make sure that we notice an important aspect of
the novel's realism. The origin of love and the nature of misfortune
are central to the novel's truthful and ordinary materials. The
authorial commentary provokes a comparison with other less realistic
examples of her art, and by admitting artifice proclaims reality and
offers truth.

The necessarily lavish commentary in *Northanger Abbey* is almost
entirely technical, but it does include a few generalizations which
move outside the themes of novels in general and her novel in particular, though they are usually embedded in the technical commentary. They broaden its scope, while lightening its tone. Playful or
ironic, they are almost always part of the comparison of 'real' and
conventional heroines, like the observation on Catherine's improvement in looks: 'To look *almost* pretty, is an acquisition of higher
delight to a girl who has been looking plain the first fifteen years of her
life, than a beauty from her cradle can ever receive.' (*NA*, p. 15) This
candid but friendly remark shades into the more caustic description of
her mind as 'about as ignorant and uninformed as the female mind at
seventeen usually is' and ends with the more trivial question: 'for
what young lady of common gentility will reach the age of sixteen
without altering her name as far as she can?' (*NA*, p. 19) These comments sustain the author's presence and attractively blend truths with
satires.

They often combine more or less conspicuous allusions to other
novels. The moderate beauty of the heroine is one of this novel's
departures from fictional convention – or pretends to be. As in *Mansfield Park* and *Persuasion*, Jane Austen manages to subdue her
heroine's physical attraction without annihilating it. After her *début*
in the Assembly rooms in Bath, Catherine's pleasure at hearing one
compliment is compared to the gratitude of 'a true quality heroine'.
(*NA*, p. 24) The observation that Catherine's entrance into the world
is not marked by 'rapturous wonder' or any 'whisper of eager enquiry',
is an obvious allusion to the *éclat* with which Fanny Burney's heroines
enter the world and the public rooms. What may look like a neutral
remark to the modern reader, would have been more conspicuously
satirical to her contemporaries. 'My heroine' and 'our heroine' are
clever ways of sounding conventional and at the same time making
claim to reality and originality. Jane Austen makes such claims and
comparisons delicately and sportively.

Like all the other novels after *Northanger Abbey*, *Sense and Sensibility* offers more sparing use of authorial commentary. The author
has new purposes to serve. Her address is not heard at the beginning to
introduce the characters and exerts only a very faint pressure within
the impersonal narration: '. . . his will was read, and like almost every
other will, gave as much disappointment as pleasure.' (*SS*, p. 4) It is
more ironically assertive in the description of John Dashwood's child,
who 'had so far gained on the affections of his uncle, by such attractions as are by no means unusual in children of two or three years old;
an imperfect articulation, an earnest desire of having his own way,
many cunning tricks, and a great deal of noise'. Such subdued but
sardonic generalization prevails in *Sense and Sensibility*. Its author's
voice is much less volatile and playful than in *Northanger Abbey*,
where the spiteful remark about 'imbecility in a beautiful girl' stands
out as an exception, and is immediately softened by its application to
Catherine, who gets fairly sympathetic treatment from her author.

The caustic tone continues: 'He was not an ill-disposed young man,
unless to be rather cold hearted, and rather selfish, is to be ill-
disposed'; 'with as much kindness as he could feel towards any body'.
The harshest tones are reserved for the criticism of mercenariness, but
the novel forms a habit of rather sour generalization, as in the famous
dictum, 'On every formal visit a child ought to be of the party, by way
of provision for discourse', and in more reserved instances, such as
'Sir John was a sportsman, Lady Middleton a mother'. Jane Austen's

oblique irony is beginning to take over from the more open commentary of *Northanger Abbey*. Moreover, so much of the novel's action is
filtered through Elinor's consciousness that there is no position which
the author can conveniently occupy. In *Northanger Abbey*, Catherine's mind is occasionally used as a register of events and feelings, but
neither characters nor purpose make it necessary to use a steady or
consistent internal point-of-view.

The author's voice, then, is reserved for criticism. The only occasion
of the authorial 'I' is conspicuous but disconcertingly trivial, though
the triviality is the occasion for an ironic over-emphasis. The portentous introduction, 'I come now to the relation of a misfortune which
about this time befell Mrs John Dashwood', introduces an anti-climax,
to the discredit of Fanny Dashwood. But the other surprising address,
though impersonal, is warm and emphatic: 'But Elinor – how are her
feelings to be described?' (It may have taught George Eliot the
effectiveness of a sudden interruption of open sympathy, and so lie
behind the more famous questions in *Middlemarch*: 'But why always
Dorothea?' or 'Poor Lydgate – or rather, poor Rosamond'.)

Elinor and Edward are the occasion of a warmer generalization, on
the subject of lovers' talk: 'Between them no subject is finished, no
communication is ever made, till it has been made at least twenty
times over.' But the prevailing coldness of the author's touch returns
to brush even these rational lovers, less criticized by their author than
any of her other created couples:

> . . . he did not, upon the whole, expect a very cruel reception. It was his
> business, however, to say that he *did*, and he said it very prettily. What he
> might say on the subject a twelvemonth after, must be referred to the
> imagination of husbands and wives. (*SS*, p. 366)

The generalization seems to belong more to a conventional cynicism
about courtship and marriage than to the happy ending of Elinor and
Marianne, and it is a valedictory irony which never appears after
*Sense and Sensibility*, so is the more conspicuous. The ironic, sententious summary of Lucy's career and the hardness of the farewell to
Willoughby are more clearly appropriate. But even the final summary
of the novel is, if not quite grudging, certainly limiting:

> . . . among the merits and the happiness of Elinor and Marianne, let it
> not be ranked as the least considerable, that though sisters, and living
> almost within sight of each other, they could live without disagreement

between themselves, or producing coolness between their husbands.
(*SS*, p. 380)

In *Pride and Prejudice*, in spite of Jane Austen's delight in her heroine, her direct commentary is still sober and grave, though it has lost the spite and sourness of *Sense and Sensibility*. Once more, the appreciations can be made within the novel, by Elizabeth Bennet, whose point of view prevails. It is here that we find, for the first time, the mature development of that free indirect style which allowed Jane Austen to use the third person as a sensitive register of her characters' mind, feelings and personality. But much of the commentary is dry, caustic and not playful. It is as if all the playfulness has gone into Elizabeth Bennet, leaving none over for the narrator:

> This is not the sort of happiness which a man would in general wish to owe to his wife; but where other powers of entertainment are wanting, the true philosopher will derive benefit from such as are given. (*PP*, p. 236)

> Upon the whole, therefore, she found, what has sometimes been found before, that an event to which she had looked forward with impatient desire, did not in taking place, bring all the satisfaction she had promised herself. (*PP*, p. 237)

Sometimes it is neutral, as in this curt avoidance of description:

> It is not the object of this work to give a description of Derbyshire, nor of any of the remarkable places through which their route thither lay; Oxford, Blenheim, Warwick, Kenelworth, Birmingham, &c. are sufficiently known. (*PP*, p. 240)

At the end the author's solitary 'I' appears: 'I wish I could say, for the sake of her family, that the accomplishment of her earnest desire in the establishment of so many of her children, produced so happy an effect as to make her a sensible, amiable, well-informed woman for the rest of her life.' (*PP*, p. 385) It is not, as in *Sense and Sensibility*, that we feel ourselves in the presence of an occasional superfluity of irony, but rather that the author has withdrawn as far as possible, reserving her commentary and using her most neutral tones.

In *Mansfield Park* the author's ironic voice is much more pervasive; it is much wittier here and in the last two novels. The ironic beginning is especially satiric and generalized. Fanny Price is soon to take over much of the point of view, but irony makes its presence felt throughout the novel. There is also an occasional marked use of the tentative 'probably' or 'perhaps' to suggest a provisional or detached attitude of author to character. But while the author disclaims knowledge, she feels free to express neighbourly pity: 'Poor woman!' she says of Mrs Price, 'she probably thought change of air might agree with many of her children.' (*MP*, p. 11) The second 'probably' is rather different, not so much admitting a lack of knowledge of the heroine as headaches and heartaches: 'The state of her spirits had probably had its share in her indisposition. . . .' The third act of dissociation is entirely comic, a discreet 'perhaps': 'Sir Thomas, after a moment's thought, recommended Speculation. He was a Whist player himself, and perhaps might feel that it would not much amuse him to have her for a partner.' (*MP*, p. 239) The rhetorical question about a heroine's feelings appears again, offering another model for George Eliot: 'And Fanny, what was *she* doing and thinking all this while? and what was *her* opinion of the newcomers?' (*MP*, p. 48) We have left the neutral tones of *Pride and Prejudice* and the sour tones of *Sense and Sensibility* for something more like the volubility of *Northanger Abbey*. There is a special warmth here for the heroine, who is – as has long been noticed – 'my Fanny'. The author's voice is exclamatory at times, and freely personal. At the beginning of Volume Three, the author intervenes to mark the awful occasion of Sir Thomas's return: 'How is the consternation of the party to be described? To the greater number it was a moment of absolute horror. Sir Thomas in the house!' *MP*, p. 175) But nearly all the interesting interventions are made on Fanny's behalf. Jane Austen feels more solicitous for her than for any of the other heroines, because, as Mary Lascelles has sensitively explained, Fanny begins her career in the novel as a child, but also perhaps because of that charmlessness with which her author first endows her and for which she may feel the responsibility of a parent imaged in his children. The solicitude is never sentimental and it is tempered by irony and amusement:

> . . . for although there doubtless are such unconquerable young ladies of eighteen (or one should not read about them) as are never to be persuaded into love against their judgment by all that talent, manner, attention, and flattery can do, I have no inclination to believe Fanny one of them, or to think that with so much tenderness of disposition, and so much taste as belonged to her, she could have escaped heart-whole from the courtship. . . . (*MP*, p. 231)

She had all the heroism of principle, and was determined to do her duty; but having also many of the feelings of youth and nature, let her not be much wondered at if, after making all these good resolutions on the side of self-government, she seized the scrap of paper on which Edmund had begun writing to her, as a treasure beyond all her hopes. . . .

(*MP*, p. 265)

The author affectionately admits that her heroine is made of common clay. On one occasion there is a sharp comment which intrudes its feeling jarringly:

How much time she might, in her own fancy, allot for its dominion, is another concern. It would not be fair to enquire into a young lady's exact estimate of her own perfections. (*MP*, p. 331)

The last chapter makes the fullest use of direct commentary since *Northanger Abbey*. There is the sense of the author's self-knowledge: 'Let other pens dwell on guilt and misery. I quit such odious subjects as soon as I can, impatient to restore every body, not greatly in fault themselves, to tolerable comfort, and to have done with all the rest.' There is also the sense of her affection, though it is expressed in a curiously conjectural way, as if the feeling in 'my Fanny' demanded the convention of biographical reality: 'My Fanny indeed at this very time, I have the satisfaction of knowing, must have been happy in spite of every thing. She must have been a happy creature in spite of all that she felt or thought she felt, for the distress of those around her.' The moral commentary is feeling and vigorous. The author gravely asks of Mrs Rushworth: 'What can exceed the misery of such a mind in such a situation?' speaking not of remorse but of Henry Crawford's reproaches 'as the ruin of all his happiness in Fanny'. She is harsh about Mrs Rushworth: 'The indignities of stupidity, and the disappointments of selfish passion, can excite little pity.' Her remark on the double standard, 'In this world, the penalty is less equal than could be wished', probably possesses the distinction of being Jane Austen's only direct social criticism. It is followed by the reserved 'without presuming to look forward to a juster appointment here-after', which hints, albeit negatively, at the author's only recorded wish in the novels for social reform. The end is playful, ironic and evasive:

I purposely abstain from dates on this occasion, that every one may be at liberty to fix their own, aware that the cure of unconquerable passions, and the transfer of unchanging attachments, must vary much as to time in different people.—I only intreat every body to believe that exactly at the time when it was quite natural that it should be so, and not a week earlier, Edmund did cease to care about Miss Crawford, and became as anxious to marry Fanny, as Fanny herself could desire. (*MP*, p. 470)

*Emma* is the most self-effacing of the novels, for obvious reasons. It has been called a detective story, and the authors of detective stories, like their detectives, must lie low and keep secrets. The free indirect style allows the author to register slight hints and suggestions which the knowing reader sooner or later discovers. As we follow the track of the author, on second and later readings, it is to find that she has always played fair. The clues are present, but not too obtrusive until we look for them, for example: 'She then repeated some warm personal praise which she had drawn from Mr Elton.' There are also pervasive pressures of irony, more subdued than in any other novel. We are kept largely, though not entirely, within Emma's point of view. The author even keeps out of the introduction, which is straight and frank, presenting a striking contrast to the ironic first sentences of *Pride and Prejudice* and *Mansfield Park*:

> The real evils indeed of Emma's situation were the power of having rather too much her own way, and a disposition to think a little too well of herself; these were the disadvantages which threatened alloy to her many enjoyments. The danger, however, was at present so unperceived, that they did not by any means rank as misfortunes with her. (*E*, pp. 5-6)

The reservations of 'seemed to unite some of the best blessings' and other similar hints are not enigmatic, since the situation is so frankly outlined. Even Mr Woodhouse is described straightforwardly, without ironic indirectness: 'though everywhere beloved for the friendliness of his heart and his amiable temper, his talents could not have recommended him at any time'. This is dry, but clear. Its impact is not delayed.

Generalization is sparse, just occasionally showing through, as in the comment that Mr Weston's feeling for Miss Taylor 'was not the tyrannic influence of youth on youth' – which is not a very young remark. The free indirect style is prominent, and collaborates with plain narrative. When we are told that the privilege of exchanging any vacant evening of his own blank solitude for the elegancies and society of Mr Woodhouse's 'drawing-room and the smiles of his lovely daughter, was in no danger of being thrown away' by Mr Elton, we

have the truth placed before us as it is before Emma. The juxta-
position of Mr Elton's delights, in drawing-room and daughter, uninterrupted by even a comma, has its instructiveness. We move from
such unironic frankness to Emma's point-of-view: 'How was she to
bear the change? – It was true that her friend was going only a half a
mile from them. . . .' The sardonic tone creeps in, especially after the
factual informativeness of the first two chapters, but it is discreet:
'Altogether she was convinced of Harriet Smith's being exactly the
young friend she wanted – exactly the something which her home
required.' The free indirect style is a good medium for irony. *Emma*
preserves a habit of reticence after the secrets are out, and even at the
end the author never comes as far forward to claim her characters in
protectiveness or sympathy, nor does she say 'I'. The comic solution
which unites Emma and Mr Knightley, like the happy-ever-after, is
narrated with amusement and warmth, but from a distance. In the
novel where action is most precisely and cunningly located within the
heroine's imagination, the author is at her most reserved. There is no
English novel as dramatic and self-effacing as *Emma* until the experiments of Henry James's middle period.

In the last novel, *Persuasion*, the author's voice returns in a variety
of tone and function like that of *Mansfield Park*. Its irony is perhaps
a little more muted. The humours of Sir Walter Elliot and Elizabeth
are not introduced through loud ironies, but speak for themselves after
demure narrative: 'he could read his own history with an interest
which never failed'. This leaves us in no doubt about the author's
scorn, but it is entirely implicit.

After the third chapter has ended with Anne's musings in a favourite grove, 'a few months more, and *he*, perhaps, may be walking here',
Jane Austen's open guidance begins. Without being a serial novelist,
Jane Austen is adept at turning corners between chapters, and she
begins the fourth chapter by giving a name to that naturally anonymous pronoun repeating its italic: '*He* was not Mr Wentworth, the
former curate of Monkford, however suspicious appearances may be.'
This informative pronouncement is not greatly different from the
faintly amused commentary of *Northanger Abbey*. *Persuasion* continues the authorial dissociations of *Mansfield Park*: 'time had softened down much, perhaps nearly all of peculiar attachment to him'.
Time is allowed to tell, and the author waits, her provisional tone
refusing to make predictions about emotional survival and renewal.

The amused authorial tone is available again to observe the social changes recorded in the old-fashioned parlour of the Great House at Uppercross:

> Oh! could the originals of the portraits against the wainscot, could the gentlemen in brown velvet and the ladies in blue satin have seen what was going on, have been conscious of such an overthrow of all order and neatness! The portraits themselves seemed to be staring in astonishment.
> (*P*, p. 40)

Matter-of-fact and harsh is the report on Dick Musgrove: 'The real circumstances of this pathetic piece of family history were, that the Musgroves had had the ill fortune of a very troublesome, hopeless son, and the good fortune to lose him before he reached his twentieth year.' The bluntness offends modern sensibilities, but it is in tune with many of the harsh remarks on death, pregnancies, children and looks in the letters to Cassandra. Jane Austen may or may not redeem this cruelty when she later observes that 'Personal size and mental sorrow certainly have no necessary proportions', rhetorically absolving herself while insisting that 'there are unbecoming conjunctions . . . which ridicule will seize'. (*P*, p. 68) It is an interesting compromise between coldness and a keen anticipation of the charge of coldness. However we may judge her authorial attitude, she cannot be accused of a lack of foresight.

The free indirect style is prominent. Anne's exclamations and questions, while in the third person, are emphatically Anne's: 'Alas! with all her reasonings, she found, that to retentive feelings eight years may be little more than nothing' and 'Now, how were his sentiments to be read?' An enhancement of flexible commentary is Jane Austen's seemingly invented device of quoted indirect style, to stylize, vary or quicken the pulse of actual speech: ' "Charles had never seen a pleasanter man in his life" 'and ' "he had counted eighty-seven women go by" '. Amusement sweetened by affection enters the commentary on the heroine's feelings, in a sentence which has often been observed: 'Prettier musings of high-wrought love and eternal constancy, could never have passed along the streets of Bath, than Anne was sporting with from Camden-place to Westgate-buildings. It was almost enough to spread purification and perfume all the way.' (*P*, p. 192)

The tone becomes a little warmer towards the end, and the final chapter brings back the authorial 'I' which has been unheard since *Mansfield Park*:

Who can be in doubt of what followed? When any two young people
take it into their heads to marry, they are pretty sure by perseverance to
carry their point, be they ever so poor, or ever so imprudent, or ever so
little likely to be necessary to each other's ultimate comfort. This may be
bad morality to conclude with, but I believe it to be truth. . . . (*P*, p. 248)

Generalization supports and discriminates the individual instance,
and the author's feelings towards her characters are appreciative, full
of that esteem which she likes to chronicle. The direct address starts
the last chapter, but fades out, to let a detached summary speak for
itself, with the vivacity of the last sentences supplied by the well-
wishers within the novel.

The flexible commentary adapts itself to the particular purposes
and needs of individual novels and does not change very much with
the growth of the novelist's art. There are two kinds of generalization,
comic and serious, which run right through the novels.

Trivial generalization is, as we have seen, part of the play of satire in
*Northanger Abbey* and *Sense and Sensibility*. Even in the later novels
where commentary is quieter, it conveys a number of authorial
opinions on small matters. The comic opinions are largely concerned
with domestic matters, parents, children, marriage and courtship. The
author's reluctance to make us a present of her opinion is confirmed by
her occasional willingness to deliver opinions on unimportant matters
and to utter commonplaces. The opinions may be sardonically trivial,
like the suggestion that children should always be taken on visits to
provide subjects for conversation, or tolerantly amused, like the comment that it is in vain for a woman to fret over clothes, since no man or
woman will think the more of her for it. They may be slight but vivid,
like a generalization in *Mansfield Park* about wet Sunday evenings as
'the very time of all others when if a friend is at hand the heart must
be opened and every thing told'. An observation in *Persuasion* about
'everyone having their taste in noises' is attached to a slightly satiric
account of Lady Russell's preference for civic bustle in Bath to the
noise of children at Uppercross. *Persuasion* also contains the more
sober reflection that women's beauty is often scarcely altered for the
worse at the age of twenty-nine, or the remark that it is gratifying to
a woman 'to be assured, in her eight-and-twentieth year, that she has
not lost one charm of earlier youth'. Historical change and lack of
change make some of the commonplaces dated and some fresh. We
may feel the personal significance of certain themes, such as her sense
of the pleasures and pains of children's company, which are linked

with observations in the letters. We may feel a certain biographical weight in some opinions, especially on the subjects of age, time, and female beauty. The opinions are never gnomic or sententious; invariably attached to individual character and action, they are also invariably brief. Jane Austen's authorial commentary hardly ever enters into the feelings and passions of the characters, and never solicits or encourages the reader's sympathy, pity or admiration. Her serious generalizations are rare. Sometimes they are brief, though too firm to be called shy. She has a habit of taking a few words to move from the particular occasion towards an abstraction, then quickly returning to the novel's action. She sums up Fanny's happiness on the occasion of her coming-out ball in Mansfield in this sentence: 'Her happiness on this occasion was very much à la mortal, finely chequered.'

The unusual generalization is marked by the rare foreign phrase, and the rare visual metaphor. This is not a profound observation about the human condition, but a moving commonplace, as the French words admit with their air of quotation. The metaphorical phrase 'finely chequered', attaches itself equally to Fanny's happiness and to the mortal condition. Without leaving Fanny, the author's voice has briefly interposed, to relate the experience to other human lives. Fanny's fluctuations of feeling are evident before and during the dance, but the brief phrase makes us see them not just as the tremulous feelings of this occasion, but as typical of human blessings. Jane Austen's reserve and reticence in generalization are in marked contrast to the habits of her characters. They tend to be great generalizers, exchanging commonplaces or individual opinions which are wise, brash, amusing, ironic, or solemn. The rare occasions when the author's voice has feeling give the sense of feeling that needs to emerge.

In *Sense and Sensibility* the emergent feeling is that of an appreciative, if slightly amused, acknowledgement of the sanguine temperament, through the description of Mrs Dashwood. Here too the generalization shares a sentence with the particular comment on the character. The author briefly emerges to dwell on the pleasures of Mrs Dashwood's sensibility: 'that sanguine expectation of happiness which is happiness itself'. (*SS*, p. 8)

Similarly, she digresses briefly from the appreciation of Henry Crawford's feeling for Fanny:

The gentleness, modesty, and sweetness of her character were warmly expatiated on, that sweetness which makes so essential a part of every woman's worth in the judgment of man, that though he sometimes loves where it is not, he can never believe it absent. (*MP*, p. 294)

In *Pride and Prejudice*, when she is discussing the growth of Elizabeth's love for Darcy, she offers a judgement for our consideration:

If gratitude and esteem are good foundations of affection, Elizabeth's change of sentiment will be neither improbable nor faulty. But if otherwise, if the regard springing from such sources is unreasonable or unnatural, in comparison of what is so often described as arising on a first interview with its object, and even before two words have been exchanged, nothing can be said in her defence, except that she had given somewhat of a trial to the latter method, in her partiality for Wickham.... (*PP*, p. 279)

Here irony holds back generalization, keeping it conditional: 'If gratitude and esteem are good foundations. . . '. The author does not assert but persuades us to agree, at the same time deflating common opinion. The irony is not sharp, but grave. We are expected to assent to this experience of the heart.

In these instances, the author ventures to disclose her feelings. They are generalizations of feelings that the characters, enmeshed as they are in the act of pain, pleasure, praise, anticipation, gratitude and esteem, could not express. The author chooses to utter her feelings about acts of feeling, and so attaches the special cases to life in general, approvingly and understandingly. These are rare instances, perhaps inhibited by Jane Austen's awareness of the conventional raptures of the novel of sensibility. But in each feeling utterance of a truth of feeling, there is perhaps a little more than simple sympathy. The author's observation seems to add its own experience to the experience within the fiction. The lines of fiction and life seem to converge.

This sense of the author's desire to comment is felt as a stronger, more definite pressure in her observations on brothers and sisters in *Mansfield Park*. Once more, her voice demands to be heard, and edges its way into the descriptions of the character's feelings:

An advantage this, a strengthener of love, in which even the conjugal tie is beneath the fraternal. Children of the same family, the same blood, with the same first associations and habits, have some means of enjoyment in their power, which no subsequent connections can supply; and it must be by a long and unnatural estrangement, by a divorce which no subsequent connection can justify, if such precious remains of the earliest attachments are ever entirely outlived. Too often, alas! it is so.— Fraternal love, sometimes almost every thing, is at others worse than nothing. (*MP*, p. 234)

Other generalizations are brief, and attached to the fiction. But here the utterance takes several sentences to itself, and is more directly emotional, even rising into exclamation of feeling in 'alas!'. It is still connected to the instance of Fanny and William, enjoying the recollections of early pains and pleasures, and after it is done it returns to them: 'But with William and Fanny Price, it was still a sentiment in all its prime, and freshness. . .'. As with the image of Fanny's finely chequered happiness, the generalized truth does not digress but affirms and enlarges the fiction.

The voice of the author can sound as a personal voice, rarer, sometimes poignant, not to be wished away. Even the description of Lyme Regis seems to belong to this category of apparent personal pressures:

> . . . a very strange stranger it must be, who does not see charms in the immediate environs of Lyme, to make him wish to know it better. The scenes in its neighbourhood, Charmouth, with its high grounds and extensive sweeps of country, and still more its sweet retired bay, backed by dark cliffs, where fragments of low rock among the sands make it the happiest spot for watching the flow of the tide, for sitting in unwearied contemplation;—the woody varieties of the cheerful village of Up Lyme, and, above all, Pinny, with its green chasms between romantic rocks. . . . (*P*, p. 95)

Jane Austen usually disclaims minuteness of description and the very detail here joins with the quiet evocation of delight to give a sense of personal experience.

Jane Austen does not imagine characters who can bear a full narrative responsibility, like Robinson Crusoe, Clarissa, Jane Eyre, Lucy Snowe, David Copperfield, or Proust's Marcel. These are fictitious storytellers endowed with convenient powers of perception and expression. Some of them bear a close resemblance to the author for whom they stand, like Marcel or Lucy Snowe; some betray a fainter resemblance, like Clarissa. Resemblance to an author is itself a complex and fleeting notion, which can cover experiences, character, personality, mind and fantasy, from all of which selections are unconsciously made. Robinson Crusoe does not write the books his author writes, but he finds a writer's satisfaction in making his chronicle, and Defoe joins a literary energy with matter-of-factness, industry and piety, which we may impute to the author, and find in his other characters. Characters who are neither narrators nor even sensitive registers of consciousness may resemble the author closely, and affinities between character and author are variously discovered by friends or critics. Jane Austen has been compared to her own Anne Elliot, but this is a personal claim and perhaps a private image. The sense of an author is diffused through all the characters.

There is perhaps some justification in looking closely at the literary endowments of characters in fiction. Whatever we know or do not know about the author, we know about the authorship. We may also, as critical readers, know quite a lot about mind and style. In the novels of Jane Austen, her own powers of wit, humour, satire, irony, fun, playfulness, and controlled rhapsody are carefully distributed.

Like most other women novelists before this century, Jane Austen never writes about being a novelist. She keeps to the highroad of average experience. In one respect, her characters' society is very much more limited than hers, which was enlarged and enlivened by her authorship. However gifted her men and women, they are less gifted than their author. The women are less gifted, and also less occupied and less remarkable than their author. She stresses her heroines' lack of occupation, usually makes them clever and imaginative, but never exceptional in talent and achievement. Emma tells Harriet Smith that being a spinster is tolerable if you are rich, resourceful, and have some objects of affection, but she never suggests that authorship might help. In her recent book, *Reader, I Married Him*, Patricia Beer suggests that Jane Austen's refusal to make her women talented condemns them for a personal lack of creativity. It seems more likely that the lack of professional creativity is a deliberate attempt to define social conditions at their most representative and unexceptional. The exceptional woman proves nothing. So it is in the unexceptional woman that she finds a representative image.

But she did not resist the temptation to scatter some of her powers through her novels. As Richard Simpson [4] noticed, she liked to analyse differences of mind. She does so more thoroughly and profoundly than any other English novelist except George Eliot. Some novelists, like Dickens and Henry James, excel at varying their characters while being fairly undiscriminating about their intelligence. James may claim that there are differences in moral and aesthetic sensibility between Maggie Verver and Charlotte Stant, or Gilbert Osmond and

[4] Southam's *Critical Heritage*, op. cit., pp. 258-60.

Lord Warburton, but these are relatively refined differences, all James's characters being immensely clever. Jane Austen gives each character an almost measurable intelligence. Catherine Morland is not brilliant, but she is honest and trusts her own judgement. So she knows logical gibberish when she meets it in the flagrantly contradictory boasts of John Thorpe. Mrs Norris, who is no fool, really knows that Mr Rushworth 'is not a shining character', as she tells Sir Thomas, when he begins to register his future son-in-law's abject brainlessness. Jane Austen does one thing even better than George Eliot, for her evaluation of mind, as these last examples show, is usually registered through the response of her characters. Sometimes she tells us outright what her characters' minds are like, as with Mr Rushworth, but sometimes she leaves it to her characters. They may be sharp and superior connoisseurs of mental folly, like Mr Bennet and Elizabeth, or simply bright enough to register other intelligences. We see minds through other minds, and in the encounters of intelligence, always marked in Jane Austen's social groups, we learn about the mind observing and the mind being observed.

Among the qualities of mind dramatically analysed in her novels are those which convey some sense of an artist's experience. The refusal to write about writers encourages her to present ordinary people who possess narrative powers, wit, satire, and invention. Jane Austen may or may not be eager to say with Carlyle that every man is a poet and a narrator, but like Thomas Hardy or James Joyce, she implies it. It is less admiration than criticism of imagination and eloquence which pervades her novels. She reflects and refracts her own reading experience, both admiring and critical, in the rational praise of Henry Tilney, the more besotted thrills and identifications of Isabella and Catherine, the rapturous enthusiasm of Marianne, the indulgence of Captain Benwick and the more controlled enjoyments of Anne Elliot. In *Northanger Abbey* and *Sense and Sensibility*, she includes the response to literature in a larger critique of aesthetic feeling. Neither Catherine nor Marianne represents the perils of strong inventiveness: they suffer rather from excessive susceptibilities, Catherine to literature, Marianne to poetry, music and painting. They show a certain inability to distinguish art from life; personal imagination and self-knowledge are hampered by aesthetic saturations. Catherine's self-confessed unfixed opinions are in danger of blinding her to the nature of her environment, so that she is particularly excited by Gothic expectations and prevented from looking hard enough through appearances and at probabilities. Neither Catherine nor Marianne is in danger from free-ranging imagination but from stereotype and conformity. Marianne's raptures and ideals are strong but conventional. Her fastidious sense of style is superficial. She criticizes Sir John Middleton's clichés:

> 'I abhor every common-place phrase by which wit is intended; and "setting one's cap at a man," or "making a conquest," are the most odious of all. Their tendency is gross and illiberal; and if their construction could ever be deemed clever, time has long ago destroyed all its ingenuity.'
> Sir John did not much understand this reproof; but he laughed as heartily as if he did. . . . (*SS*, p. 45)

Sir John comes out of this little exchange rather better than the humourless and superior Marianne, whose distaste for gross and illiberal words is a bad preparation for her entrance into a gross and illiberal society. Willoughby's digression about style in the middle of his confession to Elinor draws our attention again to the dissociation of sensibility and a sense of style:

> '. . . what I felt is—in the common phrase, not to be expressed; in a more simple one—perhaps too simple to raise any emotion—my feelings were very, very painful.—Every line, every word was—in the hackneyed metaphor which their dear writer, were she here, would forbid—a dagger to my heart. To know that Marianne was in town was—in the same language—a thunderbolt.—Thunderbolts and daggers!—what a reproof would she have given me!' (*SS*, p. 325)

Jane Austen dissociates herself from not only aesthetic and literary excesses, but also from the excessive satire and criticism of superior minds.

Henry Tilney in *Northanger Abbey* has struck some readers as too unassimilated, too much the author's 'spokesman' (as Walton Litz calls him).[5] He is certainly the least criticized of Jane Austen's wits and critics, allowed to be more reliably didactic than any other character of comparable talent. He is, however, slightly criticized by Catherine for indulging his humour in the foibles of others, by his sister, for over-niceness, and perhaps by the reader, for being less than infallible in his confidence about the safety of England and the English home. But these murmurs are faint. Perhaps the novel would have benefited from some small indication that Henry hadn't

[5] Op. cit., p. 69.

sufficiently perceived his father's modern versions of Gothic villainy, but we should recognize that he is the most playful of Jane Austen's characters and she was perhaps reluctant to criticize him for that fun which Johan Huizinga has said 'resists all logical interpretation'.[6] The symmetry of *Sense and Sensibility* has also been criticized[7] and is certainly unrelieved by any golden mean. In the last four complete novels, Jane Austen avoids the detached authority of Henry Tilney's mind and the extremes of sense and sensibility. Her rule in the mature novels is to charm and amuse by powers of wit, imagination and satire, but at the same time to assimilate the wits, critics and satirists into the moral action and subject them most severely to critical judgement. Wit, imagination and satire are set free, suspected, tried, and found wanting.

Such thorough criticism seems to be new in the English novel. There is the long history of burlesque and criticism of sensibility, in novels like Charlotte Lennox's *The Female Quixote*. A warning against sensibility may even be sounded within Gothic novels, like that given by her father to the heroine of Mrs Radcliffe's *The Mysteries of Udolpho*, though the warning can't be said to go far into the action. Further back are Sterne's travesties of fictional forms and his 'Cervantick' humour, which, like Charlotte Lennox's, remind us that behind three centuries of English fiction looms the brilliantly comic self-analysis of imagination in *Don Quixote*. Jane Austen is unusual in her serious and fundamental criticism of the powers, not the weaknesses, of imagination. Only Cervantes looked as deeply into the imagination. He looked at madness. She looks at sanity.

She looks at the sane imagination, and finds it imperfect. Every artist knows the pleasure of confident powers. Elizabeth Bennet shares with her father the self-indulgent joys of the comic spirit. In Mr Bennet they are over-developed, the consolations of a disappointed mind which falls back on superior condescension, the superiority and complacency of the sense of humour. It seems right that Jane Austen, whose sense of humour is always ebullient in her fiction, and also her letters, even when she is ill and dying, should attend to the dangers of this most flattering sense. It is not until E. M. Forster's *A Room with a View* that we get such another warning against humour, once again from a comic writer who knew all about it. In Elizabeth the self-

---

[6] *Homo Ludens* (London, 1949; Paladin edition, 1970), p. 21.

[7] Stuart Tave has a refreshingly new interpretation, op. cit., Chap. iii.

delighting comic spirit is still young, unembittered and springy, but the congeniality of the father and the daughter is all too clear, making its own delicate implications about environment and heredity. In the foreground is the analysis of the comic energy which is a reflection of the author's mind. Mr Bennet and Elizabeth care too much for style and intelligence and enjoy mocking its absence. (They are both capable of laughing at themselves.) What they find most funny in Mr Collins is the satisfaction of a style so adequate to the hollowness of the man. Mr Bennet also finds his wife funny, though there is some sourness as well as self-indulgence in the deliberately obscure irony he addresses to her. Elizabeth, significantly, doesn't find her funny. But the comic sense can err, and the style isn't invariably an index of the man. Darcy, as well as Mr Collins, is pompous, but there is more to Darcy than his social and linguistic pomposity conveys. There is less to Wickham than meets the charmed eye and ear. Elizabeth and Mr Bennet, satirists diverted by follies, not crimes, are subject to the perils of satiric self-satisfaction. An eye for folly can easily be blind to crime, which is better at hiding itself than folly. A pride in the powers of mind and style can be deceived by mere cleverness and mere style, whether in words, vivacity, or looks. Henry James was to snare Strether by Parisian appearances, so alluring after the unaesthetic dullness of Woollett, but Jane Austen was first to show that the visual sense can run to seed. She makes one of her most perceptive links, between a susceptibility to style and a susceptibility to personal appearance. The novelist herself relies heavily on correlations of looks and style, in Mr Collins, Mr Rushworth, and Mr Rushworth's great house, and she is especially alert to the snags and traps of appearances.

The critique of a sense of style continues in *Mansfield Park*. Henry and Mary Crawford are endowed with charm, wit, and vivacity. Their charm is conventional, their wit insensitive, their vivacity self-engrossed. Their charm, wit and vivacity are greedy and reach out for people. Mary's graceful ease and fluency depend almost entirely on the assured reporting of social commonplaces; she holds what is generally held.[8] Her wit is superficial, and never notices its audience. Her vivacious turns of speech may be cultivated and literary, 'North or South, I know a black cloud when I see one', but are there to show off and persuade. Henry is also civilized in his uses of literature: he adroitly uses Shakespeare to draw Fanny. He knows how to vary his

8 Babb, op. cit., pp. 156-7.

bait, entertaining Julia Rushworth with amusing stories, and Maria
by flattery and *double-entendre*: 'I do not like to see Miss Bertram so
near the altar.' Henry Crawford anticipates Emma's imaginary
portrait of Frank Churchill, able to be all things to all men, being
enough of a chameleon to be able to adapt his playing for different
audiences. He is painfully but appropriately punished by being
required to go through with his act, as he never had to with the
amateur performance which was never staged. Henry performs his
lover's vows with a difference.

Jane Austen does not rely on these warning images, but follows
through the logic of her argument with positive illustration. Up to
now her novels have been utterly conventional, in making a correla-
tion of virtue with charm and good looks. Every eighteenth-century
novelist had done as much. (In *Camilla* Fanny Burney has the
virtuous Eugenia who is disfigured and deformed, though she gives
her a subordinate role.) Jane Austen manages to suggest something of
an Ugly Duckling quality in Fanny, while making her, as Mary Crawford says, 'pretty enough'. Before she 'comes out' her looks attract no
attention. In *Persuasion* Jane Austen restores Anne Elliot's bloom,
after getting something of the same initial effect of comparison with
prettier girls, but Anne's charm and elegance are felt. Fanny is not
only less beautiful than her cousins and Mary Crawford, she is less
charming. She thinks everything out earnestly and carefully, even in
public, and never says anything just for fun or playfulness. Her
rhapsodies show her fervour, but also solemnity. Jane Austen is anything but committed to the absolute moral distrust of fun for fun's
sake, as her letters show on every page, but in Fanny she insists relent-
lessly that virtue need not be attractive. Mary's charm and Fanny's
charmlessness set a trap for the average sensual reader drawn to
vivacity, wit and flirtatiousness. It is a trap that many readers –
possibly more men than women – have fallen into, though some
emerge again.

Emma's elations of wit and imagination are indulged, exposed and
punished. Her wit is given its head and shows its heartlessness. It is
corrected by Mr Knightley's special form of moral chivalry, and by
Emma's own better sense. Her power is released, punished by being
mistaken, lapses, is punished again by being mistaken again, lapses,
and is punished again by remorse. Even after Mr Knightley's rebuke,
she feels chagrin at her own blindness and at seeing that she has been
the subject of somebody else's manipulative invention.

Like the novels of Richardson, Fielding, and George Eliot, Jane
Austen's novels revaluate their predecessors and influence their
successors.[9] *Northanger Abbey* tries out a representative of the author.
*Sense and Sensibility* provides no one who is at once highly rational
and highly imaginative, but the two separated extremes of reason and
enthusiasm.[10] *Pride and Prejudice* returns to another version of the
authorial character, and subjects brilliance to error, recantation and
reform. The heroine whom her author found delightful and expected
everyone else to find delightful, as they have, is succeeded by a study
of her opposite. In Fanny Jane Austen creates a division between two
aspects of the imagination, its power to charm and play and its power
to know and feel. *Emma* varies the theme, to show imagination at
its most faulty, and lazy, but still capable of feeling, reason, and self-
knowledge. Then *Persuasion* appears, the only novel where the
theme of imagination is neither pervasive nor prominent. Perhaps it
follows the five earlier novels by turning away from the theme of a
balanced imagination. The education of Elizabeth, Fanny and Emma
shows the regulation of passion and imagination by reason and solves
the local problems of being a human being in society. For these individuals, it solves problems, but the novelist works through particular
cases, in order to conduct a more general enquiry into the nature of
human and social virtue. Jane Austen moves towards an expansion of
the more artistic theme, and in *Persuasion* we lose our sense of an
author's special experience. She is also pushing beyond her previous
answer, to consider the difficulties of a character whose reason and
passion are integrated. Anne Elliot is too proficient and energetic to be
a creepmouse like Fanny. When the novel begins she has long ago
made her entry into the world. Like Elizabeth and Emma she is
intelligent, but unlike them never asserts her mind in wit. She can be
amused by herself, and by other people's defects, but takes no special
pleasure in the sense of superiority. So she is not blinkered, not elated,
not drawn to styles and appearances. Her imagination is rational, her
intelligence ardent, but she is steadily at home with her powers of
mind. She has managed to grow up among folly, pride, and affectation, without being spoilt or superior, though she has been wounded

[9] It is unsafe to say much about the order of the first three novels, since the
early versions of *Sense and Sensibility* and *Pride and Prejudice* preceded
*Northanger Abbey*, and the revision of *Sense and Sensibility* seems to have
been begun before *Northanger Abbey* was drafted.

[10] See Walton Litz, op. cit., pp. 78-80.

by conformity. Since leaving Captain Wentworth she has lived in solitude, without guides and mentors, to work out regrets and re-appraisals without violent reproach or self-pity. Her ability to say that she would not persuade as she was persuaded, but that she thinks she was right to be persuadable, is one of the most admirable efforts of self-knowledge in the novels.

Such integration does not guarantee a good life, as Jane Austen may or may not have been preserved from knowing, by her art. It is not only a matter of finding love, for as we have seen, love depends for Jane Austen, as for Rousseau, on some ideal of company or com-munity.[11] Anne's solitude is a solitude which makes uncongenial demands on her, where her relatives are likely to climb on her willingly bent back, and keep her down. She has done the right thing. To have resisted the persuasions of prudence would have been a choice of freedom, but also of danger. Anne does not choose freedom, but she does not lose passion. Hers is a perfectly bearable life, even after Captain Wentworth returns. She likes some people and tolerates others, enjoys usefulness without martyrdom. Her life in society is life in good company, but not in the best company. When Captain Went-worth returns, it is to remind her most immediately of what she has never forgotten, of that experience of his best company. *Persuasion* persuades us that someone who achieves the blend of passion and reason is still left with personal and social problems. Jane Austen separates the problem of the good imagination from the achievement of happiness. She presents a mind strong enough to grow and survive with the minimal comforts and aids. The romantic novel still saves Anne from the consequences of her choice, emphasizing not only its own conventions, but human luck or chance. It is as if the special problems of the creative mind had been left behind.

A sense of the author shows itself in the preoccupations with art and its analogues, but in *Persuasion* it disappears. *Persuasion* is the last complete novel, written in the special solitude of pain, illness and the expectation of death, but it is always dangerous to make easy correla-tions between life and art, and *Persuasion* is followed by the incom-pleted fragment of *Sanditon*, high-spirited, more socially extroverted, and returning to the burlesque of the juvenilia and *Northanger Abbey*. In the case of Jane Austen, the sense of the author is most

---

[11] Rousseau's ideal of the communion of *'âmes bien nées'* in *La Nouvelle Héloise* is more romantic and idealized than Jane Austen's.

prudently left on the safer side of biographical speculation. Up to *Persuasion* she has been concerned with the dangers of the imagination, but *Persuasion* shows us the perpetual and common difficulty of being human.